HISTORICALLY BLACK COLLEGES AND UNIVERSITIES

Their Place in American Higher Education

Julian B. Roebuck and Komanduri S. Murty

PRAEGER

Westport, Connecticut
London

Library of Congress Cataloging-in-Publication Data

Roebuck, Julian B.
    Historically black colleges and universities: their place in
American higher education / Julian B. Roebuck and Komanduri S. Murty.
        p. cm.
    Includes bibliographical references and index.
    ISBN 0–275–94267–8
    1. Afro-American universities and colleges.   2. Afro-Americans—
Education (Higher)   I. Murty, Komanduri Srinivasa.   II. Title.
LC2781.R64   1993
378.73′08996073—dc20   93–2858

British Library Cataloguing in Publication Data is available.

Library of Congress Catalog Card Number: 93–2858
ISBN: 0–275–94267–8

First published in 1993

Praeger Publishers, 88 Post Road West, Westport, CT 06881
An imprint of Greenwood Publishing Group, Inc.

Printed in the United States of America

The paper used in this book complies with the
Permanent Paper Standard issued by the National
Information Standards Organization (Z39.48–1984).

10 9 8 7 6 5 4 3 2

HISTORICALLY BLACK COLLEGES AND UNIVERSITIES

To our parents: Komanduri Krishna Murty and Komanduri Andalamma, and Henry Llewellyn Roebuck and Mary Elizabeth Wynn Roebuck, whose love and guidance fostered and supported our academic careers

CONTENTS

TABLES

PREFACE

Since the late 1950s, the presence of black students and faculty has increased on predominantly white campuses as well as at historically black colleges and universities (HBCUs). The dramatic increase of black students on white campuses has occurred with many attendant problems, as exemplified by the interracial adjustment problems occurring in the early 1990s on the campus at Stanford University. Some black and white educators maintain that the HBCUs' mission has been accomplished by providing higher education for blacks who by law and/or custom were barred from attending white private and public colleges and universities prior to 1954. They question the continued existence of HBCUs on grounds that they provide a two-tiered higher education system within an integrated society, which is counterproductive financially, philosophically, and pedagogically. On the other hand, HBCU advocates contend that racial segregation still persists and that HBCUs continue to perform functions unavailable on white campuses that are necessary for black youth. These proponents point out that HBCUs, unlike other colleges, are united in a mission to meet the educational and emotional needs of black students as well as the needs of the black community—that is, the preparation of black youth for leadership roles and professional services in the black community. The issue evolving from these two positions has been exacerbated by the ongoing ugly and provocative racial incidents on white campuses since the late 1970s.

This book addresses the HBCU issue from a broad analytical perspective, including the history and development of HBCUs; the current description, structure, and functions of HBCUs; and HBCU campus race relations as disclosed by secondary sources and by our empirical study.

The first five chapters contribute to the existing rich literature by systematizing the widely scattered data on the subject. Chapter 6 presents, for the first time, a comprehensive empirical study of race relations among black and white students and faculty on ten black and five white campuses. This study concludes that historically black colleges and universities continue to have a significant place in higher education in the United States.

Several people made this project possible. Dr. Thomas W. Cole, Jr., president of Clark Atlanta University, lent his support and encouragement to us in this endeavor. Wilson N. Flemister, Wanda Crenshaw, and Helen K. Threatt aided us in obtaining valuable archival data from the Robert Woodruff Library of the Atlanta University Center. Hugh R. Fordyce, Director of Research at the Atlanta office of the United Negro College Fund (UNCF), provided us with bibliographical material on the UNCF. The National Association for Equal Opportunity in Higher Education (NAFEO) supplied us with numerous publications and reports. Joachim Neckere, Division Director, Program Research and Surveys of the U.S. Equal Employment Opportunity Commission, Washington, D.C., kindly sent us the specially tabulated data on HBCU faculty and staff characteristics for the year 1989. William R. Scott, Professor of History at Clark Atlanta University, critiqued the historical narration in chapter 2. Estella C. Funnye, the Administrative Assistant in the Department of Criminal Justice at Clark Atlanta University, assisted us in procuring data from various institutions necessary for the preparation of HBCU profiles. Her services also proved invaluable in proofreading the manuscript. Carl H. Walker, a colleague in the Department of Criminal Justice at Clark Atlanta University, helped us with the interpretation of black culture. We acknowledge the assistance of Sophy Craze, Ron Chambers, and Lynn Flint, editors at Greenwood Publishing Group, and copyeditor Sherry Goldbecker, in finalizing the manuscript. Finally, we extend our appreciation to the student and faculty respondents without whose anonymous reports this study would not have been possible.

This book is coauthored and represents coequal efforts in all respects. There is no junior or senior author.

HISTORICALLY
BLACK COLLEGES
AND UNIVERSITIES

STUDY OBJECTIVES AND THE CASE FOR HISTORICALLY BLACK COLLEGES AND UNIVERSITIES

PURPOSES OF THE STUDY

Since the establishment of historically black colleges and universities (HBCUs) after 1865, there has been continual controversy concerning the place and role of these institutions within the larger framework of higher education in the United States. Over the years, changes have occurred in the functions and perceptions of these institutions in the minds of both blacks and whites. Though radical changes have taken place in the curricula, administrative structure, faculty and student composition, enrollment patterns, and race relations of HBCUs, their central goal—the education of black students for service and leadership roles in the black community, as well as for adjustment and success in the wider community—remains intact, despite the vicissitudes of social change, including segregation and the problems related to desegregation. The purposes of this book are (1) to address the controversy about the place of HBCUs in higher education; (2) to provide a historical perspective of HBCUs; (3) to sketch the profiles of the major HBCUs; (4) to examine the current demographics, academic programs, enrollment patterns, and faculty composition of HBCUs; (5) to review the literature on race relations on black and white campuses; and (6) to analyze race relations data gathered on fifteen southeastern black and white campuses.

ORGANIZATION OF THE BOOK

In this chapter, we delineate the thrust and scope of our study, define HBCUs, and examine the current debate about HBCUs in terms of the positions taken by their critics and proponents. The substance of this polemic sets the stage for the development of the book. Our sources were scholarly journal articles and general periodical excerpts (from 1970 to the present) that focused on the debate concerning the necessity and the viability of HBCUs.

Chapter 2, on the history of HBCUs, is divided into five periods: (1) the antebellum period (preceding the Civil War), (2) the postbellum period (1865 to about 1895), (3) the separate, but equal period (1896 to 1953), (4) the desegregation period (1954 to 1975), and (5) the modern period (1975 to the present). Sources consisted of archival materials, HBCU college catalogs, journal articles, historical texts, and historical monographs.

Chapter 3 profiles each of the major HBCUs, covering historical information, location, and physical facilities; mission statement, including purpose; governing body and administrative structure; funding source(s) and accreditation status; faculty and student composition; and curricula, degree offerings, and special academic programs. Sources were individual HBCU catalogs, National Association for Equal Opportunity in Higher Education (NAFEO) publications, United Negro College Fund (UNCF) publications, Atlanta University Center (AUC) publications, and personal communications with HBCU administrators at various institutions.

Chapter 4, on current demographics, academic programs, enrollment patterns, and faculty composition, deals with the overall academic programs offered by HBCUs and the structural characteristics of the faculty and student body. Sources were NAFEO publications, government agency documents and reports, and personal communications with the U.S. Equal Employment Opportunity Commission.

Chapter 5, which reviews the literature on campus race relations, reports the form and content of interracial and intraracial perceptions, accommodations, and conflicts among black and white students, as well as faculty, on black and white campuses. Sources were journal articles, general periodical excerpts, and student and faculty reports to investigators other than ourselves. These secondary-source reports, actually social reconstructions of interracial and intraracial interactions, were valuable in and of themselves in portraying the campus racial scene. They also aided us in constructing our research design on campus race relations, spelled out in chapter 6.

Chapter 6, on race relations on five white and ten black southeastern campuses, reports our race-relations research findings; that is, it is an empirical account of race relations as perceived by black and white students and faculty at these institutions. By "account," we mean that the actual verbal reports of students and faculty given to us during research interviews and our analysis of these reports (actually, their constructions of social reality) enabled us to reconstruct and interpret their (the social actors') recollections, observations, definitions, imputations, and explanations of campus race relations—that is, as they experienced campus

race relations themselves. No social scene can be adequately u͟
without the reports of in situ actors. At the close of this chapter, v͟
summarize and interpret our primary data (interview findings) and com-
pare them with the findings in the literature. Finally, in this chapter, we
sum up our views of HBCUs based on primary and secondary data.

HISTORICALLY BLACK COLLEGES AND
UNIVERSITIES DEFINED

Historically black colleges and universities (HBCUs) are black academic institutions established prior to 1964 whose principal mission was,
and still is, the education of black Americans. Each HBCU is legally
authorized by the state in which it is located either to be a junior college
or to provide an educational program for which a bachelor's degree is
conferred. Each must be accredited by a nationally recognized accrediting
agency or association (as determined by the secretary of the U.S. Department of Education) or be making reasonable progress toward accreditation according to such an agency or association. In sum, (1) an HBCU
must be an institution of higher learning established prior to 1964, (2) its
principal mission in the past must have been the education of black Americans, (3) its principal mission currently must be the education of black
Americans, and (4) it must be accredited or be making reasonable progress
toward accreditation by an approved accrediting body (Myers 1987). For
the purposes of this book, we also include certain institutions that were
established after 1964, but that were designated as HBCUs by the National
Association for Equal Opportunity in Higher Education (NAFEO).[1]

There are 109 HBCUs today. HBCUs do not constitute an academic
monolith because, like other colleges, they differ along several dimensions, but they share some basic characteristics that place them in a
separate educational category. They were founded and developed in an
environment unlike that surrounding other colleges—that is, in a hostile
environment marked by legal segregation and isolation from mainstream
U.S. higher education. Historically, they have served a population that
has lived under severe legal, educational, economic, political, and social
restrictions. The composition and position of the black population have
influenced the development of HBCUs, and, in turn, HBCUs have contributed much to the advancement of the black population (U.S. Department of Education 1985). In brief, HBCUs are different from other
colleges because they have maintained a very close identity with the
struggle of blacks for survival, advancement, and equality in American
society (Thompson 1978, 181). Traditionally, in comparison with other
colleges, they are poor in terms of financial resources, physical plant, and
teaching facilities; they have faced opposition from the white power struc-

ture; and they have dealt with many students who are not adequately prepared for higher education.

HBCUs are a vital national resource and have served as the fulcrum of African-American leadership. These institutions produced approximately 70 percent of all black college graduates up to 1991. Based on current trends, it is estimated that over 300,000 blacks will graduate from these institutions in the next 25 years. Though HBCUs currently enroll less than 20 percent of black undergraduates, they confer one-third of all bachelor's degrees earned by blacks. According to 1984 statistics, two HBCUs account for 40 percent of all blacks earning degrees in dentistry, two account for 22 percent of all black M.D.s, four account for 16 percent of all blacks in law, and one accounts for 82 percent of all blacks in veterinary medicine. These institutions have championed the cause of equal opportunity, have provided an opportunity for many who would not otherwise have graduated from college, and have served as custodians of the archives for black Americans and as centers for the study of black culture (NAFEO Vol. II 1991). They were originally established when segregation was mandated and now continue with predominately black enrollments on a voluntary basis.

CRITICISMS OF HBCUs

Goals, Functions, and Academic Standards

Despite the historical role of HBCUs in moving blacks into the mainstream of American life, they have been under pressure to justify their continued existence since the U.S. Supreme Court's 1954 decision in *Brown v. Board of Education*. Some black and white educators and policy makers maintain that the HBCUs' mission—to provide higher education for blacks who by law and/or custom were barred from attending white private and public colleges and universities prior to 1954—has been accomplished. Some claim that prior to the late 1960s separate sets of standards were developed for black and white colleges, but that these no longer exist; that is, black schools are being evaluated now on the same criteria as are other colleges and universities. Therefore, in a society that is striving for racial integration, the further duplication of physical facilities, academic programs, and services within a racially segregated, two-tiered higher education system is counterproductive financially, philosophically, and pedagogically (see Fleming 1984, 1–2; Harvey and Williams 1989). Still others call HBCUs anachronisms because less than 20 percent of black college-bound students currently attend them. Today some 80 percent of college-bound blacks go to integrated schools where they comprise only 7.4 percent of the total number of students (American Council on Education, *Minorities in Higher Education*, 1987).

Several among these critics define HBCUs as diploma-mill service centers for those who could not get into college anywhere else because of low Scholastic Aptitude Test (SAT) scores. Reportedly, most HBCUs provide an intellectual disservice to students and are characterized by insufficient financial resources, underpaid and incompetent teachers, a dearth of research scholars, and a semiliterate student culture (McGrath 1965; Jencks and Reisman 1968; Sowell 1972; Junod 1987). Some contend, explicitly or implicitly, that black students must be educated in white colleges if they are to compete in an integrated society (McGrath 1965; Meyers 1978; Hacker 1990). Sowell (1972), a so-called black neo-conservative, argues that many black schools have vested interests in maintaining mediocrity, that it is difficult for them to retain good faculty, and that bright students do not develop intellectually there. According to Sowell, no HBCU ranks with a decent white state university. Jencks and Reisman (1968) describe both public and private black colleges (with the exception of the "Black Ivy League" schools: Fisk University, Morehouse College, Spelman College, Dillard University, Howard University, Hampton University, and Tuskegee University) as fourth-rank schools at the tail end of academia. These critics, among others (Jones 1971; Jones and Weathersby 1978), have denounced the administrative leadership in black colleges as an in-group of mismanagers who are uninterested in academic standards, but most interested in protecting their turf.

While blacks and whites agree that HBCUs have proven themselves useful, they are now viewed by many whites and some blacks as ineffective and dispensable institutions that do not meet the academic levels of white institutions. In a poll of its subscribers in 1980, *Black Enterprise* magazine reported that 82 percent of the respondents thought HBCUs were serving a purpose that could not be met by other colleges, but that only half of this percentage hoped their children would attend a black college. Many blacks, though admiring HBCUs, prefer white institutions for themselves and their children (Branson 1987).

Emphasis on Ethnic Education

Many educators have noted a "brain drain" of bright students and faculty from HBCUs since legal integration in 1954, which supposedly has resulted in an isolated, barren black campus cultural life (Morris 1972; Thomas and McParttland 1984). Furthermore, some writers denigrate the education of black students by black educators in black schools. For example, they claim that HBCU curricula place too much emphasis on African-American cultural values and political education and not enough emphasis on educational skills and competency (Hacker 1990). Some black and white writers among these critics claim that a new universal culture is developing and that Americans of all races are short on the skills that this culture expects—whether in mathematics, reading, or geography. Therefore, they advocate that black students "act white" in order to obtain and cultivate the educational skills necessary for competition in this universal culture (Sleeper 1989). The implication is that this competency is best acquired in white schools. In a similar vein, some writers seek to diffuse the issue of any special ethnic and cultural education for blacks by blacks. They proclaim the development of a nonethnic society in the United States where ethnic and racial origins are increasingly irrelevant (Alba 1989). This may be the case for white ethnics, but it is patently unrealistic for blacks.

Financial Difficulties, Accreditation Problems, and Changed Enrollment Patterns

HBCU critics have received additional ammunition from recent HBCU financial and accreditation problems (see Simmons 1984; Jellema 1972; U.S. Department of Education 1985; Brazziel and Brazziel 1987). The shift in federal funding from college grants to loans, which began during President Ronald Reagan's first administration (actually resulting in cuts in financial aid), plays havoc with lower-class students. Approximately 80 percent of those attending black private colleges require some financial aid. In 1980, 42 percent came from families below the poverty line, and 30 percent had families earning less than $6,000 annually. In 1979–1980, only 4 percent of the students attending private schools funded by the United Negro College Fund had taken on guaranteed loans, a figure that climbed to nearly 50 percent in 1987. The shift from grants to loans is one thing for a white middle-class student, but quite another for a black lower-class one (Junod 1987).

Furthermore, others claim that the quality of education at HBCUs suffers because of the lack of federal funding and grants. Black schools rarely receive grants from the National Institutes of Health. The National Science Foundation, which was thought to have a major obligation to alleviate the lack of blacks in science, gave less than 0.4 percent of its funds to HBCUs in 1984, and not one HBCU was in the top one hundred corporate foundations grant recipients. Minority fellowship programs place few black graduate students in programs in science, engineering, and mathematics (Branson 1987).

Several HBCU detractors, and some ardent supporters, predict that within the next twenty years many HBCUs will close because of financial difficulties, lose accreditation, or lose their identities in mergers. This "passing" would be regarded as a tragedy by HBCU advocates, but for others it would be a healthy development. The latter note that the demise of black colleges was foretold in 1972 when the number of black students attending white colleges equaled the number of black students attending HBCUs (Law and Clift 1981). Overall, the civil rights movement in the 1960s produced a dramatic rise in black enrollment in white colleges because of civil rights enforcement, marches, and demonstrations and the resulting new open admissions policies (at many white institutions). The black enrollment in white colleges increased significantly after the death of Martin Luther King, Jr., in 1968. In addition, a large number of community and junior colleges were established in urban areas. Although large numbers of blacks now attend them, they were established by whites and are run by whites. They are black only in student-body racial composition (Fleming 1984). Forty-two percent of black students and fifty-six percent of Latino students enrolled in higher education institutions attend community colleges, compared to only thirty-six percent of white students (Richardson and Louis 1987).

Reduction in Degrees Awarded

Until 1954, the traditionally black institutions of higher education trained the majority of professionals, educators, and leaders in the black community. The total number of baccalaureate and higher degrees awarded by HBCUs increased from 13,000 in 1954 to 32,000 in 1974 and then declined to 28,000 by 1982. There has been a gradual decline in the number of degrees awarded by HBCUs at the baccalaureate level since 1974 and at the post-baccalaureate level since 1977 (U.S. Department of Education 1985). An estimated 60 percent of the baccalaureate degrees awarded to black students in 1988 were granted by predominately white colleges and universities, and the proportion of black students matriculating at and graduating from white institutions will probably grow in the foreseeable future (American Council on Education 1988).

RESPONSES TO THE CRITICS

HBCU advocates are aware of these caustic criticisms, some of which they would admit. They maintain, however, that the shortcomings of black colleges are the result of a social order in which the higher education of blacks has been historically constricted (by the white power structure) in order to render black institutions nothing more than second- and third-class imitations of white counterparts (Bullock 1970; Moss 1989; Goodenow 1989; Dyer 1989). HBCUs, they argue, despite their modest beginnings and discriminatory problems, have served black students with considerable effectiveness in that they have upgraded curriculum offerings and quality over the years, while maintaining a commitment to individual student development. Some HBCUs, they note, have attained high academic status (United Negro College Fund 1985; Fleming 1984).

Advocates during the civil rights movement of the 1960s were enmeshed in the problem of how to preserve HBCU identity on the one hand, while attempting to achieve integrated education on the other. By 1974, however, most black educators and black community members were convinced that the HBCUs should survive, be made stronger and more competitive, and not be merged with white institutions of higher learning. Furthermore, they wished to maintain control over what they perceived to be "their own institutions," regardless of student-body racial composition. They contended that HBCUs provide assets for black students that are unavailable and unattainable in white institutions, provide an accepting environment with emotional support (Smith 1981), serve as repositories for the black heritage; foster ethnic pride and self-esteem (Billingsley 1982; Law and Clift 1981; Lomotey 1989), enhance opportunities for the development of leadership roles (Allen 1985), furnish healthy social relationships (Fleming 1984), offer programs designed to meet the unique needs of black students and the black community (Allen 1986), and educate many black students with learning deficiencies (Allen 1987; National Commission on Testing and Public Policy 1989). Proponents explicate HBCU assets and the need for their continued existence within interrelated and overlapping topical categories.

Continuing Segregation

Proponents note that even predominantly black public schools have, for the most part, white faculties and white administrations. They contend that there is a need for more black teachers as role models at the public school and college levels and that HBCUs should graduate many of these role models. In 1989, however, fewer than 5 percent of black U.S. undergraduates were majoring in education (Hacker 1990). They also note that despite the legal integration of all schools at the secondary and college levels, white parents have done their best to ensure that their children will attend schools where they have few or no black classmates. The reaction of many blacks has been that because whites do not wish to associate with them, they should operate schools of their own (Lomotey 1989; Ehrlich 1990). Currently there are many all-black public schools in the inner cities and in the rural South. Many others throughout the United States are predominantly black, with the remaining students usually Hispanic. The National School Boards Association has published data on how many students attend schools where black, or Hispanic pupils (separately or together) account for 90 percent or more of the enrollment (see Table 1.1). In Chicago, 81 percent of black children attend such schools; in New Orleans, 84 percent; in Atlanta, 91 percent; and in Newark, New Jersey, 97 percent (Orfield and Monfort 1988). Almost two-thirds of all black students (63.3%) still attend segregated schools. In many cities there are not enough whites to make for an integrated public school system.

Table 1.1
Percentage of Black Students in "Integrated" and "Segregated" Schools in Selected Cities, 1988

City (Black Population)	"Integrated"schools: Percentage of black students in schools in which white students comprise a majority of the enrollment	"Segregated" schools: Percentage of black students in schools in which black and Hispanic students comprise 90% to 100% of the enrollment
Des Moines (6.8%)	95.5%	0.0%
Colorado Springs (5.6%)	88.6%	0.0%
San Jose (4.6%)	67.6%	0.0%
Tucson (3.7%)	63.0%	1.4%
Albuquerque (2.5%)	51.8%	2.5%
San Diego (8.9%)	26.5%	8.5%
Seattle (9.5%)	25.8%	4.5%
Fort Worth (22.1%)	22.1%	36.4%
Denver (12.0%)	19.0%	0.0%
Philadelphia (37.8%)	10.6%	73.7%
New York (25.2%)	6.8%	74.1%
Los Angeles (17.0%)	4.9%	70.0%
Dallas (29.4%)	4.6%	65.7%
Chicago (39.8%)	2.4%	81.3%
Newark (58.2%)	1.0%	96.6%

Source: National School Boards Association. The black students are in the schools not categorized as "integrated" or "segregated" according to the standards used here. Those percentages vary from 81 percent in Denver to 2.4 percent in Newark (1988).

Black students comprise more than 70 percent of those enrolled in the public schools of Illinois, New York, Mississippi, Michigan, California, New Jersey, Maryland, and Wisconsin and more than 50 percent in Arkansas, Massachusetts, Georgia, Tennessee, South Carolina, Connecticut, Missouri, Louisiana, Texas, Oklahoma, and Ohio. Furthermore, many white parents and school officials successfully use tracking methods to perpetuate segregation within so-called "desegregated" schools. Such tracking by achievement level is usually based on standardized education test results, and in schools with a white majority and a black minority, it frequently separates the races. Black students comprise 60 percent of all public school students, but make up almost 40 percent of those who are classified as mentally retarded, disabled, or otherwise deficient. Consequently, many more blacks are consigned to special education classes that segregate them from whites.

Thus, a generation after the *Brown* decision, black and white pupils walk through the same school doors, but they seldom sit alongside each other in the classroom (Hacker 1990; 1992, 164–65). The chief reasons for continued segregation in the public school system are residential segregation, tracking, and the failure of public school busing. Students usually go to school in the areas where they live.

In sum, many black and some white educators note the continuation of racism, discrimination, and segregation in the public school system; the failure of blacks to compete successfully with white students in integrated schools; the necessity of remedial courses for many college-bound black high school students; and the past and continued success of HBCUs in educating black youth and in preparing black teachers to teach black youth. Therefore, they think that HBCUs remain essential to the education of blacks in the United States for both symbolic and practical reasons (Harvey and Williams 1989).

Goals, Central Mission, and Needs

HBCUs, unlike other colleges, are united in a mission to meet the educational and emotional needs of black students. They remain the significant academic home for black faculty members and many black students (Billingsley 1982). The goals described in black college catalogs, unlike those of white schools, stress preparation for student leadership and service roles in the black community. Some black students are not prepared emotionally to succeed in white colleges and many require the conditional admission and remedial course offerings that are provided by HBCUs, but that, are not usually available in white schools. Allen (1987) argues further that HBCUs are still necessary because, among other things, they educate many black students who otherwise would not be able to obtain a college degree elsewhere. He and Hodgkinson (1985) contend that HBCUs are needed to bring still larger numbers of blacks into the nation's mainstream. Walters (1991), a black scholar, lists six specific goals for HBCUs: (1) to maintain the black historical and cultural tradition (and cultural influences emanating from the black community) by preserving and acting as a repository of material records and by encouraging scholarly accomplishments of black professors in teaching about and researching the black condition; (2) to provide key leadership in the black community because college administrators, scholars, and students have an important social role to play in community affairs (the HBCU functions as a model social organization and contributes to the resources needed for the expansion of black community activities); (3) to provide an economic function in the black community (HBCUs often have the largest institutional budget within the black community, which involves the acquisition of funds, the distribution of these funds to workers and their families and to small businesses, and the investment of these funds in economic institutions); (4) to provide black role models in the black community who can interpret the way in which social, political, or economic dynamics at the general society level impact on black people; (5) to produce graduates with special competence to deal with the problems between the minority and majority population groups; and (6) to produce black agents for specialized research, training, and information dissemination in dealing with the life environment of black and other minority communities.

Some advocates of HBCUs claim that white colleges have not met the multilayered education needs of the black population. Out of 2,000 Ph.D. degrees awarded nationally in the biomedical sciences in 1980, only 28 were earned by blacks (Meharry Medical College 1990). In 1986, only 2 percent of the faculty members in the nation's medical schools were black; only 3.6 percent of the students in white graduate business schools were black; and only 0.5 percent of the students receiving Ph.D.s were black. More blacks are currently graduating from high schools than ever before, but fewer in proportion to whites are enrolling in college. White Ivy League schools recruit vigorously for the most talented blacks, but they do not seek out black students from the inner-city schools and poor rural areas. Without HBCUs, black leaders say, blacks would have to depend on white colleges, the best of which demand high SAT scores. Blacks as a rule score low on the SAT and other college entrance tests that are white-culture-bound (Junod 1987). Moreover, some minority educators claim that the SAT is inherently biased against women, minorities, and low-income students because of built-in cultural biases and that revisions adopted for these groups are flawed. In brief, they question the use of SAT scores for college admission purposes (Becker and Weiner 1990). Furthermore, hundreds of thousands of those who graduate from high school are functionally illiterate (Junod 1987).

White colleges offer white ambiance and white values without the opportunity to achieve white identity. HBCUs, on the other hand, offer the chance to develop a healthy black identity; opportunities for the ordinary student; a place for the weak, the timid, and the militant; and a setting for black affirmation. Many claim that HBCUs can best uplift the unprepared students and simultaneously stimulate the competent ones (Fleming 1984). Frequently, black students find white universities to be hostile places where white students and faculty see them as "special admits" and beneficiaries of affirmative action. Moreover, black student adjustment at these institutions requires adherence to white cultural norms, thereby necessitating the abandonment of cultural roots. Furthermore, the selection and admission policies at many white universities result in the recruitment of black middle-class students who have been educated in white high schools and socialized in white environments. It is unlikely that such black graduates from these schools will be interested in the problems confronting poor black communities or sympathetic with the members of these communities. This situation may further widen the chasm between the black middle class and the black lower class (Smith 1981). In addition, some claim that the talents of bright black students attending white colleges are not given the extraordinary high priority required for the development of the brightest or most gifted young black students. White schools have other priorities—for example, cutthroat competition in a highly selective academic rat race. On the other hand, honors programs have been developed at HBCUs for such extraordinary students (Billingsley 1982).

Thompson (1978) maintains that blacks on black campuses, when compared with blacks on white campuses, are exposed more frequently to dedicated teachers who instill within their black students a sense of pride and personal worth. Furthermore, they experience a greater degree of personal interaction with their professors in many-sided, sustained, and personal relationships beyond the classroom—including counseling sessions and the activities of student organization sponsored by faculty. They are also oriented toward success more frequently on black campuses than on white campuses. Hemmons (1982), in a comparative study of black student attitudes on a black campus and those on a predominantly white campus, found that twice as many black students on black campuses as on white campuses felt that their school (HBCU) prepared them for membership in the American mainstream. This study also found that black students on black campuses experienced greater warmth and empathy in a viable student-teacher relationship and less racism than did their counterparts on white campus.

Success Patterns

Performance Level

Walters (1991) notes the successful performance of the HBCUs in enrolling, retaining, and graduating black students and thereby contributing a substantial portion of the black middle-class leadership. Research findings also disclose that black students fare much better on HBCU campuses than on white campuses. That is, relative to black students on black campuses, black students on white campuses have lower persistence rates (more drop out between the freshman and the senior years), lower academic achievement levels, less likelihood of enrolling in advanced degree programs, poorer overall psychological adjustment, and lower post-graduation attainments and earnings (Allen, Epp, and Haniff 1991). In fact, black students' attrition rates on white campuses are five to eight times higher than are those for white students on the same campus (Deskins 1991). Furthermore, the percentage of black high school graduates who went to college and completed at least one year did not increase from 1976 to 1987, stabilizing at a point far below the level for their white peers (U.S. Department of Education 1985). Many black educators think that this completion rate would have been higher had more been enrolled in HBCUs, rather than in white schools (personal communication from the Atlanta University Center, September 1990).

Table 1.2
Degrees Conferred by Historically Black Colleges and Universities Compared to
Total Degrees Conferred on Blacks in the United States, 1984–1985

	Bachelor's Degrees	Master's Degrees	Doctoral Degrees	Professional Degrees	Total
Degrees conferred on Blacks	57,473	13,393	1,154	3,029	75,595
Degrees conferred by Historically Black Colleges & Universities	21,467	4,213	174	942	26,796
Percentage of Degrees Conferred by Historically Black Colleges & Universities	37.3%	30.2%	15.0%	31.0%	35.4%

Source: American Council on Education, Office of Minority Concerns, Sixth Annual Status
Report (1987).

Degrees Awarded

Black schools still grant high proportions of the baccalaureate and graduate degrees earned by black students. Approximately 37 percent of the
undergraduate degrees received by blacks in the United States in 1985
were conferred by HBCUs (21,467 of a total of 57,473 were received by
blacks); 30.2 percent of the masters degrees (4,213 of 13,939); 15.0 percent
of the doctorates (174 of 1,154); 31.0 percent of first professional degrees
(942 of 3,029); and 39.6 percent of all degrees (29,943 of a total of 75,595)
(see Table 1.2). HBCUs in the southern states play an even more important
role in producing black graduates than do black schools elsewhere (U.S.
Department of Education 1985).

Less than thirty years ago over 90 percent of black students were
educated in HBCUs, whereas today they enroll less than 20 percent of
college-bound black students. They graduate, however, close to 40 percent of black students graduating from the nation's colleges (Harvey and
Williams 1989). Significantly, as of 1970, the HBCUs, despite shortages
of funds and underpaid faculties (that devote disproportionate time to
teaching, rather than to research), had graduated at the undergraduate
level 75 percent of all black American Ph.D.s, 75 percent of all black
army officers, 80 percent of all black federal judges, and 85 percent of all
black doctors (Jordan, 1975).

Post-Graduation Success

Thompson's 1986 survey of graduates of black colleges corroborates the continuing success of HBCUs in preparing blacks for effective participation in the American social system. In his three-year study of more than 2,000 alumni of these institutions, he found that nearly 90 percent of his respondents were professionals in medicine, dentistry, teaching, or law. Eight percent held white-collar jobs (for example, secretaries, salesmen, and office managers), and 3 percent were blue-collar workers (waitresses, taxi drivers, cooks, and so on). Moreover, he found that the average income of the families headed by black college graduates was $32,000—over $10,000 above the average income of families headed by non-college graduates. Thompson further reported that 50 percent of the graduates surveyed have earned a master's or doctoral degree. Approximately 10 percent of the alumni with post-baccalaureate degrees received them from Ivy League schools. This profile covers graduates of HBCUs from 1940 to 1982, with the average age being forty-three. Finally, 6 percent of the alumni reported that their high schools had adequately prepared them for college. Thompson's sample, of course, appears to be an upper-middle-class group.

Improvement in Financial Resources and Accreditation Process

HBCU advocates note that the financial resources for HBCUs have continually improved over time. For example, HBCUs received $204.8 million in 1990 under the Higher Education Act, in addition to regular financial aid and other federal funding (DeLoughry 1990). In addition, the United Negro College Fund (UNCF), a consortium of private HBCUs, has raised more than $690 million since its inception in 1944. Its current Campaign 2000 aims at raising $250 million, which will be used for scholarships, endowments, academic programs, faculty development, administration, and construction (Nicklin 1991). For further details on funding patterns, see chapter 2.

HBCU proponents also note that HBCUs have shown significant development in their accreditation process as measured by regional accreditation agencies (the Southern Association of Colleges and Schools—SACS, and the Middle States Association of Colleges and Schools—MSACS). Simmon's (1984) study of twelve HBCUs in the Middle States Association region (Bowie State College, Cheyney State College, Coppin State College, Delaware State College, Howard University, Lincoln University, Malcolm–King: Harlem College Extension, Medgar Evers College of the City University of New York, Morgan State University, Sojourner–Douglas College, and University of Maryland, Eastern Shore) found that the use of on-site visits, follow-up reports, and consultants by regional accreditation agencies has served as a catalyst for change and as a positive force in institutional improvement. Finally, as will be noted later, individual states and the federal government are continually increasing funding for HBCUs.

Social-Psychological Supports, Racial Integration, and Comfort Level

Research findings show that the general attitude on HBCU campuses, as epitomized by the faculty, administrators, and staff, is more understanding, more accepting, and less prejudiced than that on white campuses. From freshman through senior years, black students in black colleges are less likely to report instances of interpersonal stress (Fleming 1984, 18–20). There is also a general level of satisfaction and camaraderie among black students at black schools that is not found among black students on white campuses. Though the facilities (physical conditions, computers, library and research materials, and visual aids), financial resources, endowments, and range of academic programs do not approach those found on white campuses, the atmosphere is much more comforting. Black students feel more welcome at HBCUs than they do on white campuses and consequently are better able to focus on studying without racial distractions. Conversely, particularly in southern schools, they are frequently faced with alienation, stress, and at times outright hostility from white students and faculties (Allen 1987). Contrary to common practice on white campuses where many students are taught by graduate students and assistant professors, students in HBCUs are taught by designated full-time faculty members, including assistant, associate, and full professors (authors' observations).

Private and public HBCU faculties and student bodies are integrated, although a black culture prevails. Of the total faculty members employed in all HBCUs, approximately 55 percent are black, 40 percent are white, and 5 percent are composed of other minorities and foreign nationals. Among black private colleges, blacks constitute 63 percent of the faculty, while among black public colleges, they make up 51 percent. Ninety percent of the administrators in black private colleges are black, and 70 percent in black public institutions are black (Billingsley 1982; Dupre 1986). In the 1987–1988 academic year, more than one-third (38%) of the faculty at black private colleges sponsored by the UNCF were non-black. This is an enviable racial balance when compared to the extreme underrepresentation of black faculty on white campuses: Among the nation's more than 3,000 predominantly white colleges and universities, less than 4 percent of the faculty members are black. Even among those schools that have encouraged relatively large numbers of black students to enter, there has been no appreciable development of a significant cadre of black faculty members. Additionally, black colleges have always served as forums for visiting scholars, political figures, business leaders, and artists, regardless of race, creed, or religion. Many HBCUs are now actively recruiting Hispanics, Asians, and students of all races from third world countries (Harvey and Williams 1989).

The black public colleges began increasing their white enrollments in the mid-1970s because of the U.S. Supreme Court decision in *Adams v. Richardson* (1969), which mandated that institutions supported by state funding maintain a racial balance. In any case, HBCU student bodies have been racially mixed since inception. Southern private HBCUs, however, have never actively recruited white students, and, in fact (in most cases), only a few whites attend southern private HBCUs. When black institutions were founded in the late nineteenth century, their administrators and faculty were mainly white, and the leadership did not begin to shift to blacks until the mid–twentieth century. HBCU faculties today remain fully integrated (Bowles, Decosta, and Tollett 1971).

On HBCU campuses, positive black role models are present and readily available on a one-on-one basis. The intimate nature of relationships between students and faculty does not exist on white campuses, where a cooler professional relationship is maintained—if there is any relationship at all. This unique relationship, some feel, is the chief reason for the HBCUs' success. Opportunities are also available for black students to experience leadership positions in student government, fraternities, sororities, and other extracurricular organizations. Through this involvement, student-support networks may be developed, thereby fostering self-confidence, the ability to lead, and self-esteem. In contrast, on white campuses black students find themselves on the periphery of campus life (Barthelemy 1984).

Transitional Ease

The black college experience prepares students to enter and succeed in the real world beyond the black campus, which serves as a buffer zone between the segregated society they encounter through home and community and the mixed society they must enter after college. Being nurtured as adolescents in a supportive environment, free of racial tension, eases the cultural shock of movement from the black to the white world. Certain features of black campus life—a participatory ethos, an inclusive environment, an expectation of success, and an incorporation of a rich historical tradition—contribute to this passage (Harvey and Williams 1989). For example, Morehouse graduates refer to themselves as "Morehouse men." A Morehouse man embodies all that is supposedly good, noble, and strong in the African-American college male. Finally, those enrolled at HBCUs escape the campus conflict between black and white students that is frequently found on white campuses.

Black Consciousness and Culture

HBCUs emphasize the development of black consciousness and identity, black history, racial pride, and ethnic traditions. They provide an African-American culture and ambiance that many students find essential to their social functioning and mental health. Frequently, whites and many middle-class blacks either are unaware of this black cultural necessity or ignore it. Several interrelated elements of this cultural complex are

1. Language form, content, and style (black English; verbal rhythmic schemes; jazz idioms and cadence; speechifying and exaggerated embroidery; showboating, profiling, and sounding; rapping, toasting, and gaming; flattery and earthiness; realistic irony and black humor; emotive expression; aggressive loud talking; laughing; and long unstructured storytelling);
2. An extrinsic and bold black dress style;
3. Highly personalized social relationships and the need for strong affectional ties, particularly with role models and those who judge them;
4. An Afro-centric milieu and the tendency to transform social behavior settings into a familiar and exuberant mise en scène;
5. Body language cues, including physical stance, showing out, and strutting;
6. Diet and eating styles;
7. Recreational pursuits and black music (jazz, rhythm and blues, spirituals, and rap);
8. Religious form, beliefs, content, symbols, and emotional spiritual expressions—all based on a concrete and individualistic relationship with God;
9. Church services characterized by a personal interaction with the minister;
10. Everyday customs, dress, and dance style;
11. Double consciousness and racial identity (i.e., an identity of being black as well as a hyphenated American);
12. Uneasiness among whites based on feelings that one is always under scrutiny;
13. Dating patterns, practices, and preferences;
14. Artistic values, aesthetics, and expressions;
15. Political and racial attitudes, usually based on structural empowerment;
16. Emotional stimulants and responses;
17. Inner values and feelings;
18. A near deification of the mother figure; and
19. A black world view (Roebuck and Hickson 1984; Roebuck 1986; Jaynes and Williams 1989; Benjamin 1992; Jencks 1992; Jones 1992).

This African-American culture emerges from two primary sources: African cultural traits and linkages to a black heritage, and cultural traits developed as a result of racial segregation in the United States. The point is not made that all blacks share these cultural elements in a uniform communal fashion. As with other ethnic groups, there are individual differences among blacks. They exert personal choices, face a variety of social situations, and belong to different social classes. One could distinguish the isolated young and poor blacks or the professional black elite from other blacks. The point is made, however, that the foregoing set of elements composes what may be regarded as essential parts of a black ethos in the United States; that is, they are adhered to, more or less, by most American blacks.

The literature on black students attending white schools documents campus problems involving interpersonal relationships, personal identity, and black consciousness. According to Gibbs (1974), Davis and Swartz (1972), and Allen (1987), establishing a meaningful personal identity, cultivating personal relationships, and gaining social acceptance are difficult for black students on white campuses. One could argue that these adjustment problems comprise the price that has to be paid for racial integration. The price is dear, particularly for those who find adjustment on white campuses difficult, and, in any event, racial integration may be a dream only for some and undesired by others.

Personal Choice

Blacks, like whites, desire and merit options in selecting institutions of higher learning. HBCU advocates should not be required to engage in dialogue about the legitimacy of racial self-segregation. Just as different white groups have such schools as Notre Dame, Harvard, Bob Jones University, Wellesley, Brandies, Brigham Young, and so forth, blacks have HBCUs. Choice is a cherished feature of the American education system. And, in any case, HBCUs do not exclude white students or harm white society in any way. In fact, the choice of an HBCU reduces the pressure for affirmative action in white schools. HBCUs do not comprise a monolithic educational enterprise. They have varied since inception and still differ widely in curriculum, educational facilities, size, funding sources, administrative control and function, geographical location, quality, financial status, and prestige. Thus, they serve the needs of a wide range of students (Fleming 1984; Allen 1986, 1987). Though there is a so-called Black Ivy League, the supporters of black higher education have usually assumed a more egalitarian stance than have white counterparts.

Black students prefer HBCUs for a host of interrelated personal reasons, one of which is the desire to attend a school where black students and black faculty members abound. Possessing a "consciousness of kind," they prefer a black ambiance. Some seek a special kind of academic program—for example, a strong black studies program. Others choose an HBCU because of its physical proximity to their homes, and still others opt for an HBCU for financial reasons. The chances of receiving funds for specialized programs, federal aid, or philanthropic help of some kind may be greater at a particular HBCU than they are elsewhere. Many require a school with an open admissions policy and/or one offering a remedial program. Some desire, or are pressured, to go where their parents went. Some feel an HBCU will enable them to build the friendship networks necessary for future work and residence in the black community. Many go to college where their friends go.

Differences between Black Student Populations on Black and White Campuses

HBCU proponents do not maintain that all black students should attend HBCUs, but they point out that comparisons between black students on black and white campuses indicate the necessity of HBCUs for many black students. To a large extent, HBCUs enroll students who otherwise might not be able to attend college because of social, financial, or academic barriers. Black college students differ from their white peers in that their parents are urban, are less educated, work at lower-status jobs, earn less, and/or are divorced or separated more often than are white students' parents (Nettles 1988). Despite social, economic, and educational disadvantages, however, black college students have aspirations similar to or higher than those of their white counterparts. The education level of blacks who attend white colleges is generally lower than is that of their white counterparts, and, on the average, they do not perform as well academically as do whites (Allen, Epp, and Haniff 1991).

Black students on HBCU campuses share backgrounds and opportunities that differ from those of their peers (black and white) on white campuses. They lag behind in terms of family socioeconomic status; high school grades; and university faculty, facilities, available academic majors, and opportunities for advanced study (Allen, Epp, and Haniff 1991). They also tend to have lower standardized test scores and weaker high school backgrounds than do their peers on white campuses (Thomas 1984). When the psychological development of black students on black and white campuses is compared, however, students on black campuses excel. Gurin and Epps (1975) found that black students at HBCUs possessed more positive self-images, stronger racial pride, and higher aspirations than did those on white campuses. Research studies by several scholars report that when HBCU students are compared to black students on white campuses, the former perform better academically, have a greater social involvement, and possess higher occupational aspirations (Allen 1992).

HBCU proponents are aware of the academic barriers faced by black students on white campuses. Black students at HBCUs do not face admission requirements that rely on culturally and economically biased standardized tests, faculties that are dominated by white middle-class males, and high tuition rates, along with inadequate financial aid programs, dog-eat-dog competition, and denial of cultural pluralism (Allen 1992).

CONCLUSION

Though the debate continues about the viability of HBCUs, those that are stronger (in terms of educational programs, accreditation, and size of student body) are likely to continue for the foreseeable future. Several interactive aspects support this forecast: (1) Many black educators and black community members want them; (2) many HBCUs have achieved a known success, particularly with first-generation college students; (3) masses of black youth in our society have serious educational deficiencies, and many of those fortunate enough to finish high school will require diversified academic programs within different types of college settings; (4) black students, for many reasons, perform better on HBCU campuses than on white campuses (evidently, their greatest higher education need remains a basic four-year college education); and (5) public high schools, particularly those in segregated neighborhoods, need HBCU-trained teachers; students in black colleges need HBCU-trained professors; and black communities need HBCU-trained leaders and professionals. In the following chapter, the issues involved in the HBCU controversy are further examined.

NOTE

1. The National Association for Equal Opportunity in Higher Education (NAFEO) was established in October 1969 as a voluntary, independent association by historically and predominantly black colleges and universities. It is organized to articulate the need for a higher education system where race, income, and previous education are not determinants of either the quantity or the quality of higher education. This association consists of 104 black private and public institutions that are committed to this ultimate goal in terms of their resources, both human and financial. Through the collective efforts of its membership, the association promotes the widest possible sensitivity to the complex factors involved in and the institutional commitment required for creating successful higher education programs for students representing groups victimized by racism and partially neglected by other economic, educational, and social institutions in the United States. To fulfill this goal, NAFEO is geared to the following priorities: (1) to provide a unified framework representing member institutions and similar institutions in order to continue as a viable body in American society; (2) to make the case for securing increased support from federal agencies, philanthropic foundations, and private sources; and (3) to increase the participation of blacks in the leadership of education organizations (NAFEO, *Institutional and Presidential Profiles,* 1991).

2

THE HISTORY OF BLACK HIGHER EDUCATION IN THE UNITED STATES

The current problems, values, curricula, viability, and future needs of HBCUs may be best understood within a broad historical context because they are, and have been, a part of the wider education system in the United States. The history of black higher education may be divided into five periods, all of which will be discussed in this chapter.

ANTEBELLUM PERIOD

In 1860, there were approximately 4 million black slaves and 27 million whites in the United States. Ninety-two percent of the blacks resided in the South, alongside 8 million whites (Berlin 1974, 397–98). Blacks, with a few exceptions, were restricted by law from obtaining a college education in the South and by social custom elsewhere in the United States. Before the Civil War, every southern state except Tennessee prohibited the formal instruction of slaves or free blacks. While many free blacks had attended school and a number of slaves were self-taught (with the aid of whites), over 90 percent of the South's adult black population was illiterate in 1860 (Foner 1988, 196).

Following the Revolutionary War (1783), free blacks established African churches, African private schools, and African fraternal organizations in both northern and southern cities where they could worship, educate their children, and protect themselves. Some of these schools were founded by free blacks, some few by whites, and some others by freed blacks after 1865. Some were integrated, and some few were supported by sympathetic whites. By the beginning of the nineteenth century, most were segregated, and many operated clandestinely, particularly in the South, because of overt white hostility and physical destruction. Self-designated African schools were located in Richmond, Virginia (as early as 1781); Washington, D.C. (1807); Cleveland, Ohio (1820); Philadelphia, Pennsylvania (1840); and Baltimore, Maryland (in the 1840s). Many of these church-related schools, as well as literary societies, fraternal organizations, and lending libraries, were supported by occasional aid from white churches; black and white personal donations; and funds raised at black bazaars, fairs, plays, lectures, church suppers, and church parades. The chief support was black (Quarles 1985; Berlin 1974, 70–78). Some founders and leaders of these schools and organizations were black ministers, many of whom assumed dominant positions in the black communities. These African institutions provided a sense of identity as well as a means of advancement for black youth and adults. Many whites disparaged these schools because the education of blacks was illegal in the South and because these schools were considered dangerous and revolutionary, some were integrated, and most were organized and operated by free blacks (a group of 488,000 in the United States in 1860, with 226,000 in the South). To southerners, free blacks comprised an anomalous group (Berlin 1974, 74–78).

With regard to higher education, only twenty-eight blacks received baccalaureate degrees from U.S. colleges and universities prior to the Civil War. Occasionally a few institutions such as Berea College in Kentucky (established in 1855) and Oberlin College in Ohio (1833) admitted a few blacks on a selective basis. However, many received other types of "higher education" that were recognized by whites during this period: apprenticeship training (primarily in law, medicine, and the ministry), non-degree courses in colleges and universities, teacher training, university training abroad, and self-education. Two historically black private colleges that still exist were founded prior to the Civil War: Lincoln University in Pennsylvania, established in 1854 by the Presbyterian church, and Wilberforce University in Ohio, established in 1856 by the Methodist Episcopal church. These institutions were the first two to remain in their original locations, to award baccalaureate degrees, and to develop completely into degree-granting institutions (Bowles, Decosta, and Tollett 1971, 20–21). Cheyney State College (Cheyney University of Pennsylvania since 1983) was established in the early 1830s as an elementary and high school for blacks, and runaway schools were created by a Quaker group in Philadelphia (Office for the Advancement of Public Black Colleges 1985).

On the other hand, white upper- and middle-class southerners had available a wide assortment of academies, private tutors, military schools, law schools, and public and private colleges (in the South) for their higher education needs—all, of course, completely segregated (Wilson 1989). The southern masses followed the educational stance of the white power structure in opposing any kind of formal education for blacks—and cared little about education themselves. In fact, the potential danger of educated blacks to southern society became a persistent phobia (intensified after the Revolutionary era) and remains a central theme in southern history. The rationale for not educating blacks rested on two contradictory tenets: (1) Blacks are basically intellectually inferior; and (2) educated blacks will "get out of their place" and inevitably compete with whites in the economic, political, and sexual spheres (Goodenow 1989). Unless this paradoxical position is understood, the opposition of southerners to black education is incomprehensible. Wilbur J. Cash's thesis of the "Savage Ideal," proclaimed in his book *The Mind of the South* (1941), sheds light on this conundrum (King 1980).

POSTBELLUM PERIOD (1865 TO ABOUT 1895)

Five million freed blacks lived in the United States in 1865, and 92 percent of all blacks resided in the South until 1900. Toward the close of the Civil War and throughout Reconstruction (1863–1877), the responsibility for providing instruction for the mostly illiterate former slaves was shared among the federal government through its Bureau of Refugees, Freedmen, and Abandoned Lands (Freedmen's Bureau); a number of church-related missionary societies in the North, and blacks themselves. This responsibility was implicit in President Lincoln's Emancipation Proclamation of September 22, 1862; the passage in 1862 of the Fourteenth Amendment, which assured "due process"; and the passage in 1870 of the Fifteenth Amendment, which extended the franchise to black males. The federal government established the Freedmen's Bureau in 1865 as an agency for the relief of freedmen, poor whites, and refugees. Together with private northern groups (which had been sending missionaries and teachers southward in the wake of the Union armies), it provided elementary education to blacks and to poor whites on a large scale. The Freedmen's Bureau did not operate schools directly, but coordinated and financed schools in cooperation with the educational activities of northern missionary societies (Foner 1988, 96–122).

The Northern Missionary Societies

Northern missionary groups took the first steps toward developing a formal system of schools and colleges for blacks. Following the lead of the American Missionary Association (AMA) in 1861, several benevolent societies sent missionaries into the South to uplift the freed slaves and their children through religion, education, and material assistance. The AMA alone was responsible for founding seven black colleges and thirteen normal schools between 1861 and 1870. Other missionary agencies and the Freedmen's Bureau developed similar schools. The missionaries mixed social, economic, and religious goals and endeavors: saving souls, educating minds, caring for bodies, and preparing the freed slaves for their responsibilities as new citizens. Though competing among themselves regarding classroom instruction and curriculum organization, they also faced pressures from southern whites; the establishment after 1877 of a system of laws disenfranchising blacks, limits on the growth of black education, and the emphasis on vocational education (rather than a classical or liberal education). In the 1890s, the missionaries advocated black equality and the establishment of a liberal arts education for blacks (Browning and Williams 1978).

In sum, northern benevolent societies, the Freedmen's Bureau, and the southern state governments (after 1865) funded black education during the Reconstruction period (Foner 1988, 98). During this radical Reconstruction era, education provisions were enacted into the new state constitutions with the aid of black legislators. For the first time in southern history universal education was recognized as a right of all citizens. State legislators passed laws that created the position of state superintendent of education in every southern state, provided for the training of teachers, and authorized taxes in support of education. Most states, in fact, set up school funds, although blacks frequently had to pay special taxes in addition to those required of all citizens (Dyer 1989).

The southern states were mandated by law after 1865 to provide a public school education for all citizens, in keeping with the Thirteenth, Fourteenth, and Fifteenth Amendments. However, the southern power structure (planters, bankers, mill owners, and professionals) hated this task and blocked it when possible. The tax base was meager, the population was dispersed over vast areas, and neither blacks nor poor whites were considered to have any rights to an education. White lower-class southerners were considered either "trash" or "rednecks," and blacks were seen as intellectually inferior (Foner 1988, 96–122; Roebuck 1984). Therefore, the development of a public school system was slow and full of conflict.

The Black Initiative

The initiative for black schooling, as mentioned earlier, lay primarily with the blacks themselves. Southern blacks from the beginning of the Civil War had made concentrated efforts to educate themselves, despite white hostility, via informal and formal church-linked organizations. After 1865, they formed a network of so-called sabbath schools (also called African schools like their earlier counterparts in the North) which were in session throughout the week. Classes in these and other private self-supported elementary African schools met in church basements, private homes, warehouses, pool rooms, and shacks (Foner 1988, 96–102). Neither the Freedmen's Bureau nor southern whites could understand this avidity for education. Blacks desired to take full advantage of their freedom; to them, education, religion, and property were the means to gain personal respect, economic security, and racial progress.

In this endeavor, blacks formed societies and raised money as craftsmen and as day laborers to establish their private schools. They purchased land, built schoolhouses, and paid teachers' salaries. By 1869, nearly 3,000 schools serving over 150,000 students, not including many evening and private schools operated by the joint efforts of missionary societies and blacks themselves, reported to the Freedmen's Bureau. By 1870, blacks by themselves had expended over $1 million on private school education (Foner 1988, 144).

Thus, the Freedmen's Bureau (which functioned until 1870), northern missionary societies, and the freedmen themselves laid the foundation for the major black colleges and universities, such as Fisk, Morehouse, and Dillard (Raboteau 1989). Additional federal intervention to ensure the expansion of educational, economic, social, and political opportunities for emancipated blacks during Reconstruction was augmented by the enactment of the Civil Rights Acts in 1866 and 1875 and by the radical Reconstruction programs constructed by Thaddeus Stevens. Consequently, blacks entered grade school and secondary education programs at a more rapid rate (Foner 1988, chap. 6).

The Private HBCUs

During the interval from 1865 to 1890, more than two hundred black private institutions were founded in the South with the help of northern churches and missionary groups (the American Missionary Association, as well as Baptists, Methodists, Presbyterians, and Congregationalists) and the Freedmen's Bureau. Many included in their titles "normal," "college," and "university," though they were largely elementary and secondary schools. These titles nonetheless designated (prophetically) the eventual purpose they were to serve. Founded with haste and limited financial backing, many ceased to operate following 1900. Blacks played a minor role in establishing, financing, and administering these institutions which were to become, in diminished numbers, "their schools" (Jencks and Reisman 1968).

These institutions, run and staffed by northern missionaries for black students, were different from other American colleges in terms of expectations and quality of students. Most were begun to teach former slaves to read and to train black clergymen. Most became de facto teachers colleges because of the small pool of clerical students and the great demand for black teachers. However, a number—including Atlanta,

Fisk, Howard, Leland, Lincoln, Shaw, and Wilberforce—initiated college departments by or before 1872 (DuBois and Dill 1910). Forty of the private HBCUs now in existence were established between 1865 and 1890.

From a historical standpoint, some of the most important of the church schools founded in this period include Atlanta University (1865) in Atlanta, Georgia; Fisk University (1866) in Nashville, Tennessee; Talladega College (1867) in Talladega, Alabama; and Tougaloo Institute (1869) in Tougaloo, Mississippi. All four of these were established by the AMA. The Arkansas Agricultural, Mechanical, and Normal College began as a branch Normal School (two-year curriculum) in 1873 at Pine Bluff, Arkansas. Morehouse College in Atlanta, Georgia, was originally established in 1867 as the Augusta Institute in Augusta, Georgia. Morehouse was initially supported by the American Baptist Home Mission Society which was also instrumental in founding Virginia Union University (1865) in Richmond, Virginia; Shaw University (1865) in Raleigh, North Carolina; and Benedict College (1870) in Columbia, South Carolina. The Methodist Episcopal church founded Rust College (1867) in Holly Springs, Mississippi, and Morgan State College (1866), now known as Morgan State University, in Baltimore, Maryland (Law and Clift 1981).

The financial support for these newly established schools came largely from three sources: the AMA, the Freedmen's Bureau, and black church groups. The AMA, a Congregationalist-supported association, worked with the freedmen in all sorts of schools during and after Reconstruction. By 1870, it had provided financial support to 170 black colleges. The Freedmen's Bureau provided funds for a wide range of educational opportunities for blacks and poor whites. For five years it attracted teachers from the North; cooperated with missionary and religious educational organizations; and assisted newly founded institutions, including Hampton, Fisk, Berea, and Atlanta University (Goodenow 1989).

The black church groups included the African Methodist Episcopal Church and the African Methodist Episcopal Church Zion. Their church-supported schools reflected the outlook of their Christian founders, and their overriding goal was a Christian education for all students. They did not consider females as candidates for the clergy, but otherwise they were welcome. Three were founded expressly for females, including Spelman Seminary in Atlanta. In addition to Christianity, these nineteenth-century colleges sought to convey to their students high aspirational levels, a sense of social concern and responsibility, and a feeling that they should be of service to others. Education was a tool for the building of a better world (Quarles 1985). One can see by reading current HBCU catalogs that these values and aspirations still exist. Black consciousness and identity have been emphasized since the civil rights movement beginning in the 1960s.

The Public HBCUs

Sixteen of the historically black public colleges now in existence were established in the period between 1866 and 1890. Only one of these, Cheney State College (1837) in Pennsylvania, was created prior to the Civil War. Howard University, named after General O. O. Howard, the commissioner of the Freedmen's Bureau, was started by the Freedmen's Bureau and chartered by Congress in 1867 in Washington, D.C. Hampton University, originally named Hampton Normal and Agricultural Institute, was founded in 1868 by the AMA and the Freedmen's Bureau at Hampton, Virginia. Beginning with elementary and secondary programs (and stressing vocational education), it offered a bachelor's degree by 1922 and commenced graduate programs in 1956. Today it is recognized as one of the most influential schools in the history of black education. One of the first colleges to accept Native Americans and to invite African students, Hampton has world-renowned endowed chairs, supports a dance company focusing on black folklore, provides training programs in Africa, and offers a variety of publications and conferences on issues important to blacks. The Hampton library houses an outstanding collection of materials on black history. A private, coeducational, independent (controlled by a single governing body) institution, it currently combines liberal arts, teacher education, and a vocational curriculum (Sharpe 1989). For realistic reasons, we strongly endorse this type of curriculum for most black students.

All but two public HBCUs were originally listed as normal or industrial schools, and none initially conferred baccalaureate degrees. Seventeen black public colleges now in existence were established under the second Morrill Act of August 30, 1890, which paved the way for the development of legally separated black and white public colleges in border and southern states. During the period from 1890 to 1899, one black public college was either planned or founded per year in each of the seventeen southern and border states. They were unequal and did not offer four-year college programs. The legacy of the industrial, mechanical, and agricultural education of blacks in the South stems from this period, and all of the schools established under the Morrill Act offered degrees later on. Liberal arts education remained the domain of the black private colleges (Law and Clift 1981; Blackwell 1981, 11–13).

Actually, the public HBCUs were created by the southern state governments for three reasons: to get millions of dollars in federal funds for the development of white land-grant universities, to limit black education to vocational training, and to prevent blacks from attending white land-grant colleges (Browning and Williams 1978; Baker 1989). Following Reconstruction (after 1877), southern legislatures enacted a host of segregation laws, including those that excluded blacks from all the white educational institutions. Yet the region had received federal funds for designated white institutions since the passage of the first Morrill Act in 1862. In order to prevent continued discrimination against blacks in public higher education, the federal government enacted the second Morrill Act of 1890, mandating that all states had to either provide separate educational facilities for blacks or admit them to existing colleges. All southern and border states opted to establish "separate but equal" agricultural and industrial schools for blacks in order to get federal money for white land-grant colleges. These facilities were never equal, and, consequently, public HBCUs have never come close to their white counterparts financially or academically (Jencks and Reisman 1968).

Summary

Private HBCUs in this period, though largely elementary and secondary schools, turned out 1,100 college graduates by 1895. Many of these persons became prominent and assumed black leadership roles then and during the early decades of the twentieth century (Bowles, Decosta, and Tollett 1971, 33–34). These institutions were made possible by an earlier education base established by the AMA, northern church groups, the Freedmen's Bureau, and blacks themselves. Without this base, which is frequently ignored in the literature, the HBCUs could not have existed. Following the Morrill Act of August 30, 1890, and the expansion of public school education in the South during and following Reconstruction, public universities for blacks were established in several southern and border states. Later on, these institutions were to compete for students with private HBCUs.

By law, for most of this period, blacks were not permitted to attend white public or private colleges and universities. This practice foreshadowed the "separate but equal" educational system legitimized by *Plessy v. Ferguson*, discussed in the next section. Some blacks attended and graduated from northern universities during this period, as they always had. But the southern private HBCUs provided the major source of higher education for blacks during this period (Bowles, Decosta, and Tollett 1971, 34). Southerners throughout this period remained hostile toward any form of formal education for blacks, and, after 1877, white state legislatures "legally" disfranchised, discriminated against, and segregated blacks in all walks of life. The Ku Klux Klan found black schools a ready target (Goodenow 1989).

SEPARATE, BUT EQUAL PERIOD (1896 TO 1953)

The Legally Segregated System

Throughout this period more than two-thirds of the blacks in the United States still resided in the South where their status may be understood in terms of the U.S. Supreme Court's "separate but equal" decision of 1896 (*Plessy v. Ferguson*). In essence, this Court decision sanctioned and legitimized the myriad of laws stipulating the separation of the races with respect to railroad coaches, schools, churches, cemeteries, drinking fountains, restaurants—and all places of public accommodation and amusement (Franklin 1975). With regard to education, revised state constitutions and enacted state laws legally prevented black and white students from attending the same schools.

To reiterate, the southern states actually began passing segregation laws after 1877 when southerners regained control of their legislatures by voting Republican party members out. The egalitarian governmental system that had been established between 1863 and 1877 was quickly dismantled. That is, much of what the Freedmen's Bureau had accomplished was negated when the control of the social system was returned to the individual southern states. Actually, the separate schooling of black and white children was practiced on a de facto basis in schools coordinated by the Freedmen's Bureau from 1863 through 1870 in order to placate southerners. By 1890, a thoroughly racially segregated order prevailed (Foner 1988, 565–70). Within this system state legislatures spent money for whites on longer school years, on lower student-teacher ratios, and on higher salaries for teachers. In effect, blacks in the south paid for schools for whites via taxes, and not the other way around. The more black citizens in a county, the greater benefits to white students (Ayers 1992, 420–21).

This legalized segregation led to an increased pattern of underfunding for black education, even though at the time white public school facilities and programs in the South were being vastly improved by so-called populist politicians—to placate pressure groups representing poor white voters. Black public colleges also received unequal funding from state treasuries, through federal land-grant provisions, and from other federal sources. Many public HBCUs remained controlled by whites who believed in black inferiority. Some black and white administrators ruled from a strong authoritarian position (Goodenow 1989).

Within this legal framework the segregated black public schools required black teachers, and the HBCUs emerged as the primary source for black teachers. The rapid expansion of black high schools in southern urban areas set in motion a supply-demand chain in which the availability of teaching positions, supported by the state treasuries, drew more black students into HBCUs to qualify themselves for teaching positions. This interdependence between the public high schools and the HBCUs ensured a viable system that survived despite the meager and unequal resources allotted to it by the southern states. In the southern states the rate of expenditure per black pupil amounted to about one-fourth of the rate of expenditure per white pupil during this period (Bowles, Decosta, and Tollett 1971, 37).

Professional positions other than teaching and preaching were not available to blacks in the South during this era. The HBCUs educated teachers and preachers. The public school teachers (predominately female) and students expanded the system and sent more students on to HBCUs to qualify as teachers. Unlike the private HBCUs, however, the public HBCUs, were dependent on the white state governments for support. Furthermore, there were no common guidelines or standards for these completely separated white and black schools and no interaction between them. Complete control was in the hands of stingy and discriminating state governments. School segregation and the unavailability of technical and professional jobs ruled out the participation of blacks, particularly males, in the mainstream of American life. In sum, the black public school system, the private HBCUs, and the public HBCUs (founded between 1890 and 1899 under the Morrill Act of 1890) composed a closed, segregated educational world that existed through 1953 (Law and Clift 1981).

The Great Curriculum Debate

The turn of this century was marked by heated debate among conservative and radical blacks over the merits of vocational versus liberal arts education. The argument was epitomized in the divergent philosophical, political, and pedagogical views of the era's major black leaders, Booker T. Washington and W.E.B. DuBois.

Washington, a freedman born a slave in 1856 on a small farm in Virginia, was a product of Hampton Institute and founder of Tuskegee Institute, the nation's premier black vocational school (Washington 1974). Rising from slavery to the status of eminent educator and race statesman, Washington proffered an accommodation to mounting black disfranchisement and segregation in the post-Reconstruction South: in return for promises of investment in black economic development, he advocated compromise with and conciliation toward white southerners, minimized the importance of civil rights, and preached black agrarianism and practical education. Washington viewed education mainly as a utilitarian enterprise aimed at self-sufficiency and economic prosperity. He publicly acknowledged black rights to classical training, but his approbation of college education was tenuous. Suspicious of the ambitions of college-trained blacks and skeptical of the value to the freedmen of liberal arts curricula, he often characterized higher education as a means to social prominence, rather than racial progress (Harlan 1972; 1983). Concerned with the elevation of the black peasantry from plantation peonage, Washington argued that (1) black youth should be educated to appreciate the value of manual labor, to understand that work is dignified and rewarding, and (2) students should be taught practical skills, that, when coupled with Christian character, would deliver them from serfdom in the "New South."

Born free in Massachusetts in 1868 and educated at Fisk, Harvard, and

Berlin, W.E.B. DuBois was a professor at Atlanta University, noted author, political activist, and longtime editor of *Crisis Magazine*, published by the National Association for the Advancement of Colored People (NAACP). He was a harsh critic of Washington's silent submission to civic inferiority, proclaiming that it was the duty of African-American leadership to oppose all apologies for injustice and abridgments of black civil rights (DuBois 1903). He also insisted on the education of black youth according to ability. As for Washington's disdain for the liberal arts and his fervor for vocational education as the final answer to the Negro problem, DuBois viewed them as tacit acceptance of the African American's permanent industrial and political servitude. The liberal arts, he argued, formed the basis for all education systems, including industrial training. In addition, the effectual progress of blacks collectively toward intellectual, social, and political equality depended on the broad training of black men, the top 10 percent of black intellectuals, who would lead the fight against racial segregation and discrimination. For DuBois, liberal arts education was the key to the African American's social regeneration, as well as the solution to racial conflict and cooperation (DuBois 1903).

Today DuBois is frequently idolized in a fashion that denigrates Washington, but both men contributed significantly to black education. Washington established the importance of the industrial arts to black progress in modern society, while DuBois founded among African Americans a strong liberal arts tradition that combined Afro-centric scholarship with social activism. They both failed, unfortunately, to join hands in seeking solutions to the pedagogical and political dilemma of blacks at a critical juncture in African-American history.

Broader Implications

The great curriculum debate has implications for the broader national problem of educating the young, as well as for the dynamics of black education. The U.S. education system has been shaped by the dialectics of two opposing goals: (1) academic opportunity, adequacy, and equality, geared toward meeting the needs of the masses of "C" students; and (2) academic excellence, geared toward finding and educating "A" and "B" students. Generally, the country has opted for an education system tailored to the needs of the masses at both the secondary and the college levels. On the other hand, provision has always been made for "excellence" within a number of prestigious and affluent private schools and a few highly ranked state universities—that is, for those with the financial means and talents necessary to the pursuit of whatever "excellence" is. In reality, the "C" student is frequently found within the crème de la crème citadels alongside the more talented. The corollary is that many talented students, particularly those from the lower classes, attend me-

diocre schools where they can afford to go, and many average students
with means attend prestigious schools. Intellectual capacity is not necessarily correlated with financial means, social class, or race. The United
States is a highly stratified class society, and the badge of social prestige
accompanying a degree from a prestigious university, as well as an ingrained, institutional academic snobbishness, inhere in its ambiguous education system.

Organized Philanthropy

When the Freedmen's Bureau was dissolved in 1870, the northern missionary organizations remained. Whites continued to see them as destroy-
ers of southern values because they supported black education. After
1900, however, the secular philanthropic agencies began to make a greater
impact than did the religious organizations. Between 1867 and 1902, a
number of philanthropic foundations funded by wealthy white northerners
joined the older missionary groups in serving the South. By 1910, these
secular foundations were more visible than were the missionary societies.
The most important, among others, were the General Education Board
of the Rockefeller Foundation, the Southern Education Board, the Julius
Rosenwall Fund, the Phelps-Stokes Fund, and the Carnegie Foundation—
all established between 1866 and 1918 (Moss 1989).

The Peabody Education Fund, established in 1967, provides scholarships for black and white students in the public school system who are
preparing themselves for teaching. The John E. Slater Fund was established in 1882 specifically for the education of blacks. During the first
thirty years, its funds were used to assist the private and denominational
colleges in training teachers and to help public schools provide industrial
and vocational training. Thereby many private HBCUs received financial
aid. Hampton Institute and Tuskegee University also received large
grants. In 1937, this fund merged with the Negro Rural School Fund. The
aforementioned General Education Board founded by John D. Rockefeller
in 1902, contributed $63 million to Negro education until 1960, most of
which went to black colleges. The Phelps-Stokes Fund, founded in 1910,
contributed to black schools, colleges, and universities and donated funds
for black college surveys. The Julius Rosenwall Fund, founded in 1917
and liquidated in 1948, contributed funds utilized in the areas of black
education, health and medical services, and fellowships. It also made
direct contributions to black private colleges for endowments, expenses,
fellowships, and scholarships (Bowles, Decosta, and Tollett 1971, 44–46;
Quarles 1985).

Initially, white southerners were suspicious of these secular philanthropic agencies, just as they had been of the earlier missionary societies.
After 1902, however, when the General Education Board began to dom-

inate southern philanthropy and heavily influence other philanthropic associations, southerners accepted this outside help (primarily for themselves). The General Education Board assured southerners that outside philanthropic funds would be used to improve white as well as black schools, that all northern philanthropic funds would be dispensed within, and in accordance with, the segregated southern system; and that stress would be placed on industrial, rather than collegiate and professional, training for blacks. In brief, peace was made with the white supremacy system in the South. Subsequently, from 1902 to 1960 (when the General Education Board's funds were exhausted), the bulk of the philanthropy monies expended went for programs that benefited whites exclusively (Moss 1989).

The United Negro College Fund

In the early 1940s, black private colleges faced a financial crisis. Sources of support were depleted because of the Great Depression and World War II. The black private colleges were the only private colleges in the South open to blacks, and they were then educating fully half of the blacks who were in any kind of southern college. Dr. Frederick D. Patterson, the third president of Tuskegee Institute, urged that the black private colleges pool their resources and make a united appeal to the national consciousness. The resulting United Negro College Fund (UNCF) conducted its first annual campaign in 1944 with twenty-seven participating colleges and universities. In this first annual campaign, $765,000 was collected, a sum three times larger than that raised by the individual colleges in separate campaigns in previous years.

The UNCF, the first educational organization to utilize cooperative fund raising in American education, is based in New York City. Each member college president is required to spend thirty days per year organizing and running local fund-raising campaigns. In 1948, a UNCF area office, with paid staff members, was established. In 1946, the National Alumni Council was organized, marking the first time the alumni of the different private HBCUs joined together to raise funds cooperatively for all their colleges. The students of the UNCF member institutions followed the example of the alumni in 1958 and organized the National Pre-Alumni Council of the UNCF.

Since the Supreme Court's 1954 decision in the case of *Brown v. Board of Education*, one of UNCF's major goals has been to convince the black community and the public of the continued need for HBCUs. Students and alumni of the UNCF institutions were among the top leaders of the civil rights movement, but they tried to balance the UNCF's sole mission of raising funds for black colleges with their sympathy for the objectives of the movement. The money UNCF raises comes from a variety of sources: corporations, private groups, churches, and alumni all over the United States.

The last twenty years have been spent in devising new plans to collect money. Whereas in 1972 the UNCF raised $11.1 million in its annual campaign, in 1982 it collected a total of $25.8 million. In April 1990, the UNCF announced Campaign 2000: An Investment in America's Future. Walter H. Annenberg, the former publisher of *TV guide* and ambassador to Great Britain, gave a challenge gift of $50 million, requiring the UNCF to raise $200 million to be eligible to receive this gift. Since this pledge, the UNCF has received commitments and gifts in the amount of $36 million from fourteen corporations and foundations, including a $10 million pledge from the General Motors Foundation and a $6 million gift from the Exxon Education Foundation. Other donations include $5 million from the Philip Morris Companies; $4 million from E. I. du Pont de Nemours and Company; $2 million each from Citicorp and the Samuel I. Newhouse Foundation; $1.5 million from PepsiCo; $1.2 million each from Warner-Lambert Company and Johnson and Johnson; and $1 million each from the Proctor and Gamble Fund, Texaco, and the Xerox Corporation. Other donations came from the Hallmark Corporate Foundation and the Joseph E. Seagram and Sons, Inc., Fund (Nicklin 1991).

Some donors specify the programs to which their gifts should go. For example, the Andrew W. Mellon Foundation awarded $2.6 million to the UNCF in 1990 for two programs to increase the number of minority faculty members in the arts and sciences. The first program will provide twenty fellowships in each of the next three years to undergraduate students at colleges that participate in the UNCF. Students will be paired with faculty members at their institutions in order to plan supervised research projects. The second program will provide twenty year-long fellowships for each of the next three years to faculty members in the humanities at four-year member colleges of the UNCF and the American Indian College Fund. The fellowships, averaging about $24,000 each, will allow faculty members to devote a year to working full-time on their dissertations. The Mellon Foundation has also awarded a three-year grant totaling $6.6 million, to be administered by the Southern Education Foundation, to help twenty private HBCUs build the basic arts and sciences collections in their libraries (McMillen 1990).

The UNCF claims that members of minority groups will represent more than one-third of the American labor force by 2000, based on estimates by the U.S. Bureau of Labor Statistics, and that blacks will make up two-thirds of that group (Fordyce and Kirschner 1990). Since its founding as a consortium of HBCUs in 1944, the UNCF has raised more than $690 million for the support of its member institutions. The obvious success of this organization attests to the continued support of private HBCUs by the black community and the wider public. Since 1944, the UNCF has played the major role in securing financial stability for the major black private colleges and universities. Member colleges must be private, fully accredited, four-year colleges or universities. During the UNCF's initial campaign in 1944, there were twenty-seven member institutions; today there are forty-one (see Table 2.1 for a list of current UNCF member institutions).

Surveys of Black Colleges

During this extended period, many black and white educators and laypersons, though aware of black colleges, did not know what they were doing or the quality of the education they were providing. Several interest groups suggested college surveys in order to determine the educational content (industrial or liberal arts) and the quality of education existing in black colleges. Seven surveys were conducted between 1910 and 1942, two by W.E.B. DuBois, one by the Phelps-Stokes Foundation, and four by the federal government. These investigations documented the high quality of some HBCUs, particularly that of a number of private liberal arts colleges found to deserve accreditation along with white counterparts (for example, among others, Fisk, Morehouse, and Spelman). In addition to bringing national recognition to the HBCUs, these surveys fostered additional development measures. For example, they furnished individual colleges with specific recommendations for improvements and paved the way for accreditation in some cases (Fleming 1984, 6–10). The Southern Association of Colleges and Schools (SACS), founded in 1895, has worked since 1928 with HBCUs in the South in conducting surveys, establishing academic ranking mechanisms, upgrading college programs, and formalizing accreditation procedures (Bowles, Decosta, and Tollett 1971, 48–49).

Enrollment and Improvements

In 1953, the combined undergraduate enrollment in forty-seven of the black private four-year colleges was 24,173, which represented approximately 39 percent of the students enrolled in all HBCUs. By the end of this period, black private colleges were enrolling fewer students than were black public colleges. By 1930, the great majority of HBCUs had developed into full-fledged colleges, had dropped non-college courses, and were requiring all entrants to have high school diplomas. In 1953, the total enrollment in thirty-three black public four-year colleges was 37,251, comprising 61 percent of all black students enrolled in HBCUs. All regular students attending these full-fledged, public, degree-granting institutions had been admitted as high school graduates. Both private and public colleges during this period improved in terms of preparation of faculty, library holdings, curricular offerings, science laboratories, physical plant

Table 2.1
United Negro College Fund Member Institutions, 1990 (N = 41)

```
--------------------------------------------------------------------
|          Barber-Scotia College                                   |
|          Benedict College                                        |
|          Bennett College*                                        |
|          Bethune-Cookman College*                                |
|          Claflin College                                         |
|          Clark Atlanta University*                               |
|          Dillard University*                                     |
|          Edward Waters College                                   |
|          Fisk University*                                        |
|          Florida Memorial College                               |
|          Houston-Tillotson College*                             |
|          Interdenominational Theological Center*                |
|          Jarvis Christian  College                              |
|          Johnson C. Smith University                            |
|          Knoxville College*                                     |
|          Lane College*                                          |
|          LeMoyne-Owen College*                                  |
|          Livingstone College*                                   |
|          Miles College                                          |
|          Morehouse College*                                     |
|          Morris Brown College*                                  |
|          Morris College                                         |
|          Oakwood College                                        |
|          Paine College                                          |
|          Paul Quinn College*                                    |
|          Philander Smith College*                               |
|          Rust College                                           |
|          Saint Augustine's College                              |
|          Saint Paul's College                                   |
|          Shaw University*                                       |
|          Spelman College*                                       |
|          Stillman College                                       |
|          Talladega College                                      |
|          Texas College*                                         |
|          Tougaloo College*                                      |
|          Tuskegee Univeristy*                                   |
|          Virgina Union University*                              |
|          Voorhees College                                       |
|          Wilberforce University                                 |
|          Wiley College                                          |
|          Xavier University                                      |
--------------------------------------------------------------------
```

Source: The National Association for Equal Opportunity in Higher Education (NAFEO), *Fact Book on Blacks in Higher Education and in Historically and Predominantly Black Colleges and Universities*, Vol. 1, p. 175 (1991).

facilities, organization and administration, and financial base (Bowles, Decosta, and Tollett, 1971, 54–60).

By 1931, a group of thirty-one black colleges had received the approval of the American Medical Association to provide premedical courses, and SACS had agreed to establish procedures for the accreditation of black institutions. The 1930s also marked the beginning of a significant increase in graduate work at HBCUs. On the broader academic front, black literacy had risen steadily. The education level of black soldiers in World War II was markedly higher than that of their counterparts in World War I. Black education on all levels benefited directly from the Servicemen Act of 1944 (the G.I. Bill of Rights), which provided education allowances for veterans (Quarles 1985).

On the other hand, during this period the public education system for southern blacks was still beset with unequal and inferior facilities and with poorly trained teachers and administrators (relative to white counterparts), particularly in rural areas. White hostility toward black education continued unabated, and whites set up a busing system that transported their children away from blacks (Goodenow 1989).

NAACP Court Cases

In the 1930s, the NAACP carried out an education desegregation campaign, led primarily by lawyers trained at Howard University, that ended the virtual acceptance of the "separate but equal" doctrine. Between 1945 and 1954, this "separate but equal" doctrine was overturned first in graduate and professional education and then in public elementary and secondary education by *Brown v. Board of Education*, which is discussed in the next section. Through a series of successful court cases, the NAACP by 1951 had established the right of blacks, under certain conditions, to attend historically white public graduate and professional schools in the South.

To combat the assault against the "separate and unequal" policy that resulted from *Plessy v. Ferguson* (1896), several of the seventeen southern and border states either established "separate but equal" professional schools for black students or gave out-of-state tuition grants for them to study elsewhere. These measures were contrived to circumvent blacks efforts to gain admission to white public institutions. By 1933, black college graduates were increasingly demanding access to professional schools in the South. During that year, 97 percent of the approximately 38,000 black students enrolled in colleges were studying at HBCUs (Law and Clift 1981).

The NAACP and the NAACP Legal Defense and Educational Fund (LDEF) between 1935 and 1954 brought five cases before the U.S. Supreme Court that addressed the problem of equal educational opportunity for black Americans: (1) *University of Maryland v. Murray*, 165 Md. 478 (1935), (2) *Missouri ex rel. Gains v. Canada* (1938), (3) *Sipuel v. Board of Regents of the University of Oklahoma* (1948), (4) *Swett v. Painter* (1950), and (5) *McLauren v. Oklahoma Regents* (1950). The *Murray* case attacked both the principle of "separate but equal" and the policy of out-of-state tuition grants to black students. Murray had applied to the University of Maryland Law School, but was offered out-of-state tuition. He refused. The Supreme Court ruled that because no separate school of law existed for blacks in Maryland, and because attending a law school outside Maryland would result in undue hardship on Murray, the University of Maryland had to admit him to its law school. The state was ordered to desist from compelling its black students who desired graduate and professional education to accept out-of-state tuition grants in lieu of admission to state-supported graduate or professional schools. In the *Gains* case from Missouri, the Court ruled that the "separate but equal" position could not fully satisfy the demands of dual protection, that only actual identity of facilities and shared use of the same public institutions would suffice. In the *Swett* case, the court ruled that the makeshift facilities at the all-black Texas Southern University in Houston were unequal and unacceptable. Therefore, the University of Texas Law School was ordered to accept Swett (Blackwell 1981, 10–15).

These cases, though helpful, did not address the fundamental question underlying *Plessy v. Ferguson*—that is, whether state-mandated racially separate educational facilities and programs are inherently unequal. In any event, Guy Johnson estimated that, during 1952–1953, twenty-two white public institutions in the South enrolled 453 blacks for the regular academic year and 907 for the summer session. Blacks were also enrolled in nine white theological seminaries in the South during this period. An estimated 45,000 to 50,000 black students were attending northern institutions in 1953 (Johnson 1964).

Summary

In this most racially segregated era in the history of the United States, a separate, unequal, and isolated, but viable, education system was established in the South, consisting of black public schools, four-year private HBCUs, and four-year public HBCUs. Funding came from state support of the public schools and public HBCUs and from the donations of blacks and sympathetic whites, organized philanthropic sources, and the United Negro College Fund. Legal support was furnished by the NAACP, which ended the virtual acceptance of the "separate but equal" doctrine by the end of the period. Although several college surveys led to academic improvements and accreditation procedures, southern white hostility to the public education of blacks continued.

Segregation made this interdependent educational world necessary, but it did not ensure its success. Black educators and members of the black community were somewhat instrumental in developing this segregated educational enterprise, and by the end of the period, they controlled many of the private HBCUs and exerted some degree of influence over some black public schools and colleges and universities.

DESEGREGATION PERIOD (1954 TO 1975)

Brown v. Board of Education and the Civil Rights Act of 1964

On May 17, 1954, the U.S. Supreme Court ruled in the case of *Brown v. Board of Education of Topeka, Shawnee County, Kansas*, that the principle of "separate but equal" was unconstitutional. On May 24, 1954, the Court rendered three more decisions against racial segregation in higher education. Racial segregation thenceforth, in higher education as well as in public elementary and secondary education, was held unconstitutional. These Supreme Court decisions were followed by a disruptive and violent transitional interval (1955–1965), marked by massive southern resistance in the form of demurrers, stalling, and physical force. These delaying tactics were countered by black marches and demonstrations, riots, and the escalation of federal intervention to enforce court-ordered desegregation. Even then, significant desegregation did not occur until after passage of the Civil Rights Act of 1964, which empowered the U.S. attorney general to bring lawsuits on behalf of black plaintiffs and prohibited, under Title VI, the spending of federal funds (appropriated under the Elementary and Secondary Education Act of 1965 and the Higher Education Act of 1965) in segregated schools and colleges. In *Alexander v. Holmes County Board of Education* (1969), the U.S. Supreme Court ordered that all school segregation be ended immediately. The legal fight over the desegregation of schools in the South had spanned a period of fifty years, 1930–1980 (Synnott 1989).

The Higher Education Act of 1965 and *Adams v. Richardson*

Desegregation and equality of opportunity for students in higher education were greatly enhanced by the Higher Education Act of 1965 and the 1973 *Adams v. Richardson* decision. The Higher Education Act made basic education opportunity grants (BEOGs) and a variety of other financial aid programs available to disadvantaged students, which greatly increased minority enrollment in the U.S. colleges and universities. This legislation included Title III—Strengthening Developing Institutions—which was interpreted as a direct intercession favoring black colleges and universities and as a federal commitment to the survival and enhancement of HBCUs. The term "developing institutions" was incorporated into the legislation in an apparent effort to avoid designating black higher education institutions as the primary recipients of the federal assistance made available in the funding. The areas eligible for government subsidies under this act were faculty and student exchanges, faculty improvement programs, curriculum improvement, student services, a visiting scholars program, and administrative improvements. The act also identified the fundable improvement techniques that institutions could utilize—for example, cooperative arrangements with established colleges and universities and membership in consortium agreements (Thomas and McParttland 1984).

The Title III terminology provided a generic description of the HBCUs. The targeted institutions were characterized as facing problems threatening their survival, as being isolated from the mainstream of academic life, and as having strong desire and potential for a greater strength in academic accomplishment. Virtually all the HBCUs, as well as some other non-black colleges and universities, qualified for assistance under the Title III definition of a "developing institution." Although the terms "black higher education institution" and "developing institution" have not been legislatively synonymous, the Title III descriptions have become more or less conventional in reference to HBCUs. Likewise, the Higher Education Act of 1965, which provided for student financial aid programs, gave preferential treatment to "disadvantaged youth," which was interpreted as referring primarily to young blacks (Spearman 1981).

In 1970, the NAACP Legal Defense and Educational Fund brought a lawsuit (*Adams v. Richardson*) against the Department of Health, Education, and Welfare (HEW) for not enforcing Title VI of the 1964 Civil Rights Act against states that operated dual segregated public systems of higher education. Title VI of the Civil Rights Act prohibits the allocation of federal funds to segregated public schools. In July 1977, the court ordered HEW's Office for Civil Rights to develop guidelines that states with segregated systems would use when preparing desegregation plans required for compliance with Title VI. The ten states initially identified in the *Adams* decision as maintaining dual segregated systems were Arkansas, Florida, Georgia, Louisiana, Maryland, Mississippi, North Carolina, Oklahoma, Pennsylvania, and Virginia. Other states that have been site-visited since the *Adams* decision include Alabama, Kentucky, Ohio, South Carolina, Tennessee, and Texas. Though a de facto dual system of higher education still exists in the South, there has been extensive desegregation of white public colleges and universities, which has facilitated the increased presence of blacks in higher education. A substantial part of the enrollment of blacks in predominately white colleges has been in the public two-year-college sector.

The *Adams* court, in addition to mandating enforcement of desegregation laws, stipulated that states must not only achieve a better racial mix of students, faculty, and staff in public colleges (i.e., blacks on white campuses and whites on black campuses), but also increase the access and retention of minorities at all levels of higher education. The court acknowledged the role of black colleges in promoting greater educational access and higher retention rates for black students and stated that desegregation and equity efforts by predominantly white colleges should not be accomplished at the expense of or detriment to the traditional black colleges (Thomas and McParttland 1984).

Actually, the extensive desegregation of many southern school districts and colleges and universities resulted as a consequence of several combined factors: federal courts' civil rights decisions, black marches and demonstrations, federal troop action, the threat of withdrawal of federal educational grants to southern institutions, and the tying of federal education funding to nondiscriminatory practices (e.g., basic educational opportunity grants, supplemental educational opportunity grants, state student incentive grants, college work study grants, guaranteed student loans, and national direct student loans). As in the case of the second Morrill Act of 1890, federal law and money talked. It is likely that had the southern region and its school districts and colleges and universities been financially strong, the desegregation battle would have been fiercer and even more protracted. Desegregation in general has been much more successful in white colleges and universities than it has been in HBCUs because the proportion of black students enrolled in white institutions is much higher than that of white students enrolled in HBCUs. Consequently, the HBCUs, during this period, experienced enrollment declines. Despite desegregation trends, southerners of all ages have never fully accepted school desegregation psychologically at any educational level. And this does not bode well for the future of race relations in other life spheres.

Responses to Desegregation

Blacks in general accepted the *Brown* decision, as well as subsequent federal education acts, as the beginning of further acceptance of blacks and their institutions (Cohen 1974; West 1972). Some educators, however, speculated that integration would mean participation in state systems reorganized to offer services to the majority, that services designed specifically for black students would disappear, and that the existing pattern of discrimination could be perpetuated under the guise of equality (Jenkins 1952; Johnson 1954; Myers 1987). Despite these doubts, court desegregation orders brought some immediate benefits for black colleges, such as funding for physical improvements, increased financial aid for students, and a subsequent increase in student enrollments (National Center for

Education Statistics 1972; Southern Education Foundation 1972). During this period, the federal government and private philanthropic organizations commissioned fact-finding studies to gain more knowledge about black colleges in terms of physical plants, curricula, students and faculty, and financial characteristics and to develop recommendations for strengthening these colleges. The findings of these studies dramatized the black college problems and outlined the governmental support needed. These findings served as a basis for governmental funding in the late sixties and early seventies (Thompson 1973).

With the encouragement of Office for Civil Rights within HEW, states adopted several techniques to desegregate schools and to increase the enrollment of black students at white institutions and white students at historically black colleges. The goals in this period were to remove the racially identifiable symbols in order to encourage integration and to stimulate the assimilation of black students into predominately white schools. The fact that the logical end of this policy could be the elimination of black colleges was overlooked by many—though some were concerned about this possibility (Myers 1987). Furthermore, some educators claim that integration in higher education has been marred by (1) high attrition rates, which make white institutions revolving doors for too many black students; (2) the serious cultural damage that has been done to black students in the name of the best interests of all students; and (3) the increased psychological and physical endangerment to black students (Smith and Baruch 1981). The so-called goal to enroll many white students in HBCUs has failed for the most part. Though white students are accepted at all black schools, many do not feel welcomed there (Hacker 1992, 157–58).

Enrollment Patterns

Paradoxically, as black student enrollments in white colleges increased dramatically in the 1960s, the HBCUs were being strengthened. The federal government and several private foundations, following a series of black college surveys and studies, increased their financial aid to HBCUs. Moreover, strong recommendations and plans were made to further increase this aid in the future. In addition, SACS began admitting HBCUs to membership in 1957 (Fleming 1984, 7–15). Some HBCU supporters reported during this period that integration might bring to an end certain services heretofore provided by HBCUs, thus permitting discrimination to be continued under the guise of equality (Browning and Williams 1978). This concern has not been substantiated.

As has been pointed out, segregation barriers had made it virtually impossible for blacks to attend white colleges in the South prior to 1954.

Furthermore, few northern schools enrolled many blacks during this interval because of social custom, social stigma, and the belief in blacks' inferior intellectual capacity (Gurin and Epps 1975). In fact, prior to 1954, over 90 percent of black students (equaling approximately 100,000 in 1954) were educated in HBCUs. To reiterate, contemporaneous estimates indicated that less than 20 percent of black college-going students attended HBCUs in 1987 (American Council on Education, *Minorities in Higher Education*, 1987). This drastic shift in enrollment may have resulted in part from the movement of blacks out of the South to northern cities. The percentage of blacks residing in the South declined from 77 percent in 1940 to 53 percent in 1968 (U.S. Bureau of Census 1972). Probably more important, once blacks gained the opportunity and the legal right to attend white schools, they took them forthrightly.

Yet the enrollment shift to white schools could change. Over half of all blacks still reside in southern and border states. College students have a tendency to enroll near their homes, and, in any case, HBCUs still attract many students from outside the South. HBCU administrators report to the authors that many black students attending southern HBCUs are from outside the South. Moreover, northern blacks maintain very strong roots in the South and frequently urge their children to return there for higher education. Many parents return themselves at or before retirement. More important, there is evidence of a shift by black students from white schools to HBCUs, which will be commented on later.

Perhaps there is some truth in the ingrained southern folk belief that most southern migrants, black or white, eventually return to the South by choice or in a box (coffin). Southerners share this belief because of statistical data and personal observation. While the reason for this phenomenon is emotional, irrational, and inexplicable, population patterns, in fact, show that since 1975 blacks have been returning to the South from all other regions (Roseman 1989). This migration pattern may result in an increase in HBCU enrollments, depending on black students' disenchantment with white colleges and universities. HBCUs, however, will probably not regain the once predominate student enrollments they once had.

In any event, blacks are now able to enroll in all southern colleges and universities, and some of these institutions actively recruit black students for a variety of reasons—including the desire to secure increased federal funding. Recruits are usually of two kinds: those with comparatively high SAT scores, and athletes. HBCUs have always accepted white students, but they have not actively recruited them, and, with a few exceptions, few whites attend southern black colleges. These exceptions include Bluefield State and West Virginia State in West Virginia and Lincoln University in Missouri, where white students were in the majority as early as 1970 (Bowles, Decosta, and Tollett 1971, 80). Now white students account for

13.2 percent of the enrollment at Alabama A&M, 16.8 percent at Georgia's Albany State, and 17.3 percent at the University of Arkansas at Pine Bluff—all predominantly black colleges (Hacker 1992, 158).

Black Athletes

The widespread recruitment (throughout the United States) of black athletes who are sorely unprepared for college is counterproductive for all concerned: the students themselves, other students in the recruiting institution, the faculty, and the wider community, particularly the black community. Many flunk out, many drop out, many are forced out following their playing eligibility time, many never graduate, and some graduate functionally illiterate because of the support of faculty members who feel pressured by college administrators to pass them. In short, many are used as "sports mercenaries." Few reach the pros, and many who do are educationally unprepared to do anything else following a brief sports career. They would fare far better at HBCUs (Edwards 1970). Moore and Wagstaff (1974) pointed out that black athletes are exploited by some white colleges, who illegally pay for play. Edwards, in a personal communication with the authors in July 1990, claimed that the athlete situation he researched in *The Revolt of the Black Athlete* (1970) is worse now than it was then.

A 1989 survey by *The Chronicle of Higher Education* (Lederman 1991) disclosed that football and basketball players in the nation's big-time college sports programs are more than six times as likely as are other students to have received special treatment in admissions. For example, 27 percent of the football and basketball players admitted in the fall of 1989 to universities in Division I-A of the National Collegiate Athletic Association (NCAA) were characterized by their institutions as "special-authority admissions." The NCAA defines special-authority admissions as students who are accepted despite their failure to meet the colleges' regular standards. The special-authority admissions practice was not limited to football and basketball players. Approximately 18 percent of all athletes admitted in 1989 were "special admits." Therefore, athletes have a higher chance to receive special admission consideration than non-athletes.

Colleges that make intercollegiate sports a money-making business recruit black athletes who barely graduate from high school. One survey of the NCAA member institutions with the biggest sports budgets disclosed that 56 percent of their basketball players and 30 percent of their football players were black. These colleges do not recruit black students for any reason other than athletics. Among the 291 schools in the NCAA's Division I-A, blacks average only 4 percent of their student bodies. At some schools, black athletes are virtually the only black students enrolled.

Another NCAA study revealed that almost 75 percent of black Division I-A athletes failed to ever graduate; the system simply uses student athletes for as many seasons as possible. In a recent year, over 90 percent of the students barred from playing because of academic standing were black. Among black players currently on NCAA rosters, less than half have an SAT score of 700. Most black students recruited as athletes in the schools in this study are semiprofessionals and have never been students in the general sense of that term (Hacker 1992, 154–55).

Colleges widely disagree about the policies and standards that they should adopt to admit athletes. To some critics, the special admissions process results in the admission of underprepared athletes more frequently than underprepared non-athletes. Some critics propose that special admissions for athletes be eliminated altogether. The authors agree with this recommendation because colleges and universities exist to provide education, not to develop professional athletes. Some educators in higher education opt for the special admission of athletes and point out that colleges provide special admissions for all kinds of students (e.g., musicians and artists, members of minority groups, and children of alumni) (Lederman 1991). The authors take the position that these other special admits are used as a subterfuge to justify the real goal—the recruitment of semiprofessional athletes—and that the increasing emphasis on intercollegiate athletes (particularly on football and basketball) and the attendant recruiting policies weaken academic standards for all and harm black students.

MODERN PERIOD (1975 TO THE PRESENT)

The Consequences of the *Adams* Case

Since Judge Pratt's 1973 ruling in the *Adams* case, the views of HBCU supporters about this desegregation case have changed. Initially, HBCU officials thought that under this ruling the states would seek to close the black institutions as a means of promoting desegregation. As mentioned before, Judge Pratt subsequently ruled that states could not meet desegregation goals by closing black colleges, that states' desegregation plans had to include yardsticks to measure the improvement of black colleges' facilities and academic programs, and that states had to make these colleges desirable institutions for both black and white students. Though officials at black colleges maintained that the states did not follow through on all of these measures, the court-required plans did lead to significant progress. For example, state and federal funding to HBCUs has increased; a system of accountability has been created within the Department of Education (which was established in 1980) for the treatment of black colleges; civil rights groups have brought new lawsuits to enforce rulings in the *Adams* case; powerful white institutions have been prevented from taking over HBCUs by mergers; proposals to raise HBCU admission standards or graduation requirements have been blocked; and enrollments of black students on white campuses have increased, but the proportion of black students attending HBCUs has decreased (Jaschik, "Court's Desegregation Rulings," 1988).

In December 1987, Judge John H. Pratt of the U.S. District Court for the District of Columbia dismissed the *Adams* case, which had served as a linchpin for efforts to desegregate colleges in eighteen states. Judge Pratt stated that the civil rights organizations that had pursued the case no longer had enough of a legal interest to give them the right to continue the lawsuit. He also found it "entirely speculative" that the threat of a cutoff of federal funds would lead states to change. The *Adams* decision required the Office for Civil Rights (now part of the Department of Education) to obtain and monitor desegregation plans from states it determined were operating racially segregated universities and colleges. Federal aid was to be cut off from those higher education systems that did not satisfactorily prepare and carry out their plans. The desegregation plans, as mentioned earlier, set goals for recruiting minority students and faculty members to predominately white colleges and universities and for improving the facilities and programs at public black colleges (Jaschik, "Court's Desegregation Ruling," 1988). In 1988 and 1989, the Department of Education declared that seven of the states (Arkansas, Georgia, Missouri, North Carolina, Oklahoma, South Carolina, and West Virginia) were no longer operating segregated systems and scaled back its oversight of those systems. In seven other states (Delaware, Florida, Kentucky, Maryland, Pennsylvania, Texas, and Virginia), desegregation plans have expired, although the Department of Education has yet to certify the states' systems as completely desegregated. Such rulings are expected (Jaschik 1990).

Responses to the Dismissal of *Adams* Case

The states' response is that the federal government's withdrawal from enforcing the desegregation plan is long overdue because the states are better able than are their federal counterparts to develop plans for attracting minority students and faculty members to higher education. The nation's black colleges, however, have asked the federal court to reverse the dismissal of the *Adams* case and to shift the focus to the needs of public black colleges. The Department of Education fought and lost an appeal of the dismissal in 1990, and its Office for Civil Rights has declined to comment on the new NAFEO strategy, which appears to be pluralism. Some educators fear that, as a result of the dismissal, HBCUs will be closed or merged with more powerful white institutions; HBCUs will lose substantial and fair state financial support; and white legislators will favor financial support for white institutions, rather than for their black competitors. To avert the foregoing problems, supporters of black colleges say that they will have to become more politically astute and spend more time lobbying in state legislatures (i.e., exert black political muscle in black and white communities and among black and white legislators). Some state officials responded to the dismissal of the *Adams* case by saying that they would not change their educational desegregation policies. Department of Education officials have also pledged to continue to monitor state desegregation efforts. Others maintain that dismissal of the *Adams* case does not negate the legality of desegregation (Jaschik, "Court's Desegregation Ruling," 1988).

Some HBCU officials have responded to the dismissal with a separatist strategy. They view desegregation efforts as a "race mixing" policy (i.e., a policy that tries to attract black students and faculty member to predominately white institutions and vice versa) that has failed because those supervising predominately white colleges and statewide systems have made success impossible. The people in charge of desegregation were the same people who were in charge of segregation. Such efforts, the separatists claim, should be deemphasized and replaced with efforts to improve HBCUs because these are the only institutions that have consistently devoted themselves to educating black students. To them, desegregation has no value in and of itself. Moreover, the unequal education of blacks can go on as efficiently in desegregated schools as in segregated schools. These separatists claim that they initially supported desegregation plans because they thought such plans would help HBCUs obtain better facilities and equipment. Furthermore, separatists think that black colleges have lost some of their focus by trying to attract white students and, as a result, have mimicked what they cannot become. In brief, the separatists maintain that HBCUs should stress their unique roles, such as providing unprepared black students with high-quality remedial programs and all black students with a comfortable learning environment, including many black role models. On the other hand, some NAFEO supporters fear that the separatist philosophy might hurt black colleges politically. They maintain that HBCUs should press predominately white colleges to educate some black students (Jaschik, "Black Colleges," 1988). In spite of the dismissal of the *Adams* case, many black educators are primarily interested in the preservation and improvement of HBCUs and the complete desegregation of white colleges and universities.

Educational Pluralism

Several events that occurred in the late 1970s and 1980s shifted U.S. educational policy from the strict integration of colleges and universities to the encouragement of racially identifiable black colleges as part of the pluralistic system of higher education. The U.S. District Court for the District of Columbia directed the Office for Civil Rights to develop guidelines for states whereby the burden of desegregation would not fall disproportionately on historically black colleges. The historically black colleges were to be preserved and strengthened. The persistent underrepresentation of blacks in most managerial, policy-making, and professional positions (which required a college degree) and the knowledge that HBCUs are (and had been) graduating professionals at a rate all out of proportion to their numbers demonstrated the need for the improvement of all HBCUs. Furthermore, the increasing difficulties blacks were encountering on white campuses in the seventies and eighties (commented on later) resulted in increasing enrollments at HBCUs, which served as havens for black students deprived and/or rejected elsewhere. Moreover, the position taken by the executive, legislative, and judicial branches of the federal government has reinforced the acceptability and viability of HBCUs. The U.S. Supreme Court has declared constitutional the use of race-specific remedies to address the present effects of past legally enforced segregation. Therefore, to reiterate, it is constitutional to target special assistance to HBCUs.

Federal Policies Affecting HBCUs

President Reagan, in Executive Order 12320 on the historically black colleges, targeted HBCUs for special attention. In the reauthorization of the Higher Education Act of 1986, Congress passed the Historically Black College Act as Part B of Title III. This act authorizes $100 million exclusively for the historically black colleges. Under this act, Congress approved $50.7 million in the 1987 fiscal year, with at least $350,000 going to each eligible historically black college.

President Bush, in Executive Order 12677 of April 28, 1989, pertaining to HBCUs, mandated several actions intended to advance the development of human potential, to strengthen the capacity of HBCUs, to provide quality education, and to increase opportunities to participate in and benefit from federal programs. This executive order calls for the establishment in the Department of Education of an advisory commission, the President's Board of Advisors on HBCUs, which will supervise the annual development of a federal program designed to increase the participation of HBCUs in federally sponsored programs and provide advice on how to increase the role of the private sector in strengthening HBCUs. Particular emphasis will be given to providing technical, planning, and development advice to HBCUs, with the goal of ensuring the long-term viability of these institutions (*Federal Register* May 2, 1989, 54:83). Some critics claim that neither President Bush's executive order, nor a similar one signed by President Reagan, has proved to be very helpful because many of the federal agencies that could be of assistance to HBCUs—such as the Department of Defense, the Department of Health and Human Services, and the National Science Foundation—have not lent substantial assistance (Blumenstyle 1989).

In 1991, the Bush administration initiated a controversial plan that would change the way federal agencies support HBCUs. Under this plan, the HBCUs would be divided into several categories based on their missions and programs. Federal agencies planning to work with HBCUs could then focus attention and money on the category of college appropriate to the agency's needs. For example, a federal agency planning to support research could hold a competition that would be open only to black colleges designated as research institutions. Administration officials say private foundations could also use the classification system in deciding where to donate their funds. Many HBCU presidents oppose this idea, pointing out that it would allow federal government agencies and private foundations to shift money to a small subset of HBCUs (i.e., those already among the most wealthy), while overlooking other institutions. In brief, they fear a federally created "caste system" of HBCUs. This plan, critics say, would make the rich institutions richer and poor institutions poorer (Jaschik 1991).

United States v. Fordice

In June 1992, the U.S. Supreme Court's majority ruling in *United States v. Fordice* vacated the decision of the U.S. Court of Appeals for the Fifth Circuit that Mississippi had met its affirmative obligation to dismantle its prior dual system of higher education. The Court then remanded the case for further proceedings to determine the extent to which the state had violated the U.S. Constitution and Title VI by not meeting this obligation. This is probably the most important Supreme Court ruling affecting the education of blacks since the 1954 *Brown v. Board of Education* decision. In setting forth the test to be used in deciding whether a state has dismantled the discriminatory remnants of its former dual system, the Supreme Court transformed the nature of judicial and political battles affecting higher education in nineteen southern and border states. The decision rests on the position that adoption and implementation of race-neutral policies alone are not sufficient to demonstrate that a state has fulfilled its obligation to dismantle its prior dual system. College attendance (ostensibly) by choice and not by assignment does not mean that a race-neutral admissions policy has cured a system's constitutional violations; in a system based on choice, many other factors determine student attendance. Therefore, the implication that merely eliminating laws barring black students from white colleges and showing a "good faith" effort to desegregate are not enough.

The Court noted that several aspects of Mississippi's former *de jure* segregated system had survived and thus were constitutionally suspect. While stating that the court of appeals on remand should examine all policies of the university system, the Court highlighted four of the present system's policies that constitute remnants of the former system.

1. The admissions policies of Mississippi's public institutions are based on ACT scores. Yet these scores are questionable because they have not been proven to be reliable and because they discriminate against black students who score low on them. Yet Mississippi restricts automatic freshman admission to the traditionally white universities (University of Mississippi, Mississippi State University, Mississippi University for Women, and University of Southern Mississippi) on the basis of specific numerical ACT scores. [High school grades are not factored in.] The ACT scores required for automatic admission to the historically black institutions are several points lower. These differential admission standards were considered by the Court to be remnants of the dual system with a continuing segregative effect. The Court pointed out that, during the mid-1980s, more than 99 percent of Mississippi's white students were enrolled at the University of Mississippi, Mississippi State University, Mississippi University for Women, University of Southern Mississippi, and Delta State University. The student bodies of these schools remain predominately white, averaging between 80 and 91 percent white. Meanwhile, 71 percent of the state's black students attended Jackson State University, Alcorn State University, and Mississippi Valley State University, where the student bodies ranged from 92 to 99 percent black.

2. The widespread unnecessary duplication of programs was found to be a continuation of the prior dual system. Unnecessary duplication refers here to situations where two or more institutions offer the same non-essential or non-core program. All duplication of non-basic liberal arts and science courses at the bachelor's level and all duplication at the master's level and above were defined as unnecessary. Thirty-five percent of the twenty-nine undergraduate programs and 90 percent of the graduate programs at the three black colleges were found to be unnecessarily duplicated at the white universities. The Court stated that such duplication was suspect because the whole idea of "separate but equal" required duplicated programs in two sets of schools. The Court ruled that Mississippi must bear the burden of justifying the practice of having many duplicate academic programs at nearby HBCUs and white institutions before the court on remand.

3. Mississippi's system of institutional mission classification was found suspect as possibly perpetuating the state's former *de jure* dual system. The University of Mississippi, Mississippi State University, and the Uni-

versity of Southern Mississippi, the flagship institutions in the state system, were classified as "comprehensive" universities and received the most funds, offered the most advanced and specialized programs, and had the widest range of curricula. The black colleges were assigned more limited missions as "regional" and "urban" universities. The Court stated that the mission designations interfered to some extent with student choice and tended to perpetuate the prior segregated system.

4. Eight institutions (five white and three black) were first established by state law to ensure racial segregation. The Court concluded that maintaining all eight universities, instead of some lesser number, was wasteful and irrational—obviously so because four of them (two black and two white) are within thirty-five miles of one another. The Court stipulated that the issue of whether maintaining all eight institutions is educationally justifiable must be resolved.

Two points raised by the Court are of the greatest concern to the black educators who wish to maintain and improve HBCUs, while at the same time further integrating the white institutions. First, the Court did not accept the argument that historically black public colleges deserve special treatment in the desegregation process if the intent is to make them exclusively black enclaves. Moreover, the Court said that on remand the lower court must examine whether Mississippi operates eight public four-year colleges in order to perpetuate segregation. There is a real concern, therefore, that some of the nineteen southern and border states, including Mississippi, will use the Supreme Court's ruling to reduce the role of HBCUs. This could be the consequence of such steps as merging black schools into larger white schools or simply closing some black schools because they duplicate courses offered at predominantly white schools ("Opinions in Supreme Court's Decision" 1992, A19–A24; see also Jaschik 1992, A16–A18).

3

PROFILES OF HISTORICALLY BLACK COLLEGES AND UNIVERSITIES

Within the area of black higher education, private and public HBCUs have had a long and rich history. During the past 150 years, they have served hundreds of thousands of men and women who otherwise might never have received the chance for higher education. Many HBCU graduates have gone on to become leaders in their communities, and many have gained national prominence. We present the profiles of these institutions in two categories: those forming the Atlanta University Center, and the remaining HBCUs currently in operation. We first focus on the Atlanta University Center because of its unique function as a major educational hub for black students and faculty in the United States. The data for these profiles were extracted and abstracted from 1989 and/or 1990 college and university catalogs; other materials, including mission statements and institutional magazines and brochures; NAFEO's *Institutional and Presidential Profiles of the Nation's Historically and Predominantly Black Colleges and Universities* (1991); and the American Council on Education's *American Universities and Colleges* (1987).

THE ATLANTA UNIVERSITY CENTER

The Atlanta University Center, a small, non-profit corporation, is the oldest and largest consortium of black private higher education institutions in the world. Its six contiguous campuses, located less than a mile from downtown Atlanta, form a unique arrangement of undergraduate, graduate, and professional education; Clark Atlanta University, the Interdenominational Theological Center, Morehouse College, Morehouse School of Medicine, Morris Brown College, and Spelman College comprise the center. These six independent member institutions constitute a local, national, and international resource and a national model for cooperation in higher education. These member institutions have produced many of the world's most highly esteemed African-American business, political, religious, community, and education leaders (Wymes 1992). The consortium has the dual responsibility of promoting certain coordinated operations and administering centerwide programs for all six institutions. Affiliations among the current member institutions began in 1929 when the presidents of Atlanta University, Morehouse College, and Spelman College met and signed a "contract of affiliation," a document that designated voluntary collaboration in the provision of certain student services for all three schools. In 1972, the current member institutions entered into a process of reorganization because increased enrollments, growing budgets, and expanded physical plants made operations too unwieldy to be managed under the existing affiliation agreements. In short, extreme financial pressure demanded more resource sharing and coordinated planning.

The reorganization resulted in the creation of a new legal entity, the Atlanta University Center, Inc. (AUC), with a twenty-seven-member board of trustees (fourteen of whom have no ties to the member institutions of the center) and an executive director. The executive director and his or her staff are charged with the responsibility of coordinating programs delegated to AUC (all programs involving two or more institutions). The center also provides leadership in cooperative planning for all member institutions. The executive offices of AUC are housed in the Robert W. Woodruff Library amid all six member campuses at 111 James P. Brawley Drive, Atlanta, Georgia. By coordinating, pooling, and sharing resources, AUC enables all center members to offer their students and faculty a far richer educational environment than any single institution could provide. Altogether the center oversees more than a dozen separate programs (Atlanta University Center 1987). Among the most notable cooperative ventures are the following.

1. *Robert W. Woodruff Library*: This 225,000-square-foot structure, completed in 1982, is designed to accommodate more than 1 million volumes. As of July 1, 1990, it housed a collection of 766,000 items, including books and monographs, major periodical subscriptions, microfilm, archives, and special collections. The facility also houses one of the world's most remarkable collections of documents related to the black experience in the United States and is considered a treasure by local and visiting scholars. It merges the collections of six former independent libraries and thereby eliminates the wasteful duplication of materials and personnel. The Morehouse School of Medicine maintains an independent library.

2. *Dolphus E. Milligan Science Research Institute:* The Dolphus E.

Milligan Science Research Institute (SRI) is the country's only enterprise of its kind located on a historically black campus. Named for Dolphus E. Milligan, a pioneering black scientist and graduate of Atlanta University, the SRI opened in 1982. It serves as one of the forty-two national access points for the Prophet software used by biochemists throughout the United States; administers several cooperative research programs and pools research talent, laboratories, and equipment (which would not be available on small college campuses); solicits and receives large federal research grants (e.g., from NASA and the National Science Foundation); and plays a major role in training future generations of black scientists. The SRI engages in five major types of programs: (1) projects initiated by the more than 170 science faculty members of AUC member institutions, (2) undergraduate training in primary research via cooperative research projects (including professors and students), (3) undergraduate science programs offering non-credit courses, (4) internships that place students in national laboratories, and (5) contract research at the national level by SRI scientists with particular emphasis on biochemistry (including biotechnology and genetic engineering). Support for the SRI comes from both the U.S. government and private sources. Among the most notable contracts is a 1987 $8 million grant from the National Institutes of Health (NIH), the largest grant ever made by NIH to a black institution.

3. *Dual Degree Program in Engineering:* Since 1969, this program has enabled any student to enroll in a five-year sequence of courses that leads to a science or mathematics degree from his or her undergraduate institution and an engineering degree from one of four cooperating engineering schools: Georgia Institute of Technology, Rochester Institute of Technology, Auburn University, or Boston University. Students spend the first three years at one of the center's undergraduate institutions, pursuing an approved pre-engineering curriculum that includes specially designed courses in science and mathematics. Then the last two years are spent at one of the four engineering schools. Upon completion of the five-year program, students receive undergraduate degrees in both science and engineering. The program, which provides generous scholarships, is financed almost entirely by private corporate grants. Each year the nation's major corporations vie for the services of the program's graduates. Financial support from scores of leading U.S. companies enables the program to provide more than $250,000 in scholarship aid annually to needy students. During the past thirteen years, the program has produced 194 graduates. Currently more than 600 students within the AUC are enrolled in this five-year program.

4. *Career Planning and Placement Center:* The center, established in 1970, is the result of a merger of the placement services at all AUC institutions. The combination of individual placement services in one fa-

cility provides a single location where students can meet employers and representatives of corporations, graduate and professional schools, and government agencies.

5. *Academic Computation Center:* This center, housed in the Robert W. Woodruff Library, provides computer services to students and faculty at all AUC institutions. Specialized instruction in the use of the computer is also provided for students and faculty who are working on specialized research projects.

6. *Administrative Data Processing Center:* This facility allows AUC members to avoid the high cost of purchasing administrative computers for each campus. It operates a management information system (MIS) and a cable network that links fifty-one buildings. The MIS is supported by a PRIME 9950 computer, and the communication links between the campuses and the data center are provided by a local cable network. Because this system facilitates the computerized scheduling of all courses at the member institutions, each semester thousands of students can enroll in classes on any campus. Such cross-registration gives students access to a large selection of courses and faculty.

Additional programs include a centerwide Student Crisis Center, a bookstore, and the Department of Public Safety. All of the foregoing programs exist, in great part, because of the limited resources of any one member institution. Many other colleges and universities must find ways to accomplish their goals in a cooperative and economically sound way. The development of AUC, Inc., demonstrates how a group of six black urban institutions in the South have affiliated in order to achieve academic and financial objectives. Rich in history and dedicated to traditional and culturally sensitive teaching and training, each member institution remains unique (Wymes 1992).

THE SIX ATLANTA UNIVERSITY CENTER INSTITUTIONS

Clark Atlanta University was incorporated on July 1, 1988, as a predominantly African-American, private, urban, coeducational institution offering undergraduate, graduate, and professional degrees. Clark Atlanta University is one of only two historically black private comprehensive universities in the nation that awards degrees from the bachelor's degree through the doctorate. The university is comprised of the School of Arts and Sciences and the professional Schools of Business Administration, Education, Library and Information Studies, and Social Work. Clark Atlanta University inherited the historical missions and achievements of its two parent institutions: Atlanta University and Clark College.

Atlanta University conducted its first classes in a railroad boxcar in 1865, offering primary and secondary schooling. Two years later it obtained a charter from the state of Georgia, and, by 1876, it had awarded its first bachelor of arts degree. In 1894, all education below the high school level was discontinued, and, by 1928, the university was accepting only students in the freshman and junior normal classifications. The affiliation with Morehouse and Spelman colleges in 1929 enabled the university to concentrate its energies entirely on graduate education, and it awarded its first master's degree in 1931. Since this time, Atlanta University remained exclusively a graduate institution until its merger with Clark College in 1988.

Clark College was among the first institutions established by religious denominations after the Civil War to provide black Americans in the South with formal education. It was named after Bishop Davis W. Clark, the first president of the Freedman's Aid Society of the Methodist Episcopal church, under whose auspices the institution first operated. The first class was held in 1869 in a sparsely furnished room in Clark's Chapel, the Methodist Episcopal church in Atlanta's Summerhill section. Clark changed location several times during its early years, eventually acquiring space contiguous to Atlanta University in South Atlanta in 1877. This institution offered its first college degree in 1883. It remained a private, undergraduate, coeducational, liberal arts college until its merger with Atlanta University in 1988.

The student body of Clark Atlanta University, as of 1991, includes approximately 1,000 graduate students and 2,500 undergraduates who attend classes on contiguous campuses. Clark Atlanta University offers liberal arts and professional degree programs in fourteen departments in the School of Arts and Sciences, three departments in the School of Business Administration, four departments in the School of Education, the School of Library and Information Studies, and the School of Social Work. Courses leading to the Ph.D. degree are offered in biology, chemistry, guidance and counseling, political science, and social science. The doctor of education (Ed.D.) degree is offered in educational administration, and the doctor of arts (D.A.) degree is offered in chemistry and the humanities. The educational specialist (Ed.S.) degree and the specialist in library services (S.L.S.) degree in school, public, and academic library service are offered in the School of Education and the School of Library and Information Studies, respectively. In each of the five fully accredited professional schools, the emphasis is on service and the development of liberally educated leadership. Motivating all instruction is a commitment to humane values and to the elimination of all forms of racism and injustice.

University institutes and centers include the Center for Materials Research, Center for Computational Science, Biotechnology Research Center, Center for Basic and Applied Energy Research, Institute for Community Development, Institute of Criminal Justice, Institute for International Affairs, and Center for African and American Studies. The university is now constructing the Research and Education Center for Science and Technology, a $45 million state-of-the-art facility which will house a variety of innovative programs for the education of a new generation of scholars and scientists. The university features small classes and seminars; close relationships among students, faculty, and administration; interaction among American students and the student representatives of fifty countries in Asia, Africa, South America, and the Caribbean Islands; and unusual opportunities for independent study.

The *Interdenominational Theological Center* (ITC) is one of the first institutions of its kind, bringing together the students, faculties, and assets of four independent seminaries, which represent as many denominations, into a cooperative, ecumenical, professional graduate school of religious studies. ITC was chartered in 1958 through the mutual efforts of six denominations represented by four schools of theology: (1) the Morehouse School of Religion, founded by the Baptist church in 1867; (2) the Gammon Theological Seminary, founded by the United Methodist church in 1869 as a department of religion at Clark College; (3) the Turner Theological Seminary, founded by the African Methodist church in 1885 as a department of Morris Brown College; and (4) the Phillips School of Theology, founded in 1944 by the Christian Methodist church. Two additional seminaries joined the center at later dates: The Johnson C. Smith Seminary, Inc., founded by the Presbyterian church in 1867 as a department of the Bible Institute in Charlotte, North Carolina, joined during the 1969–1970 school year; and the Charles H. Moson Theological Seminary, a Church of God in Christ, joined in 1970.

The center, located on a ten-acre plot in the heart of the AUC, is under the direction of a forty-member board of trustees. Twenty-eight come from the six participating schools; the remaining twelve are members-at-large, chosen without regard to denominational affiliation. The trustees employ the faculty and administration, set the policies, and manage the physical and financial resources of the center.

The ITC's primary mission is to provide quality theological education for the predominantly black Christian churches. To this end, its curriculum is directed toward the preparation of persons for pastoral and other ministries in black churches. Its ecumenical environment is enhanced through its multinational, multiethnic, and multiracial faculty and student body. Three hundred and ten students were registered for the 1989–1990 academic year. Five degree programs are offered: master of divinity, master of arts in Christian education, master of arts in church music, doctor of ministry, and doctor of sacred theology. The latter two degrees are offered in cooperation with the Atlanta Theological Association. The ITC is fully accredited by the Association of Theological Schools and by SACS (*ITC Catalog* 1989–1990).

Morehouse College is a predominantly independent, black, four-year, undergraduate, liberal arts college for men located on a forty-plus-acre campus within the Atlanta University Center. Founded to prepare blacks for teaching and the ministry, Morehouse began in 1867 as the Augusta Institute, in the basement of Augusta's Springfield Baptist Church. After several name and place changes, the president, Dr. John Hope, renamed the institution, now located in Atlanta, Morehouse College in 1913 in honor of Henry Lyman Morehouse (then the secretary of the American Baptist Home Mission Society). Morehouse, a charter UNCF member, was accredited by the SACS in 1957. Morehouse, as of the 1989–1990 academic year, had an enrollment of approximately 2,500 students from thirty-seven states, the District of Columbia, and fifteen foreign countries. As the nation's only historically black all-male college, Morehouse assumes as its primary mission the education of qualified and committed African-American leaders. Generally speaking, Morehouse College graduates are expected to go on to graduate or professional schools. The "Morehouse man" allegedly embodies all that is good, noble, and strong in the African-American educated male. Each student must select a major field in which he takes between twenty-four and thirty-three semester hours. He must earn a grade of "C" or higher in all required courses and electives submitted to a department to satisfy the requirement for a major. Majors are offered in the following areas: Division of Social Science; Division of the Humanities; Division of Mathematics, Natural Sciences, and Physical Science; Division of Education; and Cognitive Electives. Though recruitment efforts are generally geared toward middle-class blacks, remedial course work is required on the basis of entry placement scores (*Morehouse Catalog* 1989–1990). Morehouse is one of the three black colleges and four Georgia colleges with a chapter of Phi Beta Kappa. As of 1990, it had an enrollment of more than 2,600 students (NAFEO 1991).

Morris Brown College is a predominantly black, private, coeducational, four-year, degree-granting institution with a faculty and staff of 175 and a student body of over 1,300 students from thirty-four states and twenty foreign countries. Located on a tract of land adjacent to Clark Atlanta University, it was founded in 1881 by the African Methodist Episcopal (A.M.E.) church for the Christian education of Negro boys and girls in Atlanta. Its college department was established in 1898. The charter of incorporation in 1913 for the then Morris Brown University provided that the church-linked board of trustees should run the school and elect officers, teachers, and all other employees. The executive board continues today.

The mission of the college is to educate students in a Christian environment, thus enabling them to become fully functional persons in society. Special emphasis is placed on education for service in the black community. The college operates under an open admissions policy; however, all students upon entry must take placement tests in basic skills (English composition, mathematics, and reading). Remedial non-credit courses are required for those who need them as ascertained by the placement tests. A federally funded Special Services Program assists students with supportive academic services. Four academic degrees are offered: bachelor of arts, bachelor of science, bachelor of science in hospitality administration (H.A.D.), and bachelor of science in nursing (B.S.N.). Candidates for a bachelor's degree of any kind must complete a minimum of 124 credit hours with an average grade of "C" or better, that is, a grade point average (GPA) of at least 2.0. They must also pass a special English qualifying examination as a graduation requirement.

The faculty and course offerings are organized into thirteen departments, within which there are several majors, some of which are further divided into separate programs: biology; business education and information processing; chemistry; communications; computing and information sciences; economics and business administration; education and psychology; fine arts; music; health, physical education, and recreation; mathematics; nursing; and social science. The college also works with and under a network of federally funded programs designed to provide over 400,000 disadvantaged youth and adults the upward mobility offered by higher education, including Upward Bound, Student Support Services, Educational Talent Search, Education Opportunity Centers, and Training Programs for Leadership.

The four-year H.A.D. program requires a minimum of 128 credit hours and a minor in business administration. The H.A.D. sequence includes specific courses in food service management, quantity food production, sanitation and safety, hotel and restaurant management, rooms division management (hotel front desks and housekeeping), hospitality marketing, and meetings and conventions. What is now hospitality administration was called hotel, restaurant, and tourism administration until 1989.

The B.S.N. curriculum, when completed, certifies that the graduate is eligible to take the examination for licensing as a registered nurse (R.N.) and is qualified to perform health care services for individuals and groups in entry-level positions. The program also provides the educational preparation required for graduate study in nursing. The program has been approved by the Georgia Board of Nursing.

The curricular programs at Morris Brown provide several educational tracks. The most appealing feature to these authors is the combination of a liberal arts program with professional training—for example, in the case of H.A.D. and B.S.N. candidates. The Morris Brown curriculum, and those of other black college and university programs similar to it (for example, Tuskegee University, Tuskegee, Alabama), offers the most practical, effective, and realistic higher education opportunities to the masses of black high school graduates.

Spelman College dates from 1881 when two Boston women, members of the Women's American Baptist Mission Society of New England, started a school for black women in the basement of the Friendship Baptist Church in Atlanta. The school, initially called the Atlanta Baptist Female Seminary, moved in 1883 to its present site. Now the campus consists of more than thirty-two acres adjacent to Clark Atlanta University. In 1884, the institution was named Spelman Seminary, after Mrs. John D. (Laura Spelman) Rockefeller, in recognition of the financial support of the Rockefeller family. In 1901, the first college degrees were granted to two women, and, in early 1924, the name was officially changed to Spelman College. By the time of its affiliation in 1929 with Morehouse College and Atlanta University, Spelman was a center of cultural and intellectual activity, offering theater, music, art, and visiting lecturers. Spelman College is the nation's oldest undergraduate liberal arts college for black women and renowned for its academic excellence and the leadership and achievements of its students and alumnae.

The curriculum leads to two types of degrees: bachelor of arts and bachelor of science (for those who major in biology, biochemistry, chemistry, computer science, health science, physics, mathematics, and physical education). Its academic divisions are humanities, fine arts, social science, and natural science. One hundred twenty-four credit hours are required for graduation. A required major consists of not more than forty-two semester hours. A minimum GPA of 2.0 is required for graduation, along with a minimum of a "C" average in the major. Special programs include a dual degree major program in engineering and Afro-American studies. The educational program is designed to give students a comprehensive liberal arts background, as well as preparing them for leadership in their professional and personal lives. Though the student body has grown to 1,782, representing forty-six states, the District of Columbia, and thirteen foreign countries, Spelman attempts to retain the advantages of a small liberal arts college, while sharing the diverse resources of a large coeducational university complex. The application list for admission is long. Since 1987, Spelman's freshman classes have had the highest average SAT scores of entering students at any HBCU. In 1988, Spelman was included in *U.S. News and World Report*'s annual listing of the nation's best colleges and universities. It has 134 full-time faculty members and individualized instruction in small classes, with a balanced budget of over $20 million.

Spelman has graduated many women that can now be found in positions of responsibility and service as physicians, lawyers, social workers, public health educators, librarians, teachers, and college and university professors. Alumnae are also found in engineering, business management, and government services (*Spelman College Catalog* 1989–1990). Generally speaking, Spelman students are selected and educated on the premise that many might go on to graduate or professional schools following graduation. The school maintains an aura of exclusivity and academic excellence. In a sense, it is a sister college to Morehouse.

Morehouse School of Medicine was founded in 1975 as a medical program within Morehouse College. It was accredited as a two-year program in 1978 by the Liaison Committee on Medical Education (LCME). In July 1979, the school received authorization to begin planning for expansion to a four-year, degree-granting institution. In April 1985, the LCME granted the school full accreditation to award the M.D. degree. In July 1982, the school's first permanent facility, the Basic Medical Sciences Building, was dedicated on the school's 6.3-acre campus adjacent to Morehouse College. Morehouse School of Medicine is a national resource which was established to meet the need for more primary care physicians to serve inner city and rural areas where most minorities and poor people live. The school has the special mission of recruiting, enrolling, and training physicians who are sensitive to human needs, yet highly skilled in medicine. Morehouse School of Medicine is dedicated also to providing an academic environment in which students can pursue careers as biomedical scientists and medical educators. Eighty percent of its 150 students are female, the highest proportion of female students of any medical school in the country.

THE REMAINING HBCUs

In this section we present profiles of the eighty-three HBCUs that are not part of the Atlanta University Center for which current data are available.

Alabama Agricultural and Mechanical University, located in Huntsville, was established in 1875 as Huntsville Normal School. It offered its first instruction at the post-secondary level in the same year, offered its first instruction as a four-year college in 1939, awarded its first baccalaureate in 1941, and adopted its present name in 1969. Alabama is a public, fully accredited, coeducational, land-grant institution, with an enrollment of more than 4,000 students. The Schools of Agriculture, Environmental Science/Home Economics, Arts and Sciences, Business, Education, and Technology collectively offer over seventy undergraduate majors. Doctoral programs are offered in applied physics, plant and soil sciences, and food science. A strong research program with an operating budget of over $5 million is funded by local, federal, and private agencies. The university's Physics Department, under a contract with NASA, was involved in an experiment to test the possibilities of growing crystals in space.

Alabama State University, located in Montgomery, was first established as Lincoln Normal School, a private institution. It became the first state-supported, historically black institution in 1874, offered its first instruction at the post-secondary level and became a junior college in 1920, changed its name to Alabama State College for Negroes in 1946, and adopted its present name in 1969. For many years this was the only school of its kind in the southern states. Its aim was to provide higher education for the "Colored Race." It has grown from a teacher-training institution to a multipurpose university. Currently it enrolls over 4,000 students in its seven major units: University College, the College of Arts and Sciences, the College of Business Administration, the College of Education, the School of Music, the School of Graduate Studies and Continuing Education, and the Division of Aerospace Studies. Degree offerings range from a two-year associate's (A.A.) degree to the bachelor's and master's degrees through the educational specialist degree programs.

Albany State College, a unit of the University System of Georgia, was first established in 1903 as Albany Bible and Manual Training Institute. It changed its name to Georgia Normal and Agricultural College, offered its first instruction at the post-secondary level in 1917, and awarded its first baccalaureate degree and adopted its present name in 1943. The college, located in Albany, in southwestern Georgia, has an enrollment of more than 2,300 students. It offers traditional liberal arts programs and master's degree programs in education, criminal justice, business administration, public administration, and nursing. It also offers a special transfer degree program in engineering, leading to a degree from Georgia Tech. The college also has taken on a statewide mission with the 1989 opening of the Center for the Study of the Black Male, which currently has three satellite programs at sister institutions. Albany State is actively involved in literacy training programs and also serves as a "Partner in Excellence" to one of the four local high schools. One aim of the college is to achieve computer literacy among all personnel and students. Currently one terminal is available for every twelve students. The college foundation administers scholarship programs and seeks fund development. Students with outstanding academic records and leadership qualities are recognized through the Presidential Scholarship, an award paying up to $4,500.

Alcorn State University, located in Lorman, Mississippi, was established in 1871 as Alcorn University. It offered its first instruction at the post-secondary level and changed its name to Alcorn Agricultural and Mechanical College in 1878, awarded its first baccalaureate degree in 1882, and adopted its present name in 1974. A public land-grant university, it has an enrollment of approximately 2,900 students and more than 500 faculty and staff members. The university offers instruction in seven divisions: General College for Excellence, Agriculture and Applied Science, Arts and Sciences, Business and Economics, Education and Psychology, Nursing, and Graduate Studies. More than fifty undergraduate majors are offered. The university also offers master's degrees in elementary education, secondary education, and agriculture and the educational specialist degree in elementary education. Alcorn State is accredited by SACS. As a land-grant institution, Alcorn has an extensive research program, a cooperative extension program, and an agricultural and forestry experiment station.

Allen University, located in Columbia, South Carolina, was founded in 1870 under the auspices of the African Methodist Episcopal church. It maintains four major academic divisions: Education, Humanities, Natural Sciences, and Behavioral Sciences. Future programs will place emphasis on nutrition, gerontology, computer science, energy technology, urban studies, public administration, and adult and continuing education. Allen's alumni include many who have exemplified academic excellence as leaders in their chosen fields (e.g., it has produced ten college presidents).

Arkansas Baptist College, located in Little Rock, was founded in 1884. This four-year, historically black, church-related institution offers a liberal arts–oriented academic program leading to degrees in the natural and physical sciences, social sciences, education, and business administration. In addition, it provides several service programs, which benefit the state and the local community: a Kiddie Kollege for preschoolers, and non-credit courses through an extended career arrangement with the Arkansas Baptist Convention. It participates in the Greater Little Rock Center for Higher Education, a consortium of historically black colleges in the Little Rock area.

Barber-Scotia College, located in Concord, North Carolina, was founded in 1867 as Scotia Seminary, a preparatory school for young Negro women. It merged with Barber Memorial College and adopted its present name in 1930, offered its first instruction at the post-secondary level in 1941, awarded its first baccalaureate degree in 1945, and became coeducational in 1954. The college is an accredited, SACS four-year, liberal arts institution, historically related and affiliated with the United Presbyterian church in the United States. The college enrolls 500 students, representing over eighteen states, the U.S. Virgin Islands, and foreign countries.

Benedict College, located in Columbia, South Carolina, is a private, church-related, fully accredited, coed, SACS four-year college. It was established in 1870 as Benedict Institute, offered its first instruction at the post-secondary level in 1889, and adopted the present name and awarded its first degree in 1984. Benedict offers programs leading to the bachelor of arts, bachelor of science, and bachelor of social work degrees in thirteen different departments. Since 1973, this college has had the largest enrollment of South Carolina residents of all twenty private four-year colleges in the state. Enrolling nearly 1,500 students, it has ranked third in total enrollment among private colleges in the state. Benedict caters to the special needs of students planning careers as professionals/ paraprofessionals in government, industry, commerce, education, and church-related occupations.

Bennett College, located in Greensboro, North Carolina, is a four-year liberal arts college for women. It was founded in 1873 as a coeducational institution, offered its first instruction at the post-secondary level in 1879, awarded its first baccalaureate degree in 1885, and reorganized as a women's college in 1926. The college is affiliated with the United Methodist church and is a member of the United Negro College Fund. It offers bachelor of arts, bachelor of science, and bachelor of arts and sciences in interdisciplinary studies degrees to 600 students. Comprehensive academic advising and personal counseling services provide support systems to encourage success and promote excellence. Within the college's four academic disciplines (education, humanities, natural sciences, and social sciences), a student can concentrate in one major area, combine two or more majors for a specialized career goal, or design a non-traditional program of study. The general education core is designed to improve reading, writing, and reasoning skills. Special services, dual degree programs, and computer–assisted instruction are among the innovations that contribute to a distinctive curriculum.

Bethune-Cookman College, located in Daytona Beach, Florida, is the result of a merger in 1923 of two Florida institutions: Cookman Institute for Boys of Jacksonville, Florida, founded in 1872 by the Reverend D.S.B. Darnell; and the Daytona Normal and Industrial Institute for Girls of Daytona Beach, founded in 1904 by Dr. Mary McLeod Bethune. Both schools were established on Christian principles and at the time of their founding provided much needed rudimentary training for black boys and girls. Upon the merger in 1923, the institution became the Daytona Cookman Collegiate Institute and was operated by the board of education of the Methodist church. The name was later changed to Bethune-Cookman College. It offered its first instruction at the post-secondary level in 1932. In 1941, a four-year college degree program in liberal arts and teacher training was instituted, and, in 1943, the first group of graduates received the bachelor of science degree in elementary education. In 1960, the college became a member of SACS. This historically black, United Methodist church–related college offers the bachelor of arts degree in sixteen fields and the bachelor of science degree in twenty-four areas. It offers the master of science degree in science education, with a major in either biology education or chemistry education. It also offers preprofessional programs in dentistry, engineering, law, medicine, pharmacy, and veterinary medicine. The institutional mission is to serve the educational, social, and cultural needs of its students within a Christian framework. This private coeducational college enrolls approximately 2,500 secondary school graduates (mostly Florida residents) from diverse social, economic, and educational backgrounds. The college gives priority to teaching by continually adapting its teaching techniques to meet students' needs.

Bishop State Community College, located in Mobile, Alabama, was founded in 1927 as a branch of Alabama State College. In 1936, the college began offering a two-year curriculum as a part of its parent institution, Alabama State College. In 1965, the college became an independent junior college, and its name was changed to Mobile State Junior College. This name was changed again by legislative act in 1971 to honor its first president, Dr. S. D. Bishop. The 1985—1986 academic year marked the fiftieth year of operation, with an enrollment of nearly 2,000 students in occupational, transfer, and terminal programs.

Bowie State University, located in Bowie, Maryland, was founded in 1865 as the Industrial School for Colored Youth. It offered its first instruction at the post-secondary level in 1893, awarded its first baccalaureate degree in 1912, and changed its name to Bowie Normal and Industrial School for the Training of Colored Youth in 1925. It adopted its present name in 1963. Bowie State is a unit of the University of Maryland System. It offers twenty-seven undergraduate majors in the departments of behavioral sciences and human services; business, economics, and public administration; communications; education and physical education; humanities and fine arts; history, politics and International Studies; Natural Sciences, Mathematics, and Computer Science; and Nursing, as well as a dual degree in engineering (in conjunction with other universities). The university offers the master of education degree in six areas; the master of arts degree in counseling psychology, human resource development, administrative management (business or public administration), and organizational communications; and the master of science degree in computer science. The institution's Adler-Dreikurs Institute of Human Relations is the first fully accredited Adlerian institute in the United States. It serves as a regional university for south central Maryland.

Carver State Technical College, located in Mobile, Alabama, was founded in 1962 and is named after Dr. George Washington Carver. This two-year public college is accredited by SACS. It offers the following associate's degree programs: office systems technology, medical and legal secretarial technology and word processing, auto body repair and refinishing, barbering and hair styling, brick masonry and concrete finishing, culinary arts, electrical appliance repair, plumbing and pipefitting, tailoring and alterations, and welding technology. Carver State also offers a G.E.D. readiness course to members of the Mobile community in cooperation with the Mobile County Public School System.

Central State University, located in Wilberforce, Ohio, was originally a part of Wilberforce University. It obtained its independent institutional status in 1947. This four-year public university enrolls approximately 2,500 undergraduate students in the traditional degree programs within the Colleges of Arts and Sciences, Business Administration, and Education. Other programs include a certificate program in African and Afro-American studies, an interdisciplinary program in the allied health fields, and an optional cooperative education program. In addition, majors in computer science (mathematics), computer information systems (business administration), water resources management, and manufacturing engineering are offered. The new construction on the campus includes the Paul Roberson Cultural and Performing Arts Center, a Library/College of Education Building, and Galloway/Alumni Tower.

Cheyney University of Philadelphia, now located in Cheyney, Pennsylvania, was founded in Philadelphia in 1837 by Richard Humphreys, a Philadelphia Quaker. Chartered as the Institute for Colored Youth in 1842, it moved to Cheyney in 1902 and changed its name to Cheyney Training School for Teachers in 1913. The school was purchased by the state and named State Normal School in 1921. It offered its first instruction at the post-secondary level in 1931, awarded its first baccalaureate degree in 1932, became Cheyney State College in 1959, and adopted its present name in 1982. This oldest historically black college is a public four-year institution. Cheyney offers thirty-three academic programs leading to the bachelor of arts and bachelor of science degrees, including business administration, medical technology, mathematics, computer science, education, industrial technology, hotel/restaurant and institutional management, broadcast/cable television communications technology, and social relations. It affords a Center for Excellence in Education, Center for Excellence in Industrial Technology and Engineering, Center for Excellence in Life Sciences, and Center for Excellence in Mathematics and Computer Science. Cheyney, as a member of the Pennsylvania state system of higher education, is accredited by MSACS.

Claflin College, located in Orangeburg, South Carolina, was founded by two Methodist laymen and offered its first instruction at the post-secondary level in 1869. It merged with Baker Theological Institute and awarded its first baccalaureate degree in 1870. It is associated with the United Methodist church. This four-year, private, liberal arts college offers majors to approximately 850 students in art, biology, business administration, chemistry, education, English, health and physical education, mathematics, music education, religion and philosophy, and social sciences. Claflin's mission is to prepare students for achieving a better life, not just for making a living.

Coahoma Community College, located in Clarksdale, Mississippi, was established in 1949. This two-year, multiethnic, coeducational, public institution offers a curriculum leading to the associate in arts and associate in science degrees and vocational certificate programs. The college offers general and preprofessional education, in addition to vocational-technical programs. Coahoma is accredited by SACS and by the Board for Community and Junior Colleges, formerly the Junior College Commission.

Coppin State College, located in Baltimore, Maryland, was established as a teacher training program housed in Douglas High School. It offered its first instruction at the post-secondary level in 1900, became Fannie Jackson Coppin Normal School in 1926, became a four-year college and changed its name to Coppin Teachers College in 1930, awarded its first baccalaureate degree in 1942, and adopted its present name in 1967. A part of the University of Maryland System, it has the unique mission of focusing on the needs and aspirations of the people of the inner city. It offers majors in computer science, nursing, management science, criminal justice, early childhood and elementary education, special education, and physical education for the handicapped within the Divisions of Arts and Sciences, Education, Nursing, Graduate Studies, and Continuing Education. Coppin's position in the University of Maryland System will allow it to expand its dual degree and certification programs with the university beyond the existing ones in dentistry, engineering, pharmacy, and social work. Coppin's alumni are found in middle- and higher-level administrative positions in criminal justice, education, nursing, and social services. Coppin is in a real sense Baltimore's "community school."

Delaware State College, located in Dover, was chartered and incorporated as the State College for Colored Students in 1891. It offered its first instruction at the post-secondary level in 1892 and awarded its first baccalaureate degree in 1893. This publicly supported, four-year, land-grant institution enrolls approximately 2,600 students. As an accredited residential/commuter college, it offers bachelor of arts, bachelor of science, and bachelor of technology degrees for students in the following areas: nursing, social work, economics, business administration, and education. Master's degrees are offered in curriculum and instruction, business administration, social work, special education, chemistry, biology, physics, and science education. Its new program in airway science, which is one of the few in the country recognized by the Federal Aviation Administration, offers the bachelor of science degree. Another new curriculum option is the program in hotel/restaurant management, which offers the bachelor of science degree in home economics. A cooperative engineering program is offered in collaboration with the University of Delaware. Off-campus bachelor's degree programs in elementary education, social work, and occupational teacher education are now being offered in Sussex County, Delaware. Delaware State is also actively involved in research.

Denmark Technical College, located in Denmark, South Carolina, was founded in 1947. This two-year, public, residential institution is accredited by SACS. It was an all-black trade school for twenty-one years before becoming, in 1969, a member of the South Carolina technical education system of sixteen colleges. The college offers seventeen associate's degree programs, eight diploma programs, and eleven technical certificate programs to 700 students. The institution is the only South Carolina technical college maintaining a residential campus.

Dillard University, located in New Orleans, Louisiana, was founded in 1869 by the American Missionary Association of the Congregational church and the Freedman's Aid Society of the Methodist Episcopal church as Union Normal School. This private, non-sectarian, coeducational, undergraduate, liberal arts college was named in the honor of James Hardy Dillard, whose distinguished service in the education of blacks in the South forms an important chapter in the history of American education. In 1930, it merged with New Orleans University and Straight College (both established in 1869). Dillard offered its first instruction at the post-secondary level in 1935 and awarded its first baccalaureate degree in 1937. Dillard has an enrollment of 1,625 students and is related to the United Church of Christ and the United Methodist church. Dillard is accredited by SACS, the Department of Education of Louisiana, the National Nursing Accrediting Service, the University Senate of the United Methodist church, and the National Association of Schools of Music. It offers majors in more than thirty areas within the Divisions of Education, Humanities, Natural Sciences, Nursing, Social Sciences, and Business Administration, leading to the bachelor of arts, bachelor of science, and bachelor of science in nursing degrees.

Edward Waters College, located in Jacksonville, Florida, was founded in 1866 as Brown Theological Institute. It changed its name to Brown University in 1874, offered its first instruction at the post-secondary level and adopted its present name in 1891, and awarded its first baccalaureate degree in 1980. This oldest HBCU in the state of Florida is an accredited, liberal arts, coeducational, private, four-year college and is affiliated with the African Methodist Episcopal church. The college enrolls 650 students in both day and evening courses. The institutional mission is to equip its students with the tools necessary for achieving upward social and economic mobility in today's society.

Elizabeth City State University, located in Elizabeth City, North Carolina, was founded in 1891 as Elizabeth Colored Normal School. It offered its first instruction at the post-secondary level in 1937, changed its name to Elizabeth City State Teachers College and awarded its first baccalaureate degree in 1939, and adopted its present name in 1969. This four-year public institution has been a unit of the sixteen-campus University of North Carolina System since 1972. Currently it offers degrees in geology, physics, accounting, criminal justice, industrial technology, political science, music merchandising, computer science, and middle grades education. The university has an interracial, international faculty of 125 instructors and over 1,600 students.

Fayetteville State University, located in Fayetteville, North Carolina, was founded as Howard School in 1867. It changed its name to State Colored Normal and Industrial School in 1916, offered its first instruction at the post-secondary level and changed its name to State Normal School for the Negro Race in 1921, awarded its first baccalaureate degree in 1943, and adopted its present name in 1969. It has been a part of the University of North Carolina System since 1972. Fayetteville State is the second oldest state-supported institution in North Carolina and one of the oldest teacher education institutions in the South. This four-year public institution offers associate's degrees in twenty-five disciplines, bachelor's degrees in twenty-six disciplines, and master's degrees in business administration and supervision, special education, biology, and history and master of arts degrees in teaching. It is accredited by SACS and has a multiethnic student body of nearly 3,300.

Fisk University, located in Nashville, Tennessee, was established as Fisk School in 1865. It incorporated and adopted its present name in 1867, offered its first instruction at the post-secondary level in 1871, and awarded its first baccalaureate degree in 1875. Its purpose was to educate and train young men and women, irrespective of color. The Fisk Jubilee Singers were students who traveled in the United States and Europe from 1871 to 1878. They built the Fisk tradition in music and art and introduced the spiritual as an American art form. Fisk offers undergraduate degrees in twenty-one major areas of study and course work leading to the master's degree in four fields of study. In 1930, Fisk became the first HBCU to gain full accreditation by SACS and was the first such institution to be placed on the approved list of the Association of American Universities (1933) and the American Association of University Women (1948). In 1952, Fisk was granted a charter for the establishment of a chapter of the Phi Beta Kappa Honor Society, Delta of Tennessee. The Department of Chemistry is on the approved list of the American Chemical Society. Fisk is a member of the National Association of Schools of Music, American Association of Schools of Music, and American Association of Colleges for Teacher Education. Fisk ranks among the foremost liberal arts colleges in the United States.

Florida Agricultural and Mechanical University, located in Tallahassee, was founded in 1887 as the State Normal College for Colored Students. It became a land-grant institution in 1891, offered its first instruction at the post-secondary level in 1905, awarded its first baccalaureate degree in 1910, and adopted its present name in 1953. This four-year public institution offers undergraduate and graduate programs to 8,500 students. Though an HBCU, the university recruits qualified students from all racial, ethnic, religious, and national groups. It operates on a 419-acre campus with physical facilities valued at $119 million and has faculty and staff of nearly 1,100. Programs are offered through twelve schools and colleges:

Arts and Sciences; Education; Engineering Sciences, Technology, and Agriculture; Pharmacy and Pharmaceutical Sciences; FAMU/FSU College of Engineering and Schools of Allied Science; Architecture; Business and Industry; General Studies; Journalism, Media, and Graphic Arts; Nursing; and Graduate Studies, Research, and Continuing Education. Graduate degree offerings include master of agriculture; master of business administration; master of education; master of science in school/community psychology, education, agricultural education, and pharmaceutical sciences; and doctor of philosophy in chemical engineering and mechanical engineering.

Florida Memorial College, located in Miami, is the result of a 1941 merger of two Florida institutions: the Florida Baptist Institute, founded in 1879 in Live Oak under the auspices of the American Baptist Home Mission Society; and Florida Baptist Academy, founded in 1892 at Jacksonville, but subsequently moved to St. Augustine in 1918 as Florida Normal and Industrial Institute. It awarded its first baccalaureate degree in 1945. The school was renamed Florida Memorial College in 1963, and, in September 1968, it was moved to Miami. This four-year, undergraduate, coeducational, liberal arts college with approximately 1,500 students is supported by its Baptist church–related constituency. Though an HBCU, it has a multiracial faculty and student body and is committed to equal educational opportunity for all. It offers bachelor of science and bachelor of arts degrees. Its Airway Science Program offers the bachelor of science degree, leading to careers in aviation, with concentrations in airway science management, airway computer science, air traffic control, and aviation data processing. This program is recognized by the Federal Aviation Administration.

Fort Valley State College, located in Fort Valley, Georgia, was founded in 1895 as Fort Valley High and Industrial School. It changed its name to Fort Valley Normal and Industrial School in 1932, offered its first instruction at the post-secondary level and became Fort Valley State College in 1939, and awarded its first baccalaureate degree in 1941. This four-year, liberal arts, land-grant institution is a unit of the University System of Georgia. The Fort Valley High and Industrial School, chartered in 1895, and the State Teachers and Agricultural College of Forsyth, founded in 1902, were consolidated in 1939 to form Fort Valley State College. Its mission is the education of students for professional, technical, and scholarly careers. The college is strongly committed to teaching, while also pursuing research, service, and scholarly activity. It offers over forty undergraduate majors and five graduate programs to nearly 2,000 students. Recently added degree offerings are computer science, ornamental horticulture, agricultural economics, veterinary science, agribusiness, criminal justice, electronic engineering technology, mass communications, and commercial design. It has a U.S. Agency for International Development (USAID) grant which supports project activities in Africa and in the Caribbean.

Grambling State University, located in Grambling, Louisiana, was founded by Charles P. Adams in 1901. This multipurpose, state-supported, coeducational institution enrolls nearly 6,000 students. The original purpose of the institution was to teach students how to make a living, to improve methods of farming, to prepare and preserve food, to improve health and sanitary conditions, to buy land and build homes, and to live with people. These purposes were achieved through industrial education patterned after that of Tuskegee Institute. Grambling State offers programs in liberal arts, science and technology, education, business, nursing and social work. Preliminary training is available for medicine, law, and dentistry, and opportunities for cooperative education are provided in some colleges and schools. Non-credit continuing education programs serve the citizens of Grambling and northern Louisiana. New emphasis in Grambling State's graduate school curriculum has been placed on the doctor of education in developmental education degree. Grambling State is accredited by SACS and the National Council for Accreditation of Teacher Education. Grambling's motto is "Everybody Is Somebody."

Hampton University, located in Hampton, Virginia, was founded in 1868 by General Samuel Chapman Armstrong, a twenty-nine-year-old Union brigadier general and the son of missionary parents. He had been assigned by the Freedman's Bureau to help solve the problems of thousands of former slaves who had gathered behind Union lines on the Virginia Peninsula. He founded, with the aid of the American Missionary Association, Hampton Normal and Agricultural Institute to train selected young men and women to teach and lead their people by example and in this way to build up an industrial system for blacks. It offered its first post-secondary instruction in 1922, awarded its first baccalaureate degree in 1926, added a graduate program in 1928, and adopted its present name in 1930. Hampton offers forty-one undergraduate and nine master's degrees. Hampton is Virginia's only coeducational, non-denominational four-year, private college. It serves over 5,000 students and has a student-faculty ratio of 16:1. Degrees offered include bachelor's degrees in airway science; architecture; engineering; radio, television, and print journalism; communications disorders; computer science; and marine science. Both bachelor's and master's degrees are offered in business administration and in nursing. Twenty-eight schools and institutions are outgrowths of Hampton. Hampton alumni have founded ten institutions, including Tuskegee University, St. Paul's College, and Bowling Green Academy.

Harris-Stowe State College, located in St. Louis, Missouri, was founded in 1857 by the St. Louis public schools as St. Louis Normal School for Women—and thus became the first public teacher education institution west of the Mississippi River and the twelfth such institution in the United States. It offered post-secondary education since its founding, became a four-year institution in 1919, and awarded its first baccalaureate degree in 1924. The college that exists today has had several predecessor institutions which through the years expanded and merged; the resulting institution became a member of the State of Missouri System of Higher Education in 1979. In 1924, the college received accreditation from the North Central Association of Schools and Colleges. In 1981, it received state approval for a new degree program, the bachelor of science in urban education. Harris-Stowe State has always been in the forefront of teacher education. The college is organized for two main purposes: the education of teachers through accredited, four-year, teacher degree programs, and the development of non-teaching urban education specialists through a unique and innovative four-year program that is especially designed for this new professional. In addition, the college provides three academic support programs: the honors program, the subject matter minors program, and the developmental program.

Howard University, located in Washington, D. C., was founded as a private university in 1867 by act of the U.S. Congress. It offered its first post-secondary education in 1867 and awarded its first baccalaureate degree in 1872. It is one of the two HBCUs in the country that qualify as comprehensive universities. Howard was named after General Oliver Otis Howard, commissioner of the Freedmen's Bureau. It has been coeducational and multiracial since its inception. The university is composed of eighteen fully accredited schools and colleges with a total faculty of 1,900, including the largest concentration of black scholars and black P.h.D.s at any single institution of higher education. More than 11,000 students from every state and nearly one hundred foreign countries are enrolled in the university. The university has grown from a single frame building to a main campus of more than 89 acres, a 22-acre West Campus on which the School of Law is located, a 22-acre School of Divinity campus, and a 108-acre tract of land in Beltsville, Maryland, used for research in the physical and biological sciences. The university was recently ranked a Level-One Research Institution by the Carnegie Foundation. The schools and colleges of the university are supported by nine research centers and institutes. Howard offers nearly 200 areas of academic concentration leading to bachelor's, master's and doctoral or professional degrees. The institution's facilities include a state-of-the-art undergraduate library; specialized collections in a library system that has 1.8 million bound volumes; a comprehensive laser chemistry laboratory; a modern 500-bed hospital; a 150-room full-service hotel; a commercial radio station, WHUR-FM; and a public television station, WHMM. To date, Howard University has awarded approximately 64,500 degrees. Howard is probably the most prestigious HBCU in the country.

Hinds Junior College, located in Utica, Mississippi, was founded in 1903 by Dr. William H. Hotzclaw. It is a public, two-year, coeducational institution which offers twenty-one vocational-technical programs and thirty-two academic programs to nearly 1,000 students. To determine and provide for the educational needs of students, the institution emphasizes an interdisciplinary curriculum.

Jackson State University, located in Jackson, Mississippi was founded in 1877 by the American Baptist Home Mission Society. It offered its first instruction at the post-secondary level in 1921, awarded its first baccalaureate degree in 1924, and adopted its present name in 1974. It is the state's designated urban university within the state university system. It has an enrollment of more than 7,000 students and a faculty of over 400. The university is comprised of five schools: Education, Science and Technology, Liberal Studies, Business, and the Graduate School—which collectively offer forty undergraduate degrees, thirty-two master's degrees, and nine specialist degrees in education. Two doctoral degree programs are offered, including the only doctorate in early childhood education in the state of Mississippi and among the nation's HBCUs. Jackson State is accredited by SACS.

Jarvis Christian College, located in Hawkins, Texas, was founded in 1912 as Jarvis Christian Institute. It adopted its present name and offered its first post-secondary instruction in 1937 and awarded its first baccalaureate degree in 1939. This is a four-year, private, coeducational, church-related college. A small college with less than 1,000 students, it enrolls 60 percent of its students from the state of Texas. Jarvis offers sixteen majors/specializations and nineteen minors/specializations within four academic divisions: Business Administration, Education, Science and Mathematics, and Humanities and Social Science. The Division of General Studies is responsible for the general education curriculum, which all students must complete. The college's Advanced Summer Enrichment Program (ASEP) is a six-credit-hour course emphasizing communications and mathematics, the skills that are recognized as the most essential for success in college.

Kentucky State University, located in Frankfurt, was chartered in May 1886 as the State Normal School for Colored Persons. It offered its first instruction at the post-secondary level in 1887 and awarded its first baccalaureate degree in 1929. It became a land-grant college in 1890 and a university (under its present name) in 1972. In 1973, the first graduate students enrolled in its School of Public Affairs. The university's mission and its academic emphasis have changed many times. Teacher training, educational and vocational training, industrial training, and liberal arts education are among the curricula that have been offered. By the mid-1970s, Kentucky State had become a small comprehensive university. It is a coeducational, liberal arts institution with a multicultural and racially balanced student body of 2,250 and a faculty of 150. As one of Kentucky's two land-grant institutions, its role within Kentucky's public higher education system is to excel as a small university with the system's lowest student-faculty ratio. It provides extensive community education programs, and its graduate center offers master's degree programs. Central to Kentucky State's twenty-eight baccalaureate programs are its liberal studies requirements, which provide students with the intellectual tools necessary in today's world. It offers predentistry, prelaw, premedicine, pre-engineering, preoptometry, and preveterinary medicine programs and ten occupation-oriented associate degree programs. The Whitney M. Young, Jr., College of Leadership Studies is unique in U.S. public higher education. In its Great Books Program, students study classic works of literature, history, philosophy, mathematics, and science in seminars and tutorials. The university is accredited by SACS and offers accredited social work, teacher education, nursing, and music programs. It also operates a Cooperative Extension Program and a Community Research Service Program.

Knoxville College, currently a four-year, coeducational college located in Knoxville, Tennessee, was originally established as McKee School for Negro Youth in 1863. It adopted its present name in 1875, offered its first post-secondary instruction in 1877, and awarded its first baccalaureate degree in 1883. It has been affiliated with the United Presbyterian Church of North America since 1875. Knoxville is accredited by SACS. Among its distinguished alumni are ambassadors and college presidents. Currently enrolling over 1,300 students of diverse backgrounds and cultures, the college stimulates students of demonstrated academic abilities and assists others in overcoming precollege deficiencies.

Lane College, located in Jackson, Tennessee, was founded in 1882 by the Colored (Christian) Methodist Episcopal church as the C.M.E. High School and became Lane College in 1896. The college's J. K. Daniels Library houses over 90,000 printed volumes. The college enrolls over 500 students representing twenty-five states, with the majority coming from Tennessee and the bordering states, and several foreign countries. A faculty-student ratio of about 1:17 has been maintained over the last few years. The primary purpose of Lane College is to train students to possess the will, desire, and capability to benefit from the experiences that are offered. The instructional program is organized into five major divisions: General Studies, Humanities, Natural and Physical Sciences, Social Sciences, and Education. The bachelor of arts degree is awarded to students whose major fields are communications, elementary education, English, history, music, religion, and sociology. The bachelor of science degree is awarded to students whose major fields are biology, business, chemistry, mathematics—computer science, physical education and health, computer science, and engineering. Preprofessional training is offered in medicine, dentistry, nursing, and law. Developmental programs are available in reading, English, and mathematics.

Langston University, located in Langston, Oklahoma, was established on March 12, 1897, as the Colored Agricultural and Normal University. It offered its first post-secondary instruction in 1897, awarded its first baccalaureate degree in 1901, and adopted its present name in 1941. Its original purpose was to instruct both male and female colored persons in the art of teaching various branches pertaining to a common school education and in the fundamental laws of the United States. This land-grant institution is an integral part of the Oklahoma State System for Higher Education, providing both lower- and upper-division undergraduate programs in thirty-six fields organized within five divisions: Allied Health and Nursing, Applied Sciences, Arts and Sciences, Business, and Education and Behavioral Sciences. The institution also offers graduate programs leading to the master's degree in teaching English as a second language, bilingual/multicultural education, elementary education, and urban education. The university's American Institute for Goat Research, established in 1984, continues to attract research scientists, agricultural specialists, and others on the state, national, and international levels. The university enrolls over 2,800 students from thirty-six states and ten foreign countries.

Lawson State Community College, located in Birmingham, Alabama, was founded in 1972 by the Alabama State Board of Education as a two-year state community college. This institution is the only predominantly black state-supported institution in central Alabama that serves the special needs of the black community, many of whom are low-income and female students. Enrolling over 2,000 students, Lawson State offers fifteen programs within its academic and technical divisions, leading to associate in arts, associate in science, and associate in applied science degrees.

LeMoyne-Owen College, located in Memphis, Tennessee, was formed by the merger of LeMoyne College (founded in 1862) and Owen College (founded in 1946) in the fall of 1968. LeMoyne College was a 100-year-old institution established by the American Missionary Association, an arm of the Congregational church, which offered its first post-secondary instruction in 1924, became a four-year institution in 1930, and awarded its first baccalaureate degree in 1932. Owen College was a junior college founded in 1954 by the Tennessee Baptist Missionary and Educational Convention. LeMoyne-Owen is a private, four-year, coeducational, liberal arts college with the ultimate purposes of preparing its students to uplift the race and inculcating religious values. Though a non-sectarian school, the college's tradition of service to the community is rooted in Christian motivation and commitment. Endowment support is contributed by two church-sponsored organizations, the United Church Board for Homeland Ministries of the United Church of Christ and the Tennessee

Baptist Missionary and Educational Convention. Course offerings are administered through six academic divisions: Arts and Humanities; Business and Management; Lifelong Learning; Natural Sciences, Mathematics, and Computer Science; Social and Behavioral Sciences; and Teacher Education, leading to bachelor of arts, bachelor of business administration, and bachelor of science degrees. A charter member of the United Negro College Fund, the college is fully accredited by SACS; its social work program is pursuing accreditation by the Council on Social Work Education and has been admitted to candidacy. Its student body is less than 1,000.

Lewis College of Business, located in Detroit, Michigan, was founded in 1929 by Dr. Violet T. Lewis to provide post-secondary business science education to urban dwellers unable to obtain training from private or public institutions. It began in a storefront in Indianapolis, Indiana. This private junior college is fully accredited by the North Central Association of Colleges and Schools. As the oldest black college in Michigan, Lewis awards the associate of arts degree in accounting, business administration, computer science, conference and court reporting, and secretarial sciences (executive, legal, and medical). All 614 students currently enrolled participate in the Cooperative Education Program, which reinforces classroom theory with experimental learning. Lewis's mission is to provide opportunities for educational freedom and justice to those who would find these difficult to obtain elsewhere.

Lincoln University, located in Jefferson City, Missouri, was founded in 1866 by the 62d and 65th U.S. Colored Infantry Units as Lincoln Institute. It offered its first post-secondary instruction in 1877. In 1879, the school formally became a state institution, and under the second Morrill Act of 1890, it became a land-grant institution. It awarded its first baccalaureate degree in 1891. In 1921, the state legislature passed the bill introduced by Walthall M. Moore, the first black to serve in that body, whereby the school name became Lincoln University. A board of curators was created by the same legislature to help govern the university. Graduate instruction began in 1940, with majors in education and history and minors in English, history, and sociology. The School of Journalism was established in 1942. Since the 1954 U.S. Supreme Court decision in *Brown v. Board of Education*, the university has moved forward with the process of racial integration, and today it stands as one of the effective models of multicultural higher education in the United States. This comprehensive, multipurpose institution of higher education is accredited by the North Central Association of Colleges and Schools. Its nursing program is accredited by the National League of Nursing, and its music program is accredited by the National Association of Schools of Music. This university, with a faculty of 145 full-time members, enrolls over 3,000 in its fifty-five degree programs (forty-four undergraduate and eleven graduate).

Its off-campus and continuing education services benefit government workers, other full-time workers, and incarcerated persons, and it works with less developed countries through the U.S. Agency for International Development. In 1983, the National Trust for Historic Preservation designated seven buildings on the Lincoln University campus as an historic district.

Lincoln University, located in Lincoln University, Pennsylvania, was founded in 1854 as Ashmun Institute. It offered its first instruction at the post-secondary level in 1854, changed its name to Lincoln University in 1866, awarded its first baccalaureate degree in 1868, and adopted its present name in 1972. Lincoln is the first institution to provide higher education in arts and sciences for male youth of African descent. During the first one hundred years of its existence, Lincoln graduates comprised approximately 20 percent of the black physicians and more than 10 percent of the black attorneys in the United States. Its alumni have headed thirty-six colleges and universities and many prominent churches. Ten of its alumni have served as U.S. ambassadors or mission chiefs and as heads of state. Many are federal, state, and municipal judges, and several others have been mayors or city managers. Founded in the midst of slavery, its motto has always been "If the Son shall make you free, ye shall be free indeed." It currently serves more than 1,200 students.

Livingstone College, located in Salisbury, North Carolina, was founded in 1879 by the African Methodist Episcopal Zion church as Zion Wesley Institute. It offered its first post-secondary instruction in 1880 and awarded its first degree and adopted its present name in 1887. This accredited, four-year, coeducational, liberal arts institution was named after David Livingstone, a legendary explorer, missionary, and philanthropist. As a non-sectarian undergraduate college, Livingstone offers programs leading to the bachelor of arts and bachelor of science degrees. Its Hood Theological Seminary provides professional training for the ministry leading to the master of divinity and master of religious education degrees. The college has a current enrollment of more than 500 students, and its alumni number over 5,000.

Mary Holmes College, located in West Point, Mississippi, was founded in 1892 by the Board of Freedmen of the Presbyterian Church, now known as the Presbyterian Church (U.S.A.). Mary Holmes is known for offering assistance to disadvantaged and first-generation college students through the Upward Bound and special service programs. This private, two-year, coeducational school offers both liberal arts and career studies programs leading to associate's degrees. It enrolls more than 500 students, 90 percent of which come from Mississippi and the neighboring states. About 84 percent of its graduates transfer to senior colleges and universities, and many of them later enter graduate and professional schools.

Meharry Medical College, located in Nashville, Tennessee, was founded in 1876 as the Medical Department of Central Tennessee College. Its mission was to educate health professionals for the black community. The institution became an independent medical college in 1915. In 1886, the Department of Dentistry was established, and, in 1910, the George Hubbard Hospital, the major clinical teaching facility, was opened. Meharry has been cited as a "national resource" by the Robert Wood Johnson Foundation for its role in educating minority health professionals. It has trained one-third of the black physicians and dentists practicing in the United States today. Meharry graduates comprise 40 percent of the black faculty at U.S. medical schools and about 25 percent of the black faculty at U.S. dental schools. Graduates serve as health care providers in forty-eight states and twenty-two foreign countries. Currently Meharry operates the Schools of Medicine, Dentistry, Graduate Studies, and Allied Health, as well as the teaching/research West Basic Sciences Center, Community Mental Health Center, Comprehensive Health Services Center, International Health Science Center, and Hubbard Hospital. The institution emphasizes the provision of primary care in medically underserved areas and biomedical research in areas of concern to underserved populations. A World Health Organization (WHO) Center now operates within its international unit.

Mississippi Valley State University, located in Itta Bena, was founded in 1946 in the heart of the Mississippi Delta. The nation's youngest minority public university, it was originally established and chartered as Mississippi Vocational College. It awarded its first baccalaureate degree in 1953 and adopted its present name in 1974. Mississippi Valley State has nearly 2,000 students, 125 faculty members, and 8,500 alumni. It offers more than 700 different courses and awards undergraduate degrees in seventeen areas. Master's degrees are also offered in elementary education and environmental health. It has an Air Force Reserve Officers' Training Corps (ROTC) detachment and an outstanding band, which has performed at the Indianapolis 500, the Rose Bowl, the U.S. presidential inauguration, and Disney World. It also offers the state's first nationally accredited art and environmental health programs and has produced national athletic champions.

Morgan State University, located in Baltimore, Maryland, was first established in 1867 as the Centenary Biblical Institute (1867–1890) by the Baltimore Conference of the Methodist Episcopal church to train young black men as ministers for their congregations. From 1890 to 1939, it was known as Morgan College, and its mission was to prepare black persons of good moral standing for public school teaching and other careers. It awarded its first baccalaureate degree in 1895. It remained private and church controlled, but its governing board was expanded to include prominent citizens in the black community. Morgan State College (1939–1975) was created in 1939 when the institution was purchased from the Methodist Episcopal church by the state of Maryland. As a state-supported college, governance passed to an independent board of trustees from 1939 to 1967 and to the State Board of Trustees of State Colleges from 1967 to 1975. The school's mission during this period was expanded from teacher training to a balanced liberal arts education. Morgan State College became Morgan State University in 1975 and changed from being a predominately negro college to being a multiracial university. The university, however, retains its historical commitment to train black students in the liberal arts, selected professions, and graduate studies. Now one of the three black degree-granting institutions in the state, Morgan State has become Maryland's first urban-oriented institution, with programs leading to undergraduate liberal arts, preprofessional, and professional degrees and to master's and doctoral degrees emphasizing teaching, research, and public service. Morgan State's campus is located in the northeastern section of Baltimore, surrounded by residential communities. Isolated, yet easily accessible to the heart of downtown, Morgan State enjoys the advantages of both a suburban location and proximity to urban life. In 1975 a new library was opened, providing an ample facility for housing and preserving volumes, as well as research and cultural artifacts that support instructional programs. The campus is currently being enhanced with the construction of a building to house the School Science Complex and the renovation of the physical education instructional center. As a doctorate-granting institution in Maryland and the only public institution with an urban mandate, Morgan State's programs of teaching, research, and public service creatively address the learning needs of persons and institutions within cities. Morgan State has a total population of 4,419 students (3,798 undergraduate and 621 graduate) and 213 full-time faculty. Its offerings include forty undergraduate majors and areas of concentration; preprofessional studies in pharmacy, dentistry, medicine, medical technology, and law; and twenty-five graduate majors leading to master of arts, master of science, master of business administration, master of architecture, and doctor of philosophy in urban educational leadership degrees.

Morris College, located in Sumter, South Carolina, was founded in 1908 by the Baptist Educational Missionary Convention for "the Christian and Intellectual Training of the Black Youth." The majority of the "founding fathers" were poor and without any formal learning, but they possessed the Christian faith and a zeal to provide for others the educational opportunities they themselves were denied. Initially Morris College provided schooling at the elementary, high school, and college levels. It offered its first instruction at the post-secondary level in 1911, and, in 1915, the bachelor of arts degree was conferred on the first two graduates. This institution discontinued its elementary school in 1930, its high school in 1946, and its "normal" program in 1979. From 1930 to 1932, the school operated only as a junior college, but it resumed its four-year program in 1933. The word "Negro," which appeared in the original certification of incorporation, was eliminated on August 14, 1961, thereby opening enrollment to students of all ethnic groups. Currently this four-year, coeducational, liberal arts college has an enrollment of more than 600 students, is owned and operated by the Baptist Educational and Missionary Convention of South Carolina, and is fully accredited by SACS. The college offers bachelor of arts, bachelor of fine arts, and bachelor of science degrees. Course offerings are organized into six divisions: Education; General Studies; Humanities; Natural Sciences and Mathematics; Business Administration; and Social Sciences, History, and Pre-law Studies. Degrees are offered in English, history, liberal studies, political science/history, religious education, social studies, liberal-technical studies, sociology, fine arts, biology, business administration, mathematics, early childhood education, elementary education, health science (school health and community health), and health and recreation. An Army ROTC program is also included in the college's curriculum. From its beginning the college has been a center for training ministers and teachers. Many black youth who otherwise would never have attended college have received the benefits of higher education at this school. Many communities and state agencies have utilized the facilities of the college to carry their programs of general welfare and social uplift. Morris is one the few senior colleges operated solely under black auspices, and, as such, it represents the distinct contribution of blacks to American education and society.

Norfolk State University, located in Norfolk, Virginia, was founded as the Norfolk unit of Virginia Union University, a junior college. It offered its first post-secondary instruction in 1935, became a four-year institution in 1956, awarded first baccalaureate degree in 1958, and adopted its present name in 1979. Today, it is an SACS-accredited, four-year, coeducational, urban institution, consisting of nine schools that offer seven associate's, fifty bachelor's, and fifteen master's degree programs to nearly 8,000 students. Classroom buildings include a communications center with laboratories for television and a 1000-watt FM radio station, a life science center with a planetarium, a new ROTC/physical education and basketball arena complex, and a technology center. The other campus structures include a library, a fine arts and music center, two dining facilities, and six dormitories. Norfolk State's programs are nationally accredited by American Corrective Therapy Association, National Accrediting Agency for Clinical Laboratory Sciences, National League for Nursing, Council on Social Work Education, National Association of Schools of Music, American Medical Records Association, American Dietetics Association, American Psychological Association, and the Committee on Allied Health Education.

North Carolina Agricultural and Technical State University, located in

Greensboro, was founded in 1891 as A & M College for the Colored Race. It offered its first instruction in Raleigh as an annex of Shaw University in 1890, moved to its present location in 1893, awarded its first baccalaureate degree in 1896, and adopted its present name in 1967. This comprehensive land-grant university became a part of the North Carolina State System in 1972. Its academic programs are offered through seven schools and the College of Arts and Sciences. The technology/engineering and high-tech program was developed on a strong liberal arts base. Other programs include business, nursing, education, and agriculture. Its teaching and research programs in animal science are related to the School of Veterinary Medicine. North Carolina A&T leads the nation in the graduation of black engineers and has one of the two nationally accredited accounting programs at black universities in the nation. The university's alumni include a long list of distinguished black leaders and role models: for example, the late astronaut Dr. Ronald McNair; the Reverend Jesse Jackson; New York Congressman Edolphus Town; Major General Charles D. Bussey (ret.), chairman of the A&T Board of Trustees; North Carolina Associate Supreme Court Justice Henry E. Frye; and Brigadier General Clara Adams-Endler, head of the 40,000-member Army Nurse Corps.

North Carolina Central University, now a state-supported liberal arts institution located in Durham, was chartered in 1909 as a private institution and opened to students on July 10, 1910. It was founded by its late president Dr. James E. Shepard. The university was known from its beginning as the National Religious Training School and Chautauqua, having the purpose of offering young men and women of fine character the sound academic training requisite for service to the nation. In 1923, the General Assembly of North Carolina purchased the school, and it became a public institution. It awarded its first baccalaureate degree in 1929. Following several name changes, the state legislature in 1969 designated the institution North Carolina Central University. On July 1, 1972, it became a constituent institution of the University of North Carolina. North Carolina Central enrolls more than 5,000 students within five schools: the College of Arts and Sciences, the School of Business, the School of Education, the School of Law, and the School of Library and Information Sciences. The School of Graduate Studies coordinates advanced degree programs in business, education, the arts and sciences, and library and information sciences, and a university college conducts summer, evening, continuing education, and extension programs. The university's black student enrollment is the second largest among North Carolina's forty-eight senior colleges and universities, and its white enrollment is larger than nine of the state's private senior colleges. Its library collection of more than 600,000 volumes is the seventh largest in the state. The university provides, through its Learning Resource Center, a centralized pool of educational media and services for all university departments. The center's staff are available to teachers and students for consultation and help in the selection, use, and production of instructional materials. The facilities of the center include a recording studio, a photographic darkroom, a graphic preparation room, a closed-circuit television studio, a maintenance and preview room, and a film library.

Oakwood College, located in Huntsville, Alabama, was founded in 1896 as Oakwood Industrial School. It changed its name to Oakwood Manual Training School in 1904, offered its first post-secondary instruction in 1917, became a senior college and adopted its present name in 1944, and awarded its first baccalaureate degree in 1945. Today it is a four-year, historically black, coeducational, liberal arts school, owned and operated by the General Conference of Seventh Day Adventists. Oakwood's mission is to provide a quality education within a Christian framework for persons reflecting demographic, economic, cultural, and educational diversity. It is accredited by SACS, the National Council for the Accreditation of Teacher Education, the Council of Social Work Education, and the Seventh Day Adventist Board of Regents. Oakwood grants bachelor of business, bachelor of social work, bachelor of arts, bachelor of science, bachelor of general studies, associate of arts, and associate of science degrees. Curricula are available in natural science and mathematics, behavioral and social sciences, humanities, religion and theology, and applied sciences and education. Other course offerings include nursing and various professional curricula and one and two-year courses—particularly in health sciences, engineering, and law. Oakwood enrolls 1,233 students "for service to humanity and to God" through the harmonious development—mentally, physically, and spiritually—of the whole person.

Paine College, located in Augusta, Georgia, was founded in 1882 by the Christian Methodist Episcopal church and the United Methodist church as Paine Institute in the honor of Bishop Robert Paine. It offered its first post-secondary instruction in 1891, awarded its first baccalaureate degree in 1895, and adopted its present name in 1903. Its original purpose was to train ministers and teachers following the Civil War. However, there were no public schools for blacks at that time, and Paine continued to provide secondary education as well as college work for its students. In 1945, when the first public high school for blacks was opened in Augusta, Paine discontinued its preparatory and high school programs. Throughout its history, Paine has been a distinctively Christian college. Paine College is historically biracial in its administration and faculty, and, although the student body has been historically black, the college encourages enrollment of all racial and ethnic groups. The college seeks to emphasize and enhance the black experience as part of the total education process. This private, four-year, coeducational, liberal arts institution offers majors in biology, business administration, chemistry, early childhood education, English, history, mass communication, mathematics, middle grades education, music education, psychology, religion and philosophy, and sociology to nearly 600 students. Special programs include the preprofessional sciences program.

Paul Quinn College, located in Dallas, Texas, was founded in 1872 in a one-room building in Austin, Texas, by a group of African Methodist circuit riders who saw a need for a trade school to teach newly freed slaves blacksmith, carpentry, tanning, saddlery, and other skills. In May 1881, the college, named in the honor of Bishop William Paul Quinn, was chartered by the state of Texas and moved to Waco. Paul Quinn is the oldest liberal arts college established by blacks west of the Mississippi River. Currently the college provides special counseling, guidance services, and an expanded academic program for all who seek higher education. Twenty degree programs in ten areas are offered at the bachelor's level. In cooperation with Baylor University and Texas State Technical Institute, Paul Quinn offers thirty other degree programs. Special programs are offered in the areas of social work, computer science, business administration, chemical technology, medical technology, and the usual liberal arts areas. The archives of the African Methodist Episcopal church are housed on the first floor of the Johnson Library–Learning Resources Center. These archives contain materials on the African Methodist Episcopal experience in Texas as well as elsewhere in the nation. The campus Ethnic Cultural Center holds the largest collection of books, art, and artifacts on the black experience in Africa and the United States on a college campus west of the Mississippi. Several non-credit courses are offered under the Paul Quinn College Continuing Education and Tenth Episcopal District Continuing Education programs. This four-year, private, coeducational institution provides a wide range of student activities and intramural and intercollegiate sports to nearly 500 students.

Philander Smith College, located in Little Rock, Arkansas, was established as Walden Seminary and offered its first instruction at the postsecondary level in 1877. It adopted its present name in 1882 and awarded its first baccalaureate degree in 1888. Today Philander Smith is a four-year, coeducational, private, liberal arts college enrolling nearly 600 students. The college was created to make education available to freedmen west of the Mississippi River. Philander Smith is one of the black colleges historically related to the United Methodist church. The Board of Higher Education and Campus Ministry of the United Methodist church have been a fiscal source for the college program. The small ratio of students to instructor allows each student to receive personal attention. The college grants bachelor of arts degrees in a number of fields and bachelor of science degrees in natural and physical science and in medical technology. The academic programs are structured in four divisions: Teacher Education, Humanities, Business, and Social Sciences. Preprofessional programs include dentistry, engineering, pharmacy, medicine, nursing, and the ministry. The school enrolls 626 students of many nationalities. For many years Philander Smith College's mission has been to educate students for "service and distinction."

Prairie View Agricultural and Mechanical University, located in Prairie View, Texas, was founded in 1876 by the Texas legislature as Alta Vista Agricultural College. Prairie View is the second oldest institution of higher education in the state of Texas. On March 11, 1878, eight young Negro men became the first of their race to enroll in a state-supported college in Texas. In its early stages Prairie View offered instruction at the elementary and secondary levels. In 1901, the school was authorized to offer a four-year course of study. The first three degrees were granted in 1902. The four- year senior college program was begun in 1919 and included training in vocational home economics, vocational agriculture, liberal arts, and mechanical arts. The name Prairie View Normal and Industrial College was changed by the legislature in 1945 to Prairie View University, and the school was authorized to offer all courses offered at the University of Texas at Austin. Prairie View was accredited by SACS in December 1958. In 1972, the institution was renamed Prairie View A&M University, and its status as an independent unit of the Texas A&M University System was confirmed. In 1981, the legislature officially recognized Prairie View as not only a general purpose university, but also a "special purpose institution," providing services to students of diverse ethnic and socioeconomic backgrounds. Prairie View's research program includes centers of the Texas Agricultural Experiment Station, the Texas Engineering Experiment Station, and the Cooperative Agricultural Research Center, with projects funded by the U.S. Departments of Agriculture and Energy and the National Aeronautics and Space Administration, among other agencies. High-energy physics research supports Texas's superconducting super collider. Its public service program includes the Cooperative Extension Service, Center for Community and Rural Development, Transportation Center, Energy Affairs Center, and International Affairs Program. The university enrolls approximately 5,800 students.

Rust College, located in Holly Springs, Mississippi, was founded in 1866 by the Freedmen's Aid Society of the Methodist Episcopal church. Its founders were missionaries from the North who opened a school in the Asbury Methodist Episcopal Church, accepting adults of all ages, as well as children, for instruction in elementary subjects. A year later the first building on the present campus was erected. In 1870, the school was chartered as Shaw University, honoring the Reverend S. O. Shaw, who made a gift of $10,000 to the new institution. In 1892, the name was changed to Rust University, in honor of Richland S. Rust of Cincinnati, Ohio, secretary of the Freedmen's Aid Society. In 1915, the name was changed to Rust College. As students progressed, high school and college courses were added to the curriculum. In 1878, two students were graduated from the college department. As public schools for Negroes became more numerous, the need for private schools decreased. In 1930, the grade school was discontinued; the high school continued to function until 1953. Today Rust College is a four-year, coeducational, accredited, liberal arts college, enrolling nearly 1,000 students. It is the only four-year, accredited, predominantly black institution of higher learning in northern Mississippi. In addition to national and regional accreditation and affiliations, Rust College is accredited by the Mississippi Association of Independent Colleges and Universities. The college confers bachelor of science, bachelor of arts, and associate in science degrees in business and economics, social and behavioral science, science and mathematics, the humanities, and mass communications. Although traditionally a senior liberal arts college, in recent years Rust has added several professional and preprofessional programs to meet its students' needs. Professional programs are offered in teacher certification, business administration, computer science and management, music, engineering, journalism, medical technology, social work, and secretarial science. Preprofessional programs include prehealth and prenursing. Among approximately 20,000 former students, many completed only their elementary or secondary education. More than 5,000, however, have graduated from the college department. The primary objective of the college is human development, which includes the physical, mental, moral, and spiritual development of the students.

Saint Augustine's College, located in Raleigh, North Carolina, was founded in 1867 as St. Augustine Normal School and Collegiate Institute. It changed its name to St. Augustine's School in 1893 and offered its first instruction at the post-secondary level and changed its name to St. Augustine Junior College in 1919. The school became a four-year institution in 1927, adopted its present name in 1928, and awarded its first baccalaureate degree in 1931. Today it is a private, four-year, coeducational, accredited, liberal arts college, closely associated with the Protestant Episcopal church. The college now offers degrees in thirty-eight distinct disciplines and emphasizes preparation for graduate studies and careers in the professions. Its recent course additions include computer science, radio broadcast journalism, and physical therapy. The college also operates a radio station, WAUG-AM, and expects to have its W68BK television station on the air soon. The college enrolls nearly 1,900 students from the Carolinas, other states, and twenty foreign countries. Seventy-two percent of the faculty hold earned doctorates, illustrating the college's dedication to academic excellence. Its distinctive educational programs include cooperative baccalaureates (1) in engineering with North Carolina State University, (2) in industrial hygiene with the University of North

Carolina at Chapel Hill, and (3) in medical technology with approved schools, and interdisciplinary programs in criminal justice, industrial hygiene, and urban affairs.

Saint Paul's College, located in Lawrenceville, Virginia, was founded in 1888 as St. Paul's Normal and Industrial School. It offered its first instruction at the post-secondary level in 1922, awarded its first bachelor's degree in 1944, and adopted its present name in 1957. Today, it is an accredited, coeducational, career-oriented, liberal arts institution affiliated with the Episcopal church. It offers degrees at the bachelor's level in fifteen areas of study for students who plan to enter graduate school, elementary and secondary school teaching, business, government, law, medicine, dentistry, social work, or theology. The college enrolls 750 students from twenty-two states, the District of Columbia, and three foreign countries. With a low student-faculty ratio, the college makes a serious effort to meet individual student needs.

Savannah State College, located in Savannah, Georgia, was established in 1890 as Georgia State Industrial College for Colored Youth. It offered its first instruction at the post-secondary level in 1926, awarded its first baccalaureate degree in 1930, and adopted its present name in 1950. The college is organized into the Schools of Business, Humanities and Social Sciences, and Sciences and Technology. It enrolls nearly 2,200 students from the United States and numerous foreign countries. It was one of the first black public land-grant colleges established by the Morrill Act of 1890 and is the oldest of the state-supported HBCUs. The college offers over thirty-six undergraduate majors; master's programs leading to master of business administration, master of public administration, and master of social work degrees; and Army and Navy ROTC programs.

Shaw University, located in Raleigh, North Carolina, was founded in 1865 as Raleigh Institute. It changed its name to Shaw Collegiate Institute in 1870, offered its first instruction at the post-secondary level in 1874, adopted its present name in 1875, and awarded its first baccalaureate degree in 1878. The private, Baptist-affiliated, liberal arts institution offers a variety of academic programs through seven major divisions, each geared toward today's key employment markets, consistent with the university's philosophy that it is possible to be liberally educated for the world of work. In addition to the usual liberal arts and science offerings, the university features specialized degree programs in speech pathology and audiology, radio-television-film, adaptive physical education (pretherapy), engineering, and computer studies. The Division of International Studies offers a major in interactional relations, with emphasis placed on Africa, the Caribbean, and the Middle East. The Center for Alternative Programs of Education (CAPE) allows students to pursue an academic degree through independent study, flexible course scheduling, and credit for prior learning experiences. The school offers CAPEs in Fayetteville and High Point, North Carolina, and in Charleston, South Carolina.

Shorter College, located in North Little Rock, Arkansas, was chartered in 1886. Shorter, a two-year, liberal arts, coeducational school, affiliated with the African Methodist church, enrolls nearly 150 students. It is accredited by the North Central Association of Colleges and Schools. The college's mission is to provide (1) quality education in a Christian atmosphere, (2) opportunities to those who may be economically and/or educationally disadvantaged, (3) a liberal arts education leading to an associate in arts or associate in science degree, (4) an open-door admission policy toward all ethnic groups, and (5) educational resources for community development.

South Carolina State College, located in Orangeburg, was founded in 1896 as the Colored Normal, Industrial, Agricultural and Mechanical College of South Carolina. It offered its first instruction at the post-secondary level in 1896, awarded its first baccalaureate degree in 1897, and adopted its present name in 1954. It is a public, coeducational, land-grant institution, with an enrollment of 4,399 students. The college offers over sixty degree programs through the Schools of Arts and Sciences, Business, Education, Engineering Technology, Graduate Studies and Continuing Education, Home Economics, and Human Services. It is the only higher education institution in the state that offers both undergraduate and graduate degrees in speech pathology and audiology and the doctor of education degree in educational administration. Currently the college awards bachelor of arts degrees in numerous fields; the bachelor of science degree in nursing; master of science degrees in education, nutritional sciences, and individual and family development; the master of education degree; and in master of arts degrees in rehabilitation counseling and speech pathology and audiology. Preprofessional programs are offered in agriculture, dentistry, medicine, optometry, and veterinary medicine.

The Southern University System, located in Baton Rouge, Louisiana, is one of the largest predominantly black public universities in the nation, with campuses in Baton Rouge, New Orleans, and Shreveport, Louisiana. The system was established by the state legislature in 1975.

Southern University–Baton Rouge, was established as Southern University in New Orleans in 1880. It offered its first post-secondary instruction in 1881 and adopted its present name in 1890. Recognized as a land-grant college in 1892, it awarded its first baccalaureate degree in 1912. Its major programs include offerings in the arts and humanities, agriculture and home economics, business, education, engineering, law, nursing, public policy and urban affairs, the sciences, naval and army ROTC, graduate studies, and other allied fields. Special emphasis is placed on liberal arts training, test sophistication, computer literacy, and career preparation.

The university maintains an environment that serves to enhance research and creative activities by faculty and students through the recognition of scholarly accomplishments and promotion of the university as a laboratory for exploration and experimentation of the higher order. Southern University–Baton Rouge now employs over 580 full-time faculty members and enrolls nearly 9,000 students.

Southern University–New Orleans was established in 1956. It offered its first post-secondary instruction the same year and awarded its first baccalaureate degree in 1963. It is a senior urban institution serving 4,000 commuters from Louisiana's largest metropolitan area by offering them baccalaureate degree programs in the liberal arts and sciences, business, education, allied health, substance abuse, social welfare, journalism, transportation, criminal justice, and technologies. A graduate program is offered in social work. Certificate programs in substance abuse and associate's degree programs in computer science, stenography, social welfare, real estate, and substance abuse are also offered. Its research and public service activities are primarily centered on the urban community. The university also operates evening and weekend programs and is fully accredited by SACS.

Southern University–Shreveport was founded in 1964. This public, two-year, coeducational, commuter community college is an integral part of the Southern University System and is accredited by SACS. The school enrolls 750 students, maintaining a faculty-student ratio of 1:15. The course offerings are organized within the Divisions of Business, Humanities, Natural Science, Social Science, and Freshman Studies. Specific offerings include developmental courses, one- and two-year career-oriented programs in technical and semiprofessional fields, two-year curricula leading to associate's degrees, and programs anticipating transfer to a four-year college or university.

Stillman College, located in Tuscaloosa, Alabama, was established as Tuscaloosa Institute in 1876 by the Presbyterian church and was incorporated as Stillman Institute in 1895, in the honor of the Reverend Charles Allen Stillman. It became a junior college in 1937, became a four-year institution and adopted its present name in 1948, and awarded its first baccalaureate degree in 1951. The private, four-year, coeducational, liberal arts college is accredited by SACS and the Alabama State Department of Education. Stillman awards bachelor of arts and bachelor of science degrees in sixteen academic areas. As a predominantly black church-related college, Stillman aims to utilize the best of its heritage by providing a Christian and intellectual environment.

Talladega College, located in Talladega, Alabama, was established as a primary school in 1867. It began normal school training in 1868, offered its first instruction at the post-secondary level in 1890, and awarded its first baccalaureate degree in 1895. Talladega provides individualized attention to students in the classroom and in the laboratory. In addition to its traditional curriculum in the liberal arts, it offers majors in most fields of interest to today's students. Talladega College, though small in size with approximately 700 students, has been cited in statistical studies for its particularly high percentage of graduates who earn science doctorates, degrees in medicine, and doctorates in other difficult disciplines. The motto for Talladega College is appropriate: "The Alpha Lyrae Vega of them all," "the brightest star" in this nation's galaxy of institutions of higher learning.

Tennessee State University, located in Nashville, was incorporated in 1909 and established as the Tennessee Agricultural and Industrial State Normal School for Negroes in 1912. It offered its first instruction at the post-secondary level in 1922, awarded its first baccalaureate degree and changed its name to the Agricultural and Industrial State Normal College in 1924, became Tennessee Agricultural and Industrial State University in 1951, adopted its present name in 1969, and merged with the University of Tennessee at Nashville in 1979. As an accredited, land-grant public institution within the Tennessee Board of Regents System, Tennessee State awards the associate's, bachelor's, master's, specialist in education, and doctoral degrees. The main campus occupies more than 500 acres in a residential area of Nashville. The Avon William Campus, also known as the Downtown Campus, is a non-residential campus. Located near the state capitol and Nashville's central business district, this campus houses the School of Business and supports the university's evening and weekend continuing education programs. It enrolls 7,300 students from a variety of cultural backgrounds representing thirty-five states and forty foreign countries. The university has competitive intercollegiate athletic programs.

Texas Southern University, located in Houston, was established as Texas State University and incorporated in 1947. It offered its first instruction at the post-secondary level the same year, awarded its first baccalaureate degree in 1948, added the School of Pharmacy in 1949, adopted its present name in 1951, and established the School of Business in 1955 and the School of Education in 1971. This public, coeducational, accredited university enrolls approximately 8,700 students and permits them to seek a wide range of undergraduate, graduate, and professional degrees, including doctorates in several programs. The university is organized into seven schools and colleges, the General University Academic Center, and an honors program. Preprofessional programs are offered in dentistry and medicine. Texans comprise approximately 78 percent of the total enrollment, 8 percent come from other parts of the United States, and 14 percent represent more than fifty nations.

Trenholm State Technical College, located in Montgomery, Alabama, is a public two-year college named after Dr. H. Council Trenholm, a well-known black leader who served as president of the neighboring Alabama State University for thirty-eight years. Trenholm is accredited by SACS, its dental assisting program is accredited by the American Dental Association, and its practical nursing program is accredited by the National League for Nursing. The emergency medical technology program at Trenholm is the only technical-college-based program in Alabama that provides training ranging from the basic to the advanced (paramedic) levels. Other programs offered by the college include associate degree or diploma programs in medical assisting, medical records technology, dental laboratory technology, accounting, secretarial/office technology, word/information processing, construction technology, electrical technology, and radio broadcasting, as well as various home economics and trades and industrial technology programs. Under a reciprocal agreement with the Community College of the Air Force, active duty and Reserve/National Guard personnel may take occupational courses at Trenholm.

Tuskegee University, located at Tuskegee, Alabama, was established in 1881 as Tuskegee Normal and Industrial Institute by Booker T. Washington and incorporated in 1893. It offered its first instruction at the postsecondary level in 1923, awarded its first baccalaureate degree in 1925, became Tuskegee Institute in 1937, and adopted its present name in 1985 upon achieving university status. Tuskegee is a coeducational, privately controlled, yet state-related, professional, scientific, and technical institution serving more than 3,400 students representing Alabama, forty other states, and fifty-four countries. Tuskegee has enrolled more than 57,000 students during its 110 years of service. Its living alumni today number more than 30,000 and are found in all parts of the nation and the world. On April 2, 1966, it became the first black college to be designated a Registered National Historic Landmark and, on October 26, 1974, the first black college to be designated a National Historic Site. Current undergraduate offerings are organized under seven major divisions: College of Arts and Sciences, School of Agriculture and Home Economics, School of Business, School of Education, School of Engineering and Architecture, School of Nursing and Allied Health, and School of Veterinary Medicine. Courses are offered leading to bachelor of arts and bachelor of science degrees. The seven major divisions offer sixty-eight degrees, including forty-five bachelor's degrees, twenty-one master's degrees, the master of architecture degree, and the doctor of veterinary medicine degree. Graduate instruction leading to the master's degree is offered in five of the seven major areas: the College of Arts and Sciences, and the Schools of Agriculture and Home Economics, Education, Engineering and Architecture, and Veterinary Medicine. The university is fully accredited by SACS, and its programs in the following professional areas are accredited by national agencies: agriculture, chemistry, dietetics, engineering, medical technology, nursing, occupational therapy, social work, and veterinary medicine. Special features of the Tuskegee program include the George Washington Carver Museum; the George Washington Carver Research Foundation, center for a variety of research projects sponsored by government agencies and private industry; the Tuskegee Archives, a center for information on the problems and history of black Americans since 1896; the Reserve Officers' Training Corps Center, and the Job Corps Program, designed to provide disadvantaged youth with useful job training and employment. Army and Air Force ROTC programs are also available. Substantial outreach service programs combine with a sizable research component to make Tuskegee a comprehensive institute. The university has a history of successfully educating black Americans to understand themselves against the background of their total heritage and the promise of their individual and collective future. A primary mission has been to prepare them to play effective professional leadership roles in society and to become productive citizens in the national and world communities.

The University of Arkansas–Pine Bluff is the second oldest state-supported institution of higher education in Arkansas and one of only two with a land-grant mission. It was created in 1873 by an act of the legislature as a branch of Arkansas Industrial University, now the University of Arkansas. Originally known as Branch Normal College, the school opened on September 27, 1875. It operated from 1927 until 1972 as Arkansas Agricultural, Mechanical, and Normal (AM&N) College, at which time it joined four other campuses to form the University of Arkansas System. The university offers degree programs in more than forty areas within the Schools of Education, Arts and Sciences, and Business and Management to more than 3,000 students.

The University of the District of Columbia, located in Washington, D.C., is the nation's only metropolitan land-grant institution of higher education. It was established in 1975 by a merger of the District of Columbia Teachers' College (established in 1851), Federal City College (established in 1966), and Washington Technical College (established in 1966) and was incorporated in 1976. It offered its first instruction at the post-secondary level in 1977 and awarded its first baccalaureate degree in 1978. The university is a commuter institution, with a student population of 11,263 and 568 full-time faculty members. Academic programs are structured under five colleges: Business and Public Management, Education and Human Ecology, Liberal and Fine Arts, Life Sciences and Physical Science, and Engineering and Technology. It also operates a Division of Graduate Studies, a Division of Continuing Education, and a University College.

The University of Maryland–Eastern Shore, located in Princess Anne, was established as Princess Anne of the Delaware Conference Academy in 1886. It became a division of the University of Maryland and changed its name to Maryland State College in 1948. The school adopted its present name in 1970 when it became a part of the University of Maryland System. Degree offerings include thirty-five bachelor's degree programs in such fields as poultry management, environmental science, airway science, hotel/restaurant management, construction management, engineering technology, physical therapy rehabilitation services, and criminal justice. Thirteen programs offer teacher certification. Master's degrees are granted in applied computer science, agriculture and extension education, guidance and counseling, and special education. Doctoral and master's degrees are offered in marine-estuarine-environmental science and toxicology. Nine preprofessional concentrations and an honors program are also available. This land-grant institution is also equipped with facilities for agriculture-related research and cooperative extension service activities for eleven counties in the state of Maryland.

The University of the Virgin Islands, located on Saint Thomas, was founded in 1962 by an act of the Virgin Islands legislature. This public, coeducational, land-grant institution offers master of arts, bachelor of arts, bachelor of science, and the associate degrees through its six academic divisions: Business Administration, Humanities, Nursing, Science and Mathematics, Social Sciences, and Teacher Education. The university's two campuses (St. Thomas and St. Croix) house the Caribbean Research Institute, Cooperative Extension Service, Agricultural Experiment Station, Bureau of Public Administration, and Reichhold Center of the Arts. The university serves 2,665 students with the support of 138 faculty members. It is accredited by the Middle States Association of Colleges and Schools. The bachelor and associate programs in nursing education are accredited by the National League for Nursing, and the Business Administration Division is a member of the Assembly of the American Association of Collegiate Schools of Business. The university is also a member of the National Student Exchange, a consortium of land-grant colleges.

Virginia State University, located in Petersburg, was established as Virginia Normal and Collegiate Institute in 1882. Alfred W. Harris, a black attorney from Petersburg, authored the bill under which the university was created. The school offered its first instruction at the post-secondary level in 1883, awarded its first baccalaureate degree in 1889, changed its name to Virginia Normal and Industrial Institute in 1902, became Virginia State College in 1946, and adopted its present name in 1979. Virginia State is the first fully state-supported, four-year black college in the United States and one of the commonwealth of Virginia's two land-grant universities. It offers degree programs in the Schools of Agriculture and Applied Sciences, Business, Education, Humanities and Social Sciences, Natural Sciences, Continuing Education, and Graduate Studies. The university offers forty-three bachelor's degree programs, twenty-four master's degree programs, and one certificate of advanced graduate studies to more than 4,000 students.

Virginia Union University, located in Richmond, was founded in 1865 to provide educational opportunities for the newly emancipated slaves. It offered its first instruction at the post-secondary level in 1865 and awarded its first baccalaureate degree and adopted its present name in 1899. This university is affiliated with American Baptist church and nurtures its students in an environment based on Christian principles. Former graduates are employed in a variety of fields, including education, medicine, theology, public service, sports, and law. This coeducational, accredited, private institution offers programs leading to either the bachelor of art or the bachelor of science degree, with options that include business administration and engineering, to 1,100 students. The School of Theology offers master of divinity and doctor of ministry degrees. The nationally recognized Kenan Project, administered by Virginia Union's Center for Teacher Effectiveness in cooperation with the university and the Richmond Public Schools, is designed to prepare high school students for college entry and successful completion of degree requirements. The project is funded by the William Kenan Charitable Trust and administered by the Southern Regional Educational Board.

Voorhees College, located in Denmark, South Carolina, was founded in 1897 as Denmark Industrial School by Elizabeth Evelyn Wright. It became Voorhees Industrial School in 1902 in honor of Ralph Voorhees, a philanthropist from Clinton, New Jersey. It offered its first instruction at the post-secondary level and changed its name to Voorhees Normal and Industrial School in 1929, adopted its present name in 1962, and awarded its first baccalaureate degree in 1969. Voorhees, a private, coeducational, liberal arts college affiliated with the Episcopal church, serves 586 students. Voorhees was the first predominately black institution in South Carolina to achieve full accreditation by SACS. Courses leading to associate's and bachelor's degrees are offered through four academic divisions: Business and Economics, Education/Humanities, Natural Sciences and Mathematics, and Social Sciences. The specific academic programs offered are accounting, business administration, office administration, secretarial science, English literature, English communications, biology, chemistry, computer science, mathematics, pre-engineering, prenursing, criminal justice, political science, social work, sociology, and prelaw.

West Virginia State College, located in Institute, was founded as West Virginia Colored Institute in 1891. It offered its first instruction at the post-secondary level and changed its name to West Virginia Collegiate Institute in 1915, awarded its first baccalaureate degree in 1919, and adopted its present name in 1929. The school attained national prominence soon after its founding as an institution of higher education for blacks, and it continues to serve as a center of black culture. The school had its origins in the second Morrill Act, passed by the U.S. Congress in 1890. It is known as a model for human relations. Of a student body that averages 4,300 per year, about 86 percent are white, 12 percent are black, and 2 percent are Asian, Hispanic, and members of other groups. West Virginia State is accredited by the North Central Association of Colleges and Schools. This land-grant, state-supported, coeducational institution seeks to develop a high level of competence in English and mathematics, an increased appreciation of the liberal arts, and an expanded awareness of and respect for the contributions of women and minorities to our society. The college's curriculum also emphasizes contemporary technology and its roots in modern science.

Wilberforce University, located in Wilberforce, Ohio, was founded in 1843 as Ohio African University by the Methodist Episcopal church and established as Wilberforce University of the Methodist Episcopal church in 1856. It changed its name to Wilberforce University in 1863, offered its first instruction at the post-secondary level in 1856, and awarded its first baccalaureate degree in 1857. Wilberforce was the first black college established in the United States and was named in honor of William Wilberforce, a great eighteenth century abolitionist. The first students were slaves and freed blacks. This private institution has a deep commitment to providing academically excellent and relevant higher education for today's youth, particularly black men and women. By keeping this commitment, Wilberforce aims at increasing the probabilities of success in college and subsequent careers for youth previously excluded from the mainstream of American society. Wilberforce offers bachelor of arts and bachelor of science degrees in twenty-one areas of concentration. It also offers the following special programs designed to meet particular student needs: basic skills development classes, freshmen honors courses, and cooperative education preparatory classes. The current student enrollment is 767, which allows a student-faculty ratio of 14:1. The university's mandatory and comprehensive cooperative education program has placed more than 10,000 students in career-oriented work assignments since its implementation in 1964, which constitutes a rate of more than 500 students per year. Wilberforce is one of the eighteen colleges in the Southwestern Ohio Council for Higher Education (SOCHE) and participates in the Consortium Cross-Registration Program.

Winston-Salem State University, located in Winston-Salem, North Carolina, was first established in 1893 as Slater Industrial Academy. It offered its first instruction at the post-secondary level and changed its name to Winston-Salem Teachers College in 1925. Winston-Salem Teachers College was the first black institution in the United States to grant degrees for teaching in the elementary grades. The school awarded its first baccalaureate degree in 1927, changed its name to Winston-Salem State College in 1963, and adopted its present name in 1969. The university is one of the sixteen constituent institutions of the University of North Carolina System. As Winston-Salem State approaches its centennial, it enjoys a tradition of excellence in teacher education, while developing its curricula in the areas of business, computer science, and accounting. This coeducational, four-year, liberal arts, public, SACS-accredited college currently offers more than thirty majors and three degree options, bachelor of arts, bachelor of science, and bachelor of administration and education through the Center for Graduate Studies.

Xavier University, located in New Orleans, Louisiana, was established as a secondary school in 1915, became a two-year normal school and offered first instruction at post-secondary level in 1917, became a four-year college in 1925, and offered its first bachelor's degree in 1922. A master's program was inaugurated in 1933. This private institution is affiliated with the Sisters of the Blessed Sacrament, of the Roman Catholic Church. This SACS-accredited school enrolls over 2,500 students representing the New Orleans area, thirty other states, and a dozen foreign countries. Xavier offers instruction in more than three dozen academic and professional fields and is comprised of a College of Arts and Sciences, a College of Pharmacy, and a Graduate School. The educational program is geared to liberal arts, and all students are required to take a core of courses in theology and philosophy, art and the humanities, communications, history, the behavioral sciences, mathematics, and the natural sciences. Xavier is widely known for its pharmacy and premed programs. The College of Pharmacy, one of the only two pharmacy schools in Louisiana, annually educates 15 percent of all black pharmacists in the United States. More than 80 percent of Xavier's premed students are accepted at medical and dental schools throughout the country.

HISTORICALLY BLACK COLLEGE AND UNIVERSITY DEMOGRAPHICS, ACADEMIC PROGRAMS, ENROLLMENT PATTERNS, FACULTY, AND STAFF

DEMOGRAPHICS

Currently there are 109 HBCUs consisting of 50 public and 59 private institutions located in fourteen southern states, three northern states, three midwestern states, the District of Columbia, and the Virgin Islands. The fifty public HBCUs (46%) include forty four-year institutions (80%) and ten two-year institutions (20%). The fifty-nine private HBCUs (54%) include forty-nine four-year institutions (83%) and ten two-year institutions (17%) (see Table 4.1 for a list of all HBCUs, giving the year founded, academic level, and public or private status). Of these 109 HBCUs, 104 are NAFEO member institutions, 93 percent of which were established by 1908. Twenty-one HBCUs are land-grant institutions (see Table 4.2 for a list of land-grant institutions).

ACADEMIC PROGRAMS

Over 450 academic programs are offered by the HBCUs in liberal arts, sciences, education, business administration, social work, law, medicine, dentistry, pharmacy, veterinary science, engineering, military science, and theology, leading to degrees including the associate's, bachelor's, master's, doctorate, and first professional degrees. In 1989, 23,246 degrees were conferred by the HBCUs, 19,449 (84%) of which were awarded to blacks and 3,797 (16%) to whites. Compared to 1976 figures, this number evidenced a 32.4 percent decline in the number of degrees awarded to blacks and a 73.2 percent increase in the number of degrees awarded to whites (NAFEO, *Factbook*, 1991, vol. II, 112).

Ten HBCUs (three public and seven private) confer first professional

Table 4.1
Historically Black Colleges and Universities

Institution	Year of founding	Level 2	4	FP	Control PU	PR
Alabama A&M University; AL	1875	–	x	–	x	–
Alabama State University; AL	1871	–	x	–	x	–
Albany State Collge; GA	1903	–	x	–	x	–
Alcorn State University; MS	1871	–	x	–	x	–
Allen University; SC	1870	–	x	–	–	x
Arkansas Baptist College; AR	1884	–	x	–	–	x
Barber-Scotia College; NC	1867	–	x	–	–	x
Benedict College; SC	1870	–	x	–	–	x
Bennett College; NC	1873	–	x	–	–	x
Bethune-Cookman College; FL	1904	–	x	–	–	x
Bishop State Jr. College; AL	1936	x	–	–	x	–
Bluefield State College; WV	1895	–	x	–	x	–
Bowie State University; MD	1865	–	x	–	x	–
Carver State Tech. Collge; AL	1962	x	–	–	x	–
Central State University; OH	1887	–	x	–	x	–
Cheyney University; PA	1837	–	x	–	x	–
Claflin College; SC	1869	–	x	–	–	x
Clark Atlanta University; GA	1988	–	x	–	–	x
Clinton Jr. College; SC	1894	x	–	–	–	x
Coahoma Comm. College; MS	1949	x	–	–	x	–
Concordia College; AL	1922	x	–	–	–	x
Coppin State College; MD	1900	–	x	–	x	–
Delaware State College; DE	1891	–	x	–	x	–
Denmark Tech. College; SC	1947	x	–	–	x	–
Dillard University; LA	1869	–	x	–	–	x
Edward Waters College; FL	1866	–	x	–	–	x
Elizabeth City State University; NC	1891	–	x	–	x	–
Fayetteville State University; NC	1867	–	x	–	x	–
Fisk University; TN	1865	–	x	–	–	x
Florida A&M University; FL	1887	–	x	–	x	–
Florida Memorial College; FL	1879	–	x	–	–	x
Fort Valley State College; GA	1895	–	x	–	x	–
Fress State Tech. Collge; AL	1963	x	–	–	x	–
Grambling St. Unviersity; LA	1901	–	x	–	x	–
Hampton University; VA	1868	–	x	–	–	x
Harris-Stowe St. College; MO	1857	–	x	–	x	–
Hinds Jr. College, Utica Campus; MS	1903	x	–	–	x	–

Table 4.1 (continued)

Institution	Year of founding	Level 2	Level 4	Level FP	Control PU	Control PR
Houstan-Tillotson College; TX	1876	-	x	-	-	x
Howard University; DC	1867	-	x	-	-	x
Interdenominational Theological Center; GA	1958	-	-	x	-	x
Jackson State University; MS	1877	-	x	-	x	-
Jarvis Christian College; TX	1912	-	x	-	-	x
J. F. Drake State Technical College; AL	1961	x	-	-	x	-
Johnson C.Smith University; NC	1867	-	x	-	-	x
Kentucky State University; KY	1886	-	x	-	x	-
Knoxville College; TN	1875	-	x	-	-	x
Lane College; TN	1882	-	x	-	-	x
Langston University; OK	1897	-	x	-	x	-
Lawson State Community College; AL	1972	x	-	-	x	-
Lemoyne-Owen College; TN	1968	-	x	-	-	x
Lewis College of Business; MI	1929	x	-	-	-	x
Lincoln University; MO	1866	-	x	-	x	-
Lincoln University; PA	1854	-	x	-	x	-
Livingstone College; NC	1879	-	x	-	-	x
Mary Holmes College; MS	1892	x	-	-	-	x
Meharry Medical College; TN	1876	-	-	x	-	x
Miles College; AL	1905	-	x	-	-	x
Mississippi Valley State University; MS	1946	-	x	-	x	-
Morehouse College; GA	1867	-	x	-	-	x
Morehouse School of Medicine; GA	1975	-	-	x	-	x
Morgan State University; MD	1867	-	x	-	x	-
Morris Brown College; GA	1881	-	x	-	-	x
Morris College; SC	1908	-	x	-	-	x
Natchez Jr. College; MS	1885	x	-	-	-	x
Norfolk State University; VA	1935	-	x	-	x	-
N. C. A&T State University; NC	1891	-	x	-	x	-
N. C. Central University; NC	1910	-	x	-	x	-
Oakwood College; AL	1896	-	x	-	-	x
Paine College; GA	1882	-	x	-	-	x
Paul Quinn College; TX	1872	-	x	-	-	x
Philander Smith College; AR	1877	-	x	-	-	x
Prairie View A&M University; TX	1876	-	x	-	x	-

Table 4.1 (continued)

Institution	Year of founding	Level 2	Level 4	Level FP	Control PU	Control PR
Prentiss Institute Jr. College; MS	1907	x	-	-	x	-
Rust College; MS	1866	-	x	-	-	x
Saint Augustine's College; NC	1867	-	x	-	-	x
Saint Paul's College; VA	1888	-	x	-	-	x
Saint Philip College; TX	1898	x	-	-	-	x
Savannah State College; GA	1890	-	x	-	x	-
Selma University; AL	1878	x	-	-	-	x
Shaw University; NC	1865	-	x	-	-	x
Shorter College; AR	1886	x	-	-	-	x
Simmons University Bible College; KY	1873	-	x	-	-	x
South Carolina State College; SC	1896	-	x	-	x	-
Southern University- Baton Rouge; LA	1880	-	x	-	x	-
Southern University- New Orleans; LA	1956	-	x	-	x	-
Southern University- Shreveport; LA	1964	x	-	-	x	-
Southwestern Christian College; TX	1949	x	-	-	-	x
Spelman College; GA	1881	-	x	-	-	x
Stillman College; AL	1876	-	x	-	-	x
Talladega College; AL	1867	-	x	-	-	x
Tennesse State University; TN	1912	-	x	-	x	-
Texas College; TX	1894	-	x	-	-	x
Texas Southern University; TX	1947	-	x	-	x	-
Tougaloo College; MS	1869	-	x	-	-	x
Trenholm State Technical College; AL	1963	x	-	-	x	-
Tuskegee University; AL	1881	-	x	-	-	x
University of Arkansas- Pine Bluff; AR	1873	-	x	-	x	-
University of the District Columbia; DC	1851	-	x	-	x	-
University Of Maryland- Eastern Shore; MD	1886	-	x	-	x	-
University of the Virgin Islands; VI	1962	-	x	-	x	-

Table 4.1 (continued)

Institution	Year of founding	Level 2	Level 4	Level FP	Control PU	Control PR
Virginia Seminary & College; VA	1888	-	x	-	-	x
Virginia State University; VA	1882	-	x	-	x	-
Virginia Union University; VA	1865	-	x	-	-	x
Voorhees College; SC	1897	-	x	-	-	x
West Virginia State College; WV	1891	-	x	-	x	-
Wilberforce University; OH	1856	-	x	-	-	x
Wiley College; TX	1873	-	x	-	-	x
Winston-Salem State University; NC	1893	-	x	-	x	-
Xavier University; LA	1915	-	x	-	-	x
Total		20	86	3	52	57

Note: FP = First Professional; PU = Public; PR = Private.

Source: The National Association for Equal Opportunity in Higher Education (NAFEO), *Fact Book on Blacks in Higher Education and in Historically and Predominantly Black Colleges and Universities,* Vol. 1, pp. 171–74 (1991).

Table 4.2
Historically Black Land-Grant Colleges and Universities

Institution	Year of Founding
Alabama A&M University; AL	1875
Alcorn State University; MS	1871
Delware State College; DE	1891
Florida A&M University; FL	1887
Fort Valley State College; GA	1895
Kentucky State University; KY	1886
Langston University; OK	1897
Lincoln University; MO	1866
N.C. A&T State University; NC	1891
Prairie view A&M University; TX	1876
Savannah State College	1890
South Carolina State College; SC	1896
Southern University-Baton Rouge; LA	1880
Tennesse State University; TN	1912
Tuskegee University; AL	1881
University of Arkansas-Pine bluff; AR	1873
University of the District Columbia; DC	1851
University Of Maryland-Eastern Shore; MD	1886
University of the Virgin Islands; VI	1962
Virgina State University; VA	1882
West Virginia State College; WV	1891

Source: The National Association for Equal Opportunity in Higher Education (NAFEO), *Fact Book on Blacks in Higher Education and in Historically and Predominantly Black Colleges and Universities,* Vol. 1, pp. 171–74 (1991).

degrees (in dentistry, medicine, optometry, osteopathy, pharmacy, podiatry, veterinary medicine, law, and theology). In 1989, they conferred 819 such degrees, 458 (55.9%) on blacks, 130 (15.9%) on whites, 56 (6.8%) on non-resident aliens, and 175 (21.4%) on others. Numerically, law degrees (408) were followed by those conferred in medicine (146), theology (119), dentistry (80), veterinary medicine (47), and pharmacy (19). This evidences a 10 percent increase over the number of first professional degrees conferred by HBCUs in 1976 (741) (computed from NAFEO, *Factbook*, 1991, vol. II, 130–32). Of the 458 first professional degrees, conferred on blacks 266 (58%) were awarded to males and 192 (42%) to females. In addition to these 458 first professional degrees awarded to blacks by HBCUs, 2,643 first professional degrees were awarded to blacks by non-HBCUs. This results in a total of 3,101 first professional degrees awarded to blacks (1,608 to males and 1,493 to females) in 1989, a 15.1 percent increase since 1976 (when 2,694 such degrees were awarded).

Twelve HBCUs (eight public and four private) confer doctorates. In 1989, they conferred 190 doctorates, 112 (58.9%) on blacks, 11 (5.8%) on whites, 38 (20.0%) on non-resident aliens, and the remaining on students whose race is unknown. Numerically, education doctorates (72) were followed by those in law (25), biological sciences (20), social sciences (24), and theology (10). This evidences a 157 percent increase over the number of doctorates conferred by HBCUs in 1976 (74) (computed from NAFEO, *Factbook*, vol. II, 1991:158). Of the 112 doctorates conferred on black, 25 (22%) were awarded to males and 87 (78%) to females. In addition to these 112 doctorates awarded to blacks by HBCUs, 959 doctorates were awarded to blacks by non-HBCUs. This results in a total of 1,071 doctorates awarded to blacks (497 to males and 574 to females) in 1989, a 11.7 percent decrease since 1976 (when 1,213 such degrees were awarded).

Thirty-eight HBCUs (thirty-one public and seven private) confer master's degrees. In 1989, they conferred 3,787 master's degrees, 2,264 (59.8%) on blacks, 871 (23%) on whites, 437 (11.5%) on non-resident aliens and 215 (5.7%) on others. Numerically, master's degrees in education (1,192) were followed by those in business and management (292), public affairs and services (236), and health professions (89). This evidences a 35 percent decrease from the number of master's degrees conferred by HBCUs in 1976 (5,841) (computed from NAFEO, Factbook, vol. II, 1991: 196–97). Of the 2,264 master's degrees conferred on blacks, 696 (30.7 percent) were awarded to males and 1,568 (69.3 percent) to females. In addition to these 2,264 master's degrees awarded to blacks by HBCUs, 11,812 master's degrees were awarded to blacks by non-HBCUs. This results in a total of 14,076 master's degrees awarded to blacks (5,200 to males and 8,876 to females) in 1989, a 30.8 percent decrease since 1976 (when 20,351 such degrees were awarded).

Eighty-five HBCUs (forty public and forty-five private) confer bachelor's degrees. In 1989, they conferred 19,225 bachelor's degrees, 15,448 (80.3%) on blacks, 1,991 (10.4%) on whites, 947 (4.9%) on non-resident aliens, and 839 (4.4%) on others. Numerically, bachelor's degrees in business and management (4,794) were followed by those in education (1,813), social sciences (1,453), computer science (1,186), and engineering (1,015). This evidences a 16.4 percent decrease from the number of bachelor's degrees conferred by HBCUs in 1976 (23,835) (computed from NAFEO, *Factbook*, 1991, vol. II: 227–32). Of the 15,448 bachelor's degrees conferred on blacks, 5,758 (37.3%) were awarded to males and 9,690 (62.7%) to females. In addition to these 15,448 bachelor's degrees awarded to blacks by HBCUs, 42,568 bachelor's degrees were awarded to blacks by non-HBCUs. This results in a total of 58,016 bachelor's degrees awarded to blacks (23,960 males and 34,056 females) in 1989, a 2.0 percent decrease since 1976 (when 59,187 such degrees were awarded).

Forty-eight HBCUs (twenty-nine public and nineteen private) confer associate's degrees. In 1989, they conferred 2,188 associate degrees, 1,167 (53.3%) on blacks, 817 (37.3%) on whites, 60 (2.7%) on non-resident aliens, and 144 (6.6%) on others. (computed from NAFEO, *Factbook*, 1991, vol. II:252–68). Of the 1,167 associate's degrees conferred on blacks 350 (30%) were awarded to males and 817 (70%) to females. In addition to these 1,167 associate's degrees awarded to blacks by HBCUs, 33,244 associate's degrees were awarded to blacks by non-HBCUs. This results in a total of 34,411 associate's degrees awarded to blacks (12,826 males and 21,585 to females) in 1989, a 28.4 percent decrease since 1981 (when 48,077 such degrees were awarded). HBCUs evidenced a decreasing trend between 1981 and 1989 as well (3.0% decrease in total degrees awarded, and 37.1% decrease in degrees awarded to blacks).

ENROLLMENT PATTERNS

HBCUs comprise about 3 percent of the total institutions of higher education in the United States and have approximately 2 percent of the total college enrollment in the United States (Patel 1988). Black enrollment in institutions of higher education increased by 5.0 percent between 1978 and 1980, decreased by 2.3 percent between 1980 and 1986, and increased by 4.4 percent between 1986 and 1988. These trends between 1978 and 1988 contributed to an overall 7.2 percent increase in black enrollment. Black male enrollment decreased by 2.2 percent during this decade, while black female enrollment increased by 14.3 percent. The proportion of blacks enrolled in institutions of higher education decreased by 0.7 percent (from 9.4 percent in 1978 to 8.7 percent in 1988).

An examination of the enrollment patterns in HBCUs from 1966 to 1989 shows a steady increase in total enrollment from 1966 to 1980 (59.6%), a

Table 4.3
Historically Black College and University Faculty by Position, Race, and Sex, 1989

Faculty Position	Black			White		
	M	F	T	M	F	T
Professors	816	327	1,143	450	130	580
Associate Prof.	927	632	1,559	599	234	833
Assistant Prof.	1,198	1,050	2,248	571	368	939
Instructors	697	799	1,496	369	431	800
Lecturers	61	88	149	27	14	41
Other Faculty	63	63	126	28	12	40
Total Full-Time	3,762	2,959	6,721	2,044	1,189	3,233
Part-Time	956	752	1,708	690	401	1,091

Faculty Position	Other			All Races		
	M	F	T	M	F	T
Professors	262	35	297	1,528	492	2,020
Associate Prof.	227	45	272	1,753	911	2,664
Assistant Prof.	256	69	325	2,025	1,487	3,512
Instructors	101	55	156	1,167	1,285	2,452
Lecturers	11	5	16	99	107	206
Other Faculty	9	2	11	100	77	177
Total Full-Time	866	211	1,077	6,672	4,359	11,031
Part-Time	126	36	162	1,772	1,189	2,961

Note: M = Male; F = Female; T = Total

Source: Compiled and computed from *1989 EEO-6 HBCUs* (information obtained through personal communications from) the U.S. Equal Employment Opportunity Commission, Washington, D.C. (May 1992).

decrease from 1980 to 1984 (2.1%), a further decrease from 1984 to 1986 (2.2%), and, finally, an increase from 1986 to 1989 (12.1%). The white enrollment at HBCUs increased from 18,389 in 1976 to 26,962 in 1989 (NAFEO, *Factbook*, vol. II, 1991, 2–32). Data on student transfers to HBCUs show that two-thirds of HBCU transfer students come from white institutions and the remaining one-third comes from other HBCUs (Patel 1988).

FACULTY COMPOSITION

In 1989, there were 11,031 full-time faculty members at HBCUs. Of these, nearly 60 percent (6,672) were males, and the remaining 40 percent (4,359) were females (see Table 4.3 for HBCU faculty composition by position, race, and sex). Of all HBCU faculty members, 39 percent were tenured; 27 percent were not tenured, but were in tenure track positions;

Table 4.4

Historically Black College and University Faculty by Tenure Status, Race, and Sex, 1989

Tenure Status	Black			White			Other		
	M	F	T	M	F	T	M	F	T
Tenured	1,568	1,070	2,638	849	343	1,192	397	73	470
Non-tenured on track	989	789	1,778	557	356	913	217	48	265
Other	1,205	1,100	2,305	638	490	1,128	252	90	342
Total	3,762	2,959	6,721	2,044	1,189	3,233	866	211	1,077

Note: M = Male; F = Female; T = Total

Source: Compiled and computed from *1989 EEO-6 HBCUs* (information obtained through personal communications from) the U.S. Equal Employment Opportunity Commission, Washington, D.C. (May 1992).

and the remaining 34 percent were of other status (see Table 4.4 for HBCU faculty composition by tenure status, race, and sex). Nearly 18 percent were full professors, 24 percent were associate professors, 32 percent were assistant professors, 22 percent were instructors, and the remaining 4 percent were lecturers and other faculty. In general, males outnumbered females, and the gender gap increased with rank (i.e., the ratio of 73 females for every 100 males at the rank of assistant professor dropped to only 32 females for every 100 males at the rank of professor). Racially, 61 percent of the faculty members were black, 29 percent were white, and the remaining 10 percent were members of other racial categories.

Black Faculty

Of the 6,721 black faculty members, 39 percent were tenured; 27 percent were not tenured, but were holding tenure track positions; and the remaining 34 percent had other academic contractual agreements. Males constituted 59 percent of tenured faculty, 56 percent of non-tenured (but on tenure track) faculty, and 52 percent of those having other faculty status. On the whole, 56 percent of all black faculty were male.

Understandably, a majority of black faculty (77%) held nine or ten-month contracts with their institutions, and some 22 percent had eleven or twelve-month contracts. Only a few faculty members were issued contracts for less than nine months by their institutions (see Table 4.5 for HBCU faculty composition by length of contract, race, and sex).

Among the black faculty, there were 1,143 full professors, 1,559 associate professors, 2,248 assistant professors, 1,496 instructors, 149 lecturers, and 126 other faculty members. The gender gap increased with rank. For example, there were more females than males in the lecturer

Table 4.5
Historically Black College and University Faculty by Length of Contract, Race, and Sex, 1989

Length of Contract	Black			White			Other		
	M	F	T	M	F	T	M	F	T
9–10 Months	2,844	2,363	5,207	1,739	1,051	2,790	671	178	849
11–12 Months	905	568	1,473	289	155	444	196	34	230
Less than 9 Months	12	7	19	4	5	9	2	0	2
Total	3,761	2,938	6,699	2,032	1,211	3,243	869	212	1,081

Note: M = Male; F = Female; T= Total

Source: Compiled and computed from *1989 EEO-6 HBCUs* (information obtained through personal communications from) the U.S. Equal Employment Opportunity Commission, Washington, D.C. (May 1992).

and instructor categories, but more males were found in the higher ranks than were females. The female underrepresentation steadily increased from a ratio of 92 females for every 100 males in the assistant professor category, to 68 females for every 100 males in the associate professor category, to only 40 females for every 100 males in the professor category. This pattern can be attributed to two possible reasons: (1) females might have entered teaching positions much later than males, in which case their supply for faculty positions at higher ranks would naturally be low; or (2) females might not be getting promoted to higher ranks at the same rate as are males, whether for justifiable reasons (less research; low publication records; unsatisfactory performance; more leaves or temporary absences from campus for various reasons, including those related to family and changes in life cycle) or for unjustifiable reasons (sex discrimination against females).

White Faculty

Males constituted 63 percent of all the white faculty at HBCUs (3,233). Of the 3,233 white faculty at HBCUs, 37 percent were tenured; 28 percent were not tenured, but were holding tenure track positions; and the remaining 35 percent had other academic contractual agreements. Males constituted 71 percent of tenured faculty, 61 percent of non-tenured (but on tenure track) faculty, and 56 percent of those having other faculty status.

As in the case of black faculty, a majority of white faculty (86%) held nine- or ten-month contracts with their institutions, and some 13 percent had eleven- or twelve-month contracts. Only nine faculty members were issued contracts for less than nine months by their institutions.

Among the white faculty, there were 580 full professors, 833 associate professors, 939 assistant professors, 800 instructors, 41 lecturers, and 40 other faculty members. The gender trends were identical to those among black faculty, but the actual gap between male and female faculty members was even higher. For example, there were only 64 white females for every 100 white males in the assistant professor category; this declined to 39 white females for every 100 white males in the associate professor category and further declined to only 29 white females for every 100 white males in the professor category. Perhaps white females do not choose to work on HBCU campuses as frequently as do white males, and/or they may not stay on these campuses throughout their career. Of course, some attrition takes place because of female withdrawal from the labor force itself, especially during child-bearing ages.

Other Faculty

Of the 1,077 faculty members of other races (i.e., those other than black and white), 866 (80%) were males, and 211 (20%) were females. Also, 43 percent were tenured; 25 percent were non-tenured, but were holding tenure track positions; and 32 percent had other academic contractual agreements. A majority (79%) held nine- or ten-month contracts and 21 percent had eleven- or twelve-month contracts; only two had less than nine-month contracts. Among this group, there were 297 full professors, 272 associate professors, 325 assistant professors, 156 instructors, 16 lecturers, and 11 other faculty members.

In addition to the above 11,031 full-time faculty members, there were 2,961 part-time faculty members at HBCUs. These part-time faculty members consisted of 956 black males, 752 black females, 690 white males, 401 white females, 126 males of other races, and 36 females of other races.

STAFF COMPOSITION

HBCUs employed 26,200 staff members in 1989; of these, 10,396 (40%) were males, and 15,804 (60%) were females. Of all staff, 12 percent were administrators, and an additional 24 percent were their assistants and deputies. Secretarial and clerical staff constituted a single major category (27%), and 94 percent of the persons in this category were female. Maintenance and service personnel was the next largest category (20%). Other categories included technical/paraprofessional workers (11%) and skilled craft workers (6%). When classified by race and gender, 34 percent of the staff were black males, 55 percent were black females, 4 percent were white males, 4 percent were white females, and 3 percent were males and

Table 4.6

Historically Black College and University Staff by Position, Race, and Sex, 1989

Staff Position	Black			White		
	M	F	T	M	F	T
Executive/Admin/ Managerial	1,590	1,272	2,862	206	80	286
Other professional (serv/support)	1,949	3,307	5,256	343	281	624
Secretarial/ clerical	412	6,021	6,433	22	485	507
Technical/ paraprofessional	972	1,541	2,513	121	137	258
Skilled crafts	1,116	72	1,188	168	57	225
Service/ maintenance	3,005	2,064	5,069	140	43	183
Total Full-Time	9,044	14,277	23,321	1,000	1,083	2,083
Part-Time	1,272	1,222	2,494	198	182	380

Staff Position	Other			Total		
	M	F	T	M	F	T
Executive/Admin/ Managerial	68	37	105	1,864	1,389	3,253
Other professional (serv/support)	127	255	382	2,419	3,843	6,262
Secretarial/ classical	15	79	94	449	6,585	7,034
Technical/ paraprofessional	59	61	120	1,152	1,739	2,891
Skilled crafts	33	0	33	1,317	129	1,446
Service/ maintenance	50	12	62	3,195	2,119	5,314
Total Full-Time	352	444	796	10,396	15,804	26,200
Part-Time	149	63	212	1,619	1,467	3,086

Note: M = Male; F = Female; T = Total.

Source: Compiled and computed from *1989 EEO-6 HBCUs*, (information obtained through personal communications from) the U.S. Equal Employment Opportunity Commission, Washington, D.C. (May 1992).

females of other races (see Table 4.6 for HBCU staff composition by position, race, and sex).

In addition to the above full-time staff, HBCUs employed 3,086 part-time staff, of whom 1,272 (41%), were black males, 1,222 (40%) were black females, 198 (6%) were white males, 182 (6%) were white females, 149 (5%) were males of other races, and 63 (2%) were females of other races.

In sum, blacks comprised by far the largest proportion of both faculty and staff, followed by whites and other races. Except for secretaries, males outnumbered females in faculty and staff categories, and this gender gap was larger among whites than among blacks. Blacks more frequently were tenured, held higher ranks, and received eleven- or twelve-month contracts than those in other racial categories. The ratio of faculty to staff exceeded 1:2, which indicates an oversized staff, especially the administrative staff (which comprised 36% of the total staff). The perception among HBCU faculty about an oversized administration is documented in the following chapters.

5

REVIEW OF THE LITERATURE ON CAMPUS RACE RELATIONS

Many campuses experience some sort of racial conflict every day arising from controversies over admission policies, racially motivated hate incidents, and curriculum content. A cross-sectional survey of young Americans of all races between the ages of fifteen and twenty-four years, entitled "Democracy's Next Generation II: A Study of American Youth on Race," discloses that youth are pessimistic about our nation's future and their ability to find good jobs and earn decent incomes. These youth see their lives as tougher than were those of their parents. Many young whites now believe that they are more likely to lose college admissions, scholarships, jobs, and promotions under the status quo than are minorities. Young blacks continue to support affirmative action policies. Whites' anger over the notion of affirmative action frequently overpowers their positive personal experiences with individual blacks. Some blacks condemn all whites on the basis of a few negative encounters with individual whites. The major controversy between black and white college students is the thorny issue of minority enrollment preferences. White students on integrated college campuses express more bigotry toward blacks than do non-college-educated whites. Black youth who have completed college remain alienated. A majority of white youth who are now in college or who have completed college and two-thirds of their black counterparts say race relations are generally bad. College-educated blacks are significantly more likely than are other young blacks to allege that blacks feel uneasy in dealing with whites. Furthermore, college-educated blacks are less likely to say they socialize with whites than are non-college-educated blacks (Kropp 1992).

Black students on white campuses are beginning to segregate themselves into social spheres separate from the rest of the campus community, despite efforts by many college administrators to integrate them into the mainstream of college life. These students also tend to stress their separateness, racial identity, and black consciousness and to seek empowerment as a minority group in order to change the academic administrative structure (Bunzel 1991; Hacker 1992, 151–52).

INTERRACIAL AND INTRARACIAL PERCEPTIONS AND ACCOMMODATIONS ON CAMPUS

Black Students on White Campuses

As mentioned before, black students report engagement, connection, acceptance, emotional support, and encouragement at HBCUs (Hemmons 1982; Allen 1992). On the other hand, on white campuses, they experience significant adjustment problems, which make it necessary for them to create their own social worlds.

Alienation Studies

Black students' more serious problems are generated by isolation, alienation, and lack of support (Allen 1985; Smith and Allen 1984). Alienation is a composite construct designating powerlessness, meaninglessness, insulation, social isolation, and racism (Moore and Wagstaff 1974; Suen 1983). Several studies (Braddock 1974; Jackson 1973; Moore and Wagstaff 1974; Schuman and Hatchett 1974; Smith 1981; Loo and Rolison 1986; Allen 1992) demonstrate this alienation.

Allen (1985), in a study of 695 black undergraduates attending six white universities in the Midwest, Southeast, Far West, and Northeast, found that nearly half the respondents (45%) believed themselves to be very little or not at all a part of campus social life. Only 12 percent reported feeling very much a part of the campus social life. Social involvement on the campus was highest among those students who claimed to have good relations with faculty, who participated in black student organization activities, and who held high positive views toward supportive services and campus race relations. Students expressing strong pro-black racial attitudes were more likely to report low social involvement. Those on southern campuses reported more favorable campus race relations than did those on campuses outside the South. The integration of these black students into campus social life was not found to be a necessary precondition for academic success, and there was no empirical support for the assumption that blacks' campus experience with whites improved their views of black-white relations. Nor did greater exposure to middle-class white culture increase their acculturation or integration into campus social networks. Good students, academically speaking, were on better terms with faculty than were poor students. Black students in southern universities evaluated the faculty and campus race relations higher than did students from other regions.

Shingles (1989) found the following from responses to interviews with 105 black students on a white southeastern land-grant university in April 1975: (1) A liberal arts education made black students more sensitive to and knowledgeable about racism in the United States, thereby enhancing their alienation (estrangement from and hostility toward the predominately white society in the United States and the institutions that serve it); (2) interracial relationships were strained and characterized by real or perceived discrimination, isolation, and limited social activities; (3) the strain between themselves and white students was greater for those who had faced racial deprivation prior to college enrollment than for those who had not experienced previous racial deprivation; (4) alienation was associated with interracial strain in their home communities; and (5) the lack of black social life on the predominately white campus led to self-debasement. In sum, a liberal arts education, along with a dissatisfaction with the university, contributed to black students' alienation from white society.

Nieves (1977), in a review of the literature on minority experiences on white campuses, found that many blacks felt they were not entitled to a college education, experienced loneliness and isolation, and suffered from cultural alienation. The research of Smith (1980) revealed similar findings. Smith and Baruch (1981) found that black students attending white universities were caught in a whirlwind of confusing racial identities, sensed a hostile milieu, and thought white students and faculty perceived all blacks as "special admits" and beneficiaries of affirmative action. Black students found that in order to adjust they must adhere quickly to white cultural norms, thereby abandoning their own cultural roots. Hostile communications from white faculty and students and a curriculum that omits or distorts black cultural contributions were constant negative reminders of their racial identities. Their efforts to counteract loneliness and alienation (by eating together, rooming together, and joining all-black social groups) were discouraged by university officials. In addition, they were frequently singled out by campus security police and asked to identify themselves and establish their right to be on campus.

Another study (Loo and Rolison 1986) found that those black students who maintained frequent and meaningful contacts with peers and faculty on white campuses reported higher levels of social integration (and therefore less alienation) than did those who did not have such contacts. Stewardt, Jackson, and Jackson (1990) conducted an alienation study among forty-six black seniors (thirty-two women and fourteen men) enrolled at a predominately white midwestern public university. All were successful students with an average high school GPA of 3.32 and a cumulative college

GPA of 2.47 on a 4-point scale. The study utilized self-administered questionnaires consisting of a student demographic questionnaire (SDQ), the fundamental interpersonal relations orientation-behavior scale (FIRO-B), and the university alienation scale (UAS). Each student completed two questionnaires, imagining themselves, first, as the only black person in an all-white campus situation and, second, as the only white person in an all-black campus situation. Study findings indicated that black students expressed a higher desire for self-inclusion and affection when they imagined themselves in an all-white campus situation than they did when in an all-black situation; that they were primarily interested in fulfilling their personal academic needs involving interaction in an all-white environment (such as receiving a degree and making the necessary professional contacts), rather than in fulfilling other personal needs that required interaction in all-black environments; that they realized the value of remaining a "stranger" in a white campus situation to protect themselves from events that might contribute to academic demise; and that they were willing to pay the alienation price required on a white campus in order to further their careers.

Pruitt and Issac (1983) found that black graduate students have a hard way to go on white campuses where old-boy networks, graduate record examinations, standardized test measures, and the selection process lessen their chances of admission and retention. Most white schools have low percentages of black students and of black faculty. Often the expectations and attitudes of white faculty lead minority graduate students to feel stigmatized. Some feel they would not have been enrolled had it not been for affirmative action requirements. Frequently, dissertation topics on minority issues are not well received. Therefore, many black students withdraw psychologically, and many drop out.

Black Students' Negative Perceptions of White Campuses and Measurement Problems

Numerous studies and published reports reveal that black faculty, as well as students, define themselves as aliens in predominantly white colleges and universities. They, too, see white campuses as hostile environments where they experience feelings of loneliness, alienation, marginality, and academic anxiety (Allen 1992). Research also notes problems of distrust and social distance between black college students and white instructors on black as well as white campuses (Levy 1967; Smith and Borgstedt 1985). Measurement in these areas of perception and the reality of the actual situations, however, has proven to be difficult. For example, Moore and Wagstaff (1974) found it difficult to determine the degree to which black students' negative perceptions mirrored institutional realities. One study of institutional responses to black students' needs reported high levels of commitment and responsiveness among administrators and faculty in four white universities (Gamson 1978).

Rice and Bonnie (1989) found that despite the fact that some white universities provide numerous institutional supports to black students—including student retention programs, black faculty, opportunities for black students and black student groups, (such as sororities and fraternities) to interact among themselves within the mainstream of campus life, a black caucus, a black culture committee, a black student government association, black affairs committees, black administrators, black history month, and so on—many still report negative reactions to white campus life. Rice and Bonnie's retention survey of 186 continuing black students (those remaining in school) showed that one-third of the students rated contacts with black faculty and professional staff, as well as social relations with white students, as fair to poor. One-fourth rated the following as fair to poor: availability of tutoring services; opportunities for financial aid, scholarships, and campus employment; one-to-one in-office advising sessions with professors; black student organizations; sense of belonging or fitting in; feeling a part of the university; and relationships with professors. On the other hand, 68 percent rated their overall educational opportunities as very good to good. Furthermore, their attrition survey of 55 former students (dropouts) found that these students had dropped out more often for personal and financial reasons than for social or academic reasons. Very few reported experiencing prejudice and/or discrimination at the university.

Dawkins and Dawkins (1980), in a study of 105 black students on the University of Maryland's College Park campus, discovered a strong relationship between academic performance in college and selected racial experiences and perceptions. The black students who did not feel that white professors were prejudiced on a personal level were more likely to have higher GPAs than were students who reported white professors to be prejudiced. Further, the frequency of contact with whites beyond essential academic transactions was positively related to grade performance. This relationship held regardless of the nature of the contact, but was stronger when the reason for contact was social or academic, rather than when related to personal conflicts with whites. Finally on this point, Hacker (1992, 134–40) found that most colleges remain committed to affirmative action programs.

White and Black Students' Attitudes toward Each Other on One Prestigious White Campus

Bunzel (1991) conducted an eighteen-month inquiry on black-white relations at Stanford University utilizing (1) in-depth interviews with fifty undergraduates (twenty whites, twenty-four blacks and six of other races) during the 1988–1989 academic year, (2) a nine-page questionnaire mailed to a sample of 862 students (half of the graduating class of 1989), (3) a report of the University Committee on Minority Issues (UCMI), and (4) informal interviews with students in their dormitories. The findings were complex, contradictory, and mixed. Only 20 percent of the black students interviewed said that Stanford was racist; roughly half of all minorities said that they had been targets of public racism on campus. Black students reported feeling like outcasts in classes, not being selected by whites for study group sessions, experiencing the on-guard behavior of whites in their presence, feeling tensions in social situations with white students, and being subjected to subconscious personal racism by whites.

A significant number of whites reported reverse discrimination (e.g., unfair affirmative action preferences for blacks in the undergraduate admissions process, devaluation by blacks because of their white skin color, discrimination in favor of blacks for campus jobs, disapproval for sitting at a black table in the dining hall and receipt of anti-white flyers). A number of blacks reported that discrimination was practiced by blacks against whites, particularly in the area of interracial dating. Among white students, 30 percent had become more suspicious of the racism of minorities and said that the struggle of blacks and other minority students was alienating a large number of whites. Of white seniors, 57 percent agreed with this statement: "I am tired of hearing about racism at Stanford." Half of the white seniors agreed that the black student leadership was made up of people "with their own political agenda who are devoted to simply seeing racism." Many whites felt alienated by the racism of blacks and observed that though the university provided extensive education on racism to improve race relations, it was to no avail. Among members of the graduating class, 63 percent said that most people on campus were fair to all racial and ethnic groups. In the main, however, campus interracial interaction did not occur at significant levels of friendship, and relationships between members of different races were often reserved and circumspect—restrained by apathy, anxiety, and peer pressure. Many students reported that they did not easily become friends with individuals of different races. Seventy percent of the students acknowledged that black and white students did not socialize to any great extent, but rather coexisted. Eighty-five percent declared that black students segregated themselves from the rest of the campus. Almost 70 percent of the black students mentioned that they felt pressure from other blacks to subscribe to a set of black positions, attitudes, and behaviors. Over 20 percent of the blacks reported feeling academically inferior to other students, and one-quarter felt less prepared for Stanford academically than did other students. Over 70 percent of the blacks thought that their competence was questioned on campus, and 40 percent thought that the faculty expected less from them than from white students. Over 70 percent of the blacks were committed to maintaining a separate identity and agreed that any university policy of color blindness would be viewed by them as a form of prejudice.

Many blacks regarded the problem of racism on campus as a struggle for power to change the system of white control. For example, they demanded more black students on the board of trustees and more black faculty members, more classes about black history and culture, and separate living quarters. Among white students, 75 percent rejected any group guilt for past or present discrimination against blacks or for any campus racial incidents. They wanted to be judged as individuals and did not think they had personally done anything to perpetuate a racist system. Seventy percent of white students agreed with the statement, "Racial tension on campus has increased in the years I have been on campus." Fifty percent of the black students reported that their experiences at Stanford had not improved their ability to interact comfortably with people of different racial and ethnic groups. One-half of the blacks and over one-third of the whites said that they were not making significant progress in interracial relations.

The most important overall finding of this significant study is that blacks believed they were winning important structural changes at Stanford, while whites were becoming increasingly disenchanted with the tactics and demands of the more active black students. These findings do not appear encouraging in light of the fact that Stanford University is nationally known for a strong commitment to the ethnic diversity of its student body and curriculum, and to the provision of large ethnic organizations, ethnic living quarters and ethnic studies, new courses on third-world philosophy, and freshmen orientation programs focusing on the minority experience. Stanford has tripled the number of black students on its campus in the past fifteen years.

Black Professors on HBCU and White Campuses

Black professors on white campuses have reportedly faced inequalities in position, promotion, tenure, and pay, as well as problems of social distance, lack of trust, and marginality (Jacques 1980, 225–26). Unlike white professors on white campuses, black professors at HBCUs are concerned primarily with conducting classroom activities, providing personal counseling, sponsoring student organizations, and participating in community services. Their interactions with students are many-sided, sustained, and personal, and they instill in their students a strong orientation toward success. They have a higher social status in the black community than do white professors in the white community (where parents frequently have a higher social status than do their children's professors). Moreover, many black faculty members at black colleges are influential local and national leaders. Black professors, unlike white counterparts, are expected to interpret the black experience for their students (Thompson 1978). The black faculty member at an HBCU who opts exclusively for research and publications runs a risk of incurring negative sanctions for not being a good citizen and not living up to the community service expectations of minority students, peers, and administrators. The black professor's role in the quest for racial equality is not complementary to the white professor's scholarship role on white campuses (Exum 1983).

Most black professors prefer to teach at HBCUs. Though there is some evidence that a few black professors moved from HBCUs to white campuses in the 1960s and 1970s, there is no such evidence for the 1980s. White colleges were not "raiding" black faculty from HBCUs during this later period. In fact, there is some question if there was ever a "brain drain." Many black professors reportedly prefer to teach at HBCUs in order to avoid what they perceive to be status ambiguities and racial conflicts at white colleges. Black faculty appear to be satisfied at HBCUs, and most have personal ties to black colleges and/or ideological commitments to the constituencies that HBCUs serve (Allen 1991). Although the number of black faculty at white colleges has increased from an estimated two hundred in 1956, it was still extremely low on white campuses (i.e., less than 5% of all faculty members) as of 1970. Based on contact with more than 3,000 black educators, Moore and Wagstaff (1974) concluded that black educators perceive themselves to be alien on white campuses. Many black professors opt for HBCUs because they feel a growing concern for other blacks, and because they think they would be lonely, depressed, ignored, and harassed on white campuses. When they do move to white campuses, it is usually for more money. Most are primarily interested in teaching and service, rather than in research and publishing, which would pose career problems on prestigious white campuses (Jones 1991). Negative reports about HBCUs by faculty members usually focus on their perceived authoritarian administration. Some black professors at HBCUs question the administration's response to faculty needs (Billingsley 1982). The authors note that similar feelings are common on white campuses.

The overwhelming number of black and white faculty members on black campuses view their work as a career, not simply as a job. Almost nine out of ten faculty members at HBCUs assert that their interaction with students, which provides them with an opportunity to have some impact on their students' lives, is their principal teaching reward. Their dissatisfactions center on what they perceive to be inadequate facilities, a dearth of equipment, inflexible and/or heavy teaching schedules, low salaries, lack of professional recognition, and too much bureaucracy (Diener 1985).

Black Student and Faculty Attitudes toward Whites on HBCU Campuses

Little research has been conducted in this area. Melish (1970), in a study of attitudes toward the white minority on a black southern campus, found that only 10 percent of the black students were hostile toward white students. Sixteen percent of the black students felt that whites were negatively motivated in deciding to attend the college (e.g., they were rejects and outcasts, they wished to feel superior and get good grades). The overwhelming number of black students defined white students (the minority) as being different and foreign. The majority of the college community saw the white students as essentially foreign students. Black students saw white instructors (the majority in a mixed faculty) as irrelevant and strange, though one-third of these students were committed to racial integration on college campuses. There were hostile splits between the white and the black faculty members. To the black instructor, a white instructor was a foreigner, a product of different schools and a different society, and, as a result, was simply not qualified to make pronouncements on the needs of black students.

Warnat (1976) suggests in a theoretical descriptive typology that the white professor on HBCU campuses generally assumes one of four roles:

1. The "Moron" is an incompetent professor who could not find a faculty position on a white campus. He functions as a faculty scapegoat and is identified as a loser inflicted on HBCUs by the white society.

2. The "Martyr" teaches on a black campus in an effort to expiate racial guilt. He flagellates himself willingly and without complaint by taking on the drudge work of educating the downtrodden. He is quite acceptable to black colleagues, who are most sympathetic to and understanding of his plight.

3. The "Messiah" makes a concerted effort to "save the damned." He expresses feelings of superiority and assumes a paternalistic attitude toward black faculty and students. He perceives his mission as "bringing in the sheep." The "Messiah" is ill received by his black colleagues and tends to foster mistrust and feelings of alienation and hostility among them toward him.

4. The "Marginal Man" incorporates a conflict of two cultures into his function. Consequently, he assumes the roles of both community member and alien. As a member of the black faculty community, he experiences cognitive dissonance from both of his worlds wherein he seeks social acceptability. The function of the "Marginal Man" is to work toward an accommodation of two cultures. In this role, he is perceived as providing a reality contact for each racial group and a communication bridge between them.

White Faculty and Students' Attitudes toward Blacks on White and Black Campuses

White Faculty

Mingle (1978), in his survey of faculty in four predominantly white universities, found that when faculty members were asked general questions about the impact of blacks on higher education and their (faculty's) attitudes toward racial issues, the overwhelming majority responded moderately, but favorably. But when the role-specific attitudes and behaviors of those who might have had the greatest impact of blacks were examined, there was a distinct shift toward non-responsive attitudes and even expressed negative perceptions. Faculty who were teaching large numbers of undergraduates in introductory courses appeared to be frustrated and pessimistic about the impact of their effort. The majority embraced a universalistic perspective, which rendered them less likely to see the university as responsible for solving racial inequities. This is not the case on black campuses.

Many studies have examined the experiences of black individuals or groups within a white majority setting. Few, however, have examined interracial relations from the perspective of whites within a black majority setting. The interactions among white and black faculty, students, and administrators on HBCU campuses may be influenced by their racial orientation and experiences within the dominant society. However, interaction among these group members is most significantly influenced by the social context of the black college—a reverse context of the dominant society. In this milieu, the social climate is one of "blacks-in-charge," whites as subordinates (Smith and Borgstedt 1985). White professors at HBCUs are keenly aware of this climate (social and formal), and they must adjust accordingly—or leave.

Smith and Borgstedt (1985), in a seminal study on campus race relations, mailed questionnaires to all native-born white faculty in a sample of six black colleges (four southern and two northern) wherein 27 percent on average were white faculty. The questionnaires were designed to explore white faculty members' perceptions of their experiences and attitudes related to their minority/majority role, as well as to gather background information related to basic demographic data, past experiences in relation to interracial interaction, and current job characteristics. Among the topics covered by the questionnaire were interactional barriers and negative stereotyping by others, social acceptance (equality and relationships), personal commitment to black education, strong white racial identification, attitudes of white friends/families about their teaching at a black college, perceived administrative career restrictions, comfort with racial differences on a black campus, openness in dealing with racial differences, conflicts in grading black students, and feeling trusted by black students. The strength of the study lies in its interactional variables which are geared toward the existence and explanation of interracial encounters between black and white faculty on an HBCU campus. Moreover, these same interactional variables will be valuable in finding out about campus race relations among the other groups of social actors (i.e., black and white students and staff on black and white campuses).

About one-third felt that the black faculty held some negative stereotypes of them. They were less likely to perceive that black students had negative perceptions of them than that black faculty or administrators did. Seventy-five percent felt they were socially accepted. Only 31 percent, however, perceived their being white as not affecting career advancement. Only 15 percent defined their present position as a chosen mission. The overwhelming majority perceived themselves as committed to the goals of the college and as supportive of the college in the community. In short, they viewed themselves as professionals, rather than as "Morons," "Martyrs," or "Messiahs." Forty percent of the white faculty alleged that their friends had made derogatory marks about their teaching in a black school. Twenty-four percent agreed that family members attached some stigma to their position, and 60 percent perceived the administration as being more rigid than counterparts at white institutions. Fifty-six percent claimed that their career advancement was limited within the college because of their race, and 44 percent said that they felt out of place in meetings where black issues were discussed. The large majority felt that black students were as willing to approach them about a problem as they were to approach black faculty; only 13 percent perceived black students as preferring black faculty. These latter two perceptions do not coincide with previous findings that black students generally prefer black teachers.

This very important study by Smith and Borgstedt did not find that social class, gender, racial attitudes, family origin, or the extent and quality of social interaction with blacks during childhood and adulthood were closely related to any adjustment factors (interactional variables) under study. Most agreed that teaching in a black college helped them to understand what it meant to be black in the United States. Over half reported positive relationships with students. Sixty-six percent reported that they found limited advancement, felt powerless in decision making, felt mistrusted at times by the black faculty, and found the administration to be authoritarian. They experienced their highest level of satisfaction with black students. Many expressed some negative feelings about the administration, claiming that many administrators saw them as "hired help," rather than as fellow professionals. This is no surprise because research elsewhere shows that whites at HBCUs are relegated to lower pay, inferior status, and subordinate authority (Jacques 1980). The authors reiterate the caveat that the relationships between professors and administrators is universally problematic in the United States. Such strain comprises an endemic academic problem.

Smith and Borgstedt (1985) also found that some relationships between white and black faculty were ambivalent. They reported conflict in equal status relationships between white and black faculty and between white and black administrators. The majority of white faculty, however, were able to make an overall adjustment and were able to cope adequately with any conflicts that stemmed from their minority role. Just as white students' perceptions of their minority experiences on black campuses have been more positive than have those of black students on white campuses, the responses of white faculty on black campuses were more positive than were those of black faculty on white campuses. This positive feeling may be due in part to a greater representation of white faculty on black colleges than that of black faculty on white campuses. The authors suggest that black faculty may be more acceptable on white campuses than white faculty are on black campus for several reasons, including, but not limited to, the following: (1) black resentment of the white power structure, (2) black awareness of racial segregation and past derogations, (3) a sense among blacks of HBCU proprietorship, (4) white guilt and wishes to atone for the past, and (5) differences in the implementation of affirmative action programs on black and white campuses.

White Students

Limited research has examined the perceptions of white students within HBCU settings. Standley (1978), in his survey of white students on black campuses, found overall positive attitudes toward HBCUs. Fewer than 10 percent felt that instructors showed racial partiality or that they had difficulty communicating with black students. White students' greatest area of conflict at HBCUs centers on extracurricular activities and personal services, reflecting interpersonal vulnerability and fear of rejection (Willie 1981). Some studies show that white male students on black campuses find this experience improves their self-concept and enables them to understand how others perceive them and their way of life. As a result of campus immersion in the black experience, most white students report that they tend to dismiss old racial stereotypes—and realize that prejudice and discrimination toward blacks continue to exist. Consequently, some think there is a need for more white students on black campuses. Less than 1.5 percent of all students enrolled in UNCF schools are white. Yet one out of every three faculty members at UNCF institutions is white or from another ethnic group. Some educators claim that white students need a more diverse faculty, which is not available on predominantly white campuses. Blacks make up less than 5 percent of the faculty members on white campuses. Desegregation in higher education, then, is beneficial to whites as well as to blacks (Willie 1991).

INTERRACIAL CONFLICT ON CAMPUS

National Mood Shift Regarding the Higher Education of Blacks

Higher education in the United States was totally segregated until a generation ago, and the desegregation of this structure has been difficult. HBCUs lost a majority of their student populations and some faculty. Some civil rights proponents, including many blacks and whites, viewed this as an unfortunate, but necessary, byproduct of the movement of erasing the color line. From a positive standpoint, the 1960s marked vigorous efforts to increase black access to higher education, and, consequently, there was a dramatic increase in the number of blacks attending predominantly white colleges and universities. The increased access to black higher education was viewed as one solution to the problem of racial inequality. During this decade public support for higher education was strong, and institutions of higher learning were expanding. Currently the country's mood pertaining to racial issues and the state of higher education has changed. The response to black demands for equality and affirmative action has become ambivalent, if not unresponsive, particularly if such demands appear to disadvantage whites in any way. There has been a decline in white support for racial social policies and programs in an economic recession. The apparent reduction of commitment to blacks and other minorities' higher education is reflected in the lower enrollment of blacks in four-year institutions in the 1980s. Desegregation brought a proliferation of black studies departments, minority student service programs, and black cultural centers on white campuses to meet the needs of black students. A cultural and ideological reaction, including a negative view of the Civil Rights Movement, has resulted from these innovations (Jones 1991; Allen 1992).

Generally speaking, white students have accepted in principle the Civil Rights Movement's drive to remove racial barriers to blacks who wished to enter white colleges. They also have accepted equal opportunity in faculty hiring and student admissions, but during the 1980s they began to express resentment of affirmative action and other measures promoting the recruitment and retention of black students on white campuses—particularly preferential measures that give black students what they consider to be unequal advantages to higher education at white students' expense. For example, some white students claim that white applicants to colleges and universities are being judged on a separate set of standards for admission than that utilized for black applicants; that many blacks in competition with them for college entrance are admitted in their stead, though the blacks have much lower SAT scores than themselves; that colleges' recruitment drives for black students are geared toward obtaining a specific racial composition of the student population involving preferential financial aid; and that blacks on white campuses make too many demands and create too much of a fuss about their identity, culture, and separateness (Jones 1991; Bunzel 1991; Hacker 1992, 135-45, 150-54).

Overt Racial Incidents on Campus

Since 1979 black students on white campuses have been increasingly ridiculed, harassed, and/or attacked by white students at provincial as well as prestigious institutions. These incidents include: (1) repeated requests by campus police to establish identity and their right to be on campus; (2) painted campus signs (e.g., "Niggers, Go Home" on an UCLA administration building); (3) swastika signs, such as the one at the University of Michigan; (4) racially debased humor as in Harvard's *National Lampoon*; (5) the throwing of black-painted bricks through dormitory windows occupied by black students at Cornell University in 1981; (6) cross burnings near black organization sites and residence halls at Purdue University and Williams College in 1980; and (7) racial slurs directed at black students on many campuses (e.g., Harvard University, Wesleyan University, Iowa State University, the University of Wisconsin, and the University of Massachusetts at Amherst) in 1980 (Jones 1991).

Ehrlich (1990) cites some 200 incidents involving ethnic or sexual bigotry from a thirty-month survey entitled "Ethnoviolence on American College Campuses," reported by the National Institute against Prejudice and Violence. Though Jews and homosexuals were among those receiving threats, black students at predominately white colleges suffered most of the harassment and punishment involved in the ethnoviolence. These incidents included cross burnings on the lawns of black residence halls; "ghetto parties" with demeaning decorations (e.g., sorority members putting on blackface); threats by white students, sometimes at gunpoint; and racial slurs made by white students and white faculty to black students. Another report published by the American Association of State Colleges and Universities (1989) disclosed a similar pattern of racial slurs and attacks against black students on white campuses (note the identification of patterns, rather than isolated incidences).

Classification of Overt Racism on Campuses

Jones (1991) classified the incidents of overt racism described in the recent literature (from January 1985 through May 1990) in four major categories: (1) spoken insults, including taunts and slurs stated in person as well as those broadcast over the radio; (2) written or pictorial insults appearing on posters and flyers, in publications, or as graffiti; (3) organized protests and reactions including demonstrations, sit-ins, and boycotts; and (4) violent activity.

Spoken Insults:

Time ("Wrong Message" 1987, 57) relates an incident in which white students in a pickup truck yelled racial slurs at blacks attending a speech by the Reverend Jesse Jackson at Northern Illinois University. Eleanor Randolph (1990, 17) reports that, in 1988, a white college fraternity was closed for hiring two black female strippers to perform while fraternity members shouted racial epithets at them. Howard (1987, 625) notes that, in October 1986, a black cadet at the Citadel (a white military college in South Carolina) was awakened by the obscene taunts of five white classmates dressed as Ku Klux Klansmen who placed a burning newspaper cross in his room. In 1989, the campus radio station at the University of Michigan, Ann Arbor, broadcast two racially pejorative jokes about blacks, telephoned in by a white student (Wiener 1989, 260). Laura Randolph (1990, 128) reports additional accounts of white students' racist derogatory broadcasts over campus stations. Frequently these racial insults have been combined with other types of racist behavior on the nation's college campuses.

Written or Pictorial Insults

Numerous reports have been filed regarding the proliferation of racially insulting graffiti on U.S. campuses in recent years. For instance, in 1986, racist graffiti was reported at Aurora University in Illinois during Holy Week (Howard 1987, 625) "Niggers, Spics, and Coons, quit complaining or get out" was spray painted on a Smith College building also in 1986. Washington (1988, 49) reports that an Oberlin College campus poster advertising the film *The Gods Must Be Crazy* was altered to read instead "The Gods Aren't Crazy, But Niggers Are!" The epithets "Nigger" and "KKK" were scrawled on the door of a black student's dormitory room at Indiana University, Bloomington, in 1988 (L. B. Randolph 1990, 128–29). The epithet "Death Nigger" was scratched onto the office door of a black academic counselor at Purdue University in 1988 (Wiener 1989, 260). In 1990, a shack bearing racial slurs was erected on the Michigan State University campus (Daubenmier 1990, 25). Also in 1990, two white fraternity pledges from the University of Mississippi were dumped on the Rust College campus, a nearby HBCU, with the words "KKK" and "We Hate Niggers" painted on their naked bodies (Gibbs 1990, 104).

A large poster reading "White Supremacy Lives! Kill All Niggers!" was paraded at Oberlin College in 1986 (Washington 1988, 49). In 1987, a "White Power" poster was found at a dormitory on the campus of New York City's Columbia University (Louis 1987, 53). In the same year, at the University of California, Los Angeles, posters appeared announcing a rally for "White students who have stood by while minority students have had their hands held." This poster carried an additional message: "Whites are prepared to fight to preserve their rights! God Bless America!!" ("Wrong Message" 1987, 57). Also in 1987, leaflets bearing the message "Get Your Black Ass Back to Africa" appeared on the University of Michigan campus, and flyers decorated with swastikas and bearing the words "Niggers, get out" were posted in campus buses at Northern Illinois University ("Wrong Message," 1987, 57). Laura Randolph (1990, 128) reports an incident in which a racist flyer was slid under the door of a dormitory lounge in which a group of black women were meeting; it declared "Open season" on "porch monkeys, jigaboos, jungle bunnies, and spooks." Louis (1987, 53) reports that a white student at the University of Michigan, Ann Arbor, constructed a computerized bulletin board for disseminating racist "jokes." In a 1989 *Dartmouth Review*, a black Dartmouth music professor was described as a cross between a welfare queen and a bathroom attendant (Wiener 1989, 260). In 1990, a cartoon critical of minority preference programs was posted on the Michigan State University campus (Daubenmier 1990, 25). At the University of Wisconsin, Eau Claire, in 1990, a racist cartoon in a campus newspaper depicted two white males (one wearing a "Cosby Show" tee shirt) painting themselves black. One character comments, "Who needs to work so hard to get a perfect GPA or money for tuition, when you have this stuff"; another character comments, "Free Tu-i-tion, here we come . . . " (Gibbs 1990, 106).

Organized Protests and Reactions

Several organized student protests occurred in the 1980s in opposition to and in support of racist policies and practices.

Demonstrations: Collison (1990) reports a three-day sit-in staged by students at Howard University to protest the appointment of Lee Atwater (then Republican National Committee chairman) to the Howard University Board of Trustees. Kantrowitz and Turque (1987, 30) have found that a series of "ugly racial incidents" and declining black enrollment at the University of Michigan led to student demonstrations and the occupation of a campus building there. In 1989, black students demonstrated at Cornell University's Bailey Hall, screaming "Off our campus, racist pig" as Louis Farrakhan (minister of the Nation of Islam) spoke (Leatherman 1989, A35). Leatherman (1989) further claims that similar scenes were enacted on more than a dozen campuses throughout the nation during 1989. Black students belonging to the Minority Students Association at Washington and Lee University in Lexington, Virginia, demonstrated against the university's Fancy Dress Ball, with a post–Civil War theme offensive to blacks, in 1989. Black students at Tulane University in New

Orleans protested against a "Debutramp Ball" at which white Tulane students paraded around the city in blackface and harassed black students. The latter two incidents are examples of black students' responses to racial incidents provoked by white students on white campuses. Wiener (1989) details numerous large demonstrations against racism involving black and white student groups during the 1980s.

Student Unions: Angered by admissions and financial aid policies that white students say unfairly favor minority students, undergraduates on some campuses are attempting to form white student unions. The students say that they are tired of being excluded from internship and scholarship programs because they are white and that they resent the special efforts colleges are making to attract and retain minority students. Leaders of these groups deny being white supremacists, but at some institutions students involved with white student unions are linked to the Ku Klux Klan (Wilson 1990). Students at some institutions have called the white student union members racist and have staged protests aimed at stopping them from meeting (Wiener 1989).

Tifft (1989) reports that one of the first white student unions was formed at Temple University in the fall of 1988 by 130 white undergraduates in order to fight affirmative action programs and to promote "White Pride." Since then, students on at least half a dozen other campuses either have established white student groups or are considering doing so. On some campuses, administrators have denounced the groups, but have allowed them to form in the name of free speech. On others, officials have refused to recognize white unions as legitimate student groups. To date, only students at Temple and at some institutions in Florida and Louisiana have formed white unions that are recognized by the institutions and are allowed to meet on their campuses and to apply for funds collected by student government organizations. White student groups have also been active at Bradley University in Illinois, Mississippi State University, Tulane University, the University of New Orleans, the University of Southwestern Louisiana, and the University of Florida. Many of the students involved in Louisiana institutions participated in the U.S. Senate campaign of David Duke, a Republican state legislator who has been denounced by Republicans and Democrats alike for his past affiliation with the Knights of the Ku Klux Klan. At the University of Nebraska at Lincoln a group calling itself The White Organization of Concerned Students distributed flyers announcing a meeting in March 1990. But more than 500 other students protested, and the white group never met at the announced site. University administrators say that they do not know who posted the flyers (Wilson 1990).

One current battleground for white student unions is on the University of Florida campus in Gainesville. Administrators there claim that white campus groups supporting white student unions are disturbing—particularly because they appear at a time when officials on many campuses are trying hard to encourage students of different racial and ethnic backgrounds to interact with each other—and that white student groups are contributing to the debate over whether students should be allowed to say and do things that may be deeply offensive to their classmates. Mark Wright, a student who heads the University of Florida's White Students Union, announced in January 1990 that many people on campus forget about freedom of speech when dealing with his group. He claims that while administrators and students have encouraged people from different cultures to be tolerant of one another's views, they have attacked the white union without finding out what it stands for. He claims that one of the union's main premises is that white students are treated differently from black students and that the administrators know this, but, in order to keep the peace, are trying to stop the union. Another group called The Coalition against Bigotry has reacted strongly against Wright's Florida student union which it says is inherently racist. This group maintains that there is no lack of white culture anywhere at the University of Florida (Wilson 1990). To date, the battle has not been won.

Members of white student unions say that their groups allow them to take pride in their heritage, but that, in doing so, they become automatically labeled as racists. On most of the campuses where white students have formed organizations, administrators say that the students were inspired by the conservative policies prompted by Ronald Reagan. These students say that they have grown up with a national leadership that has not accentuated the need for an atmosphere that is inclusive of all citizens. Some administrators fault the poor economy in states such as Louisiana, which had led to the elimination of jobs and pitted people of different races against one another. Other administrators claim that white males are frightened because women and members of minority groups are competing with them for jobs, that they increasingly realize that they no longer have their historical privileged advantage, that they also realize they are part of a generation of people who may not do as well as their fathers did, and that they are looking for scapegoats (Wilson 1990).

Impediments to Racial Conduct Regulations: Two recent decisions by two different and powerful institutions (Supreme Court and AAUP) further complicate and weaken campus speech codes that prohibit racial slurs and demonstrations: (1) codes inaugurated by some colleges and universities to prevent speech and conduct that wounds or insulates or demeans people by reason of race, gender, religion, or sexual preference; (2) college administrative policy to block white student unions. At its annual meeting in June 1992, the American Association of University Professors approved an unequivocal declaration against speech codes, after earlier considering a draft statement endorsing such codes in some circumstances. Two weeks later came yet another challenge in the form of the U.S. Supreme Court's long-awaited decision on the validity of ordinances prohibiting hate crimes, *R.A.V.v. St. Paul* (1992). The Court struck down the St. Paul, Minnesota, ordinance that bars bigoted acts, such as burning crosses and painting Nazi swastikas, that arouse anger, alarm, or resentment in others on the basis of race, color, creed, religion, or gender. Cities and states may not punish expressive conduct (even the burning of a cross on a black family's lawn) when the sanction singles out a particular message or viewpoint (O'Neil 1992).

Violent Activity

Reported incidents include racial brawls; physical attacks on black male students; verbal abuse of black students' white girlfriends, resulting in fights; the burning of black fraternity houses; Ku Klux Klan–style cross burnings in front of black sorority houses, black cultural centers, and black residence halls; the trashing of Black Student Association offices; and the destruction of black students' clothes. These incidents represent manifestations of campus racial violence nationwide (Jones 1991). As recently as April 1992, a majority of the eighty-five black students at Olivet College in Michigan left the campus less than a week after a racial brawl that involved seventy black and white students in a residence hall— and after several weeks of increased campus racial tensions. These students reportedly were worried about their personal safety ("In Brief," 1992, A5).

Affirmative Action Backlash

Some educators view the foregoing racial incidents as stemming in part from the ambiguity inherent in campus affirmative action policies and explanations. While attempting to attract minority students, admissions offices are reported to have done a poor job of explaining their equal opportunity and affirmative action policies to prospective students and their parents. Consequently, some critics maintain that the colleges are contributing to some white students' notions that they are being passed over for unqualified members of minority groups. In fact, some white students have come to believe that being black or Hispanic automatically qualifies them for college admission, and some have falsely identified themselves as minority group members on college applications. Several high school counselors report that some minority students believe they will be accepted by the colleges of their choice simply because of their minority status. Many college admissions officers admit that they do not divulge in detail their affirmation action admission policies. Some of them frequently receive telephone calls from angry white parents who think that their children are unfairly rejected for admission. Many worry that affirmative action critics will misrepresent college policies and thereby further inflame the existing tensions between white students and members of minority groups. Other critics say that institutions should make their affirmative action policies clearer. Still others hesitate to be more open because they fear such action would not please different constituencies (Hacker 1992, 125-30).

Many outsiders do not know how colleges select students, and neither students nor parents understand what colleges are trying to do. Institutions vary in their admission policies, and many take into consideration criteria other than grades or standardized test scores (e.g., ability to lead, a sense of curiosity, motivation, athletic ability, musical aptitude, physically disablity and alumni parents, as well as minority group status). Some educators believe that colleges should make explicit that the primary goal of an affirmative action policy is to gain racial and socioeconomic diversity. For example, some universities, including the University of California at Berkeley and the University of Virginia, openly practice a quota system that targets specific minority groups at the expense of others (Hacker 1992, 135–40). Some institutions judge minority students' grades and test scores differently than they do those of white students. Admissions directors at these institutions say it is unfair to expect students who do not come from white middle-class backgrounds to score as well on standardized tests as those who do. Some high school counselors say that the college admission process can be demoralizing for minority students. The attacks on affirmative action have prompted some minority students to question their abilities because they are never sure if they were accepted because of their ethnicity. This confusion has led some black students to go back to HBCUs and avoid the predominately white campuses. For example, the Black College Recruitment Association, based in Milwaukee, Wisconsin, is encouraging black students to attend HBCUs and avoid the predominately white campuses of the University of Wisconsin System. Thus, the existing ambiguous, varied, and sometimes secret admission situation leads to hostility among black and white students and parents (Collison 1992).

The authors do not agree with the critics who maintain that an educational institution's clear explanation of its affirmative action policy would allay the concerns of white students or parents. By way of any explanation, admissions offices must first distinguish between equal opportunity actions and affirmative action measures. Second, they must give the U.S. government's justification for each of the two different public policies. Neither explanation nor justification is likely to prove acceptable and, in fact, would probably further increase the animosity of students as well as parents. Equal opportunity efforts seek to correct cases where qualified applicants are denied positions, promotions, or admission to college because of prejudice and discrimination on the basis of race, religion, creed, color, or national origin. In brief, for purposes at hand, it makes for a color-blind system. Affirmative action, on the other hand, usually calls for the hiring, promotion, or admission of persons who have not met the customary criteria or who are less qualified than those judged to be qualified. In typical (but not exclusive) affirmative action cases, a basically qualified minority group member is selected over a more qualified white person. In all cases, minority students are judged by a separate set of standards. Affirmative action, in brief, facilitates racial preferences; it is, in fact, formal discrimination in favor of blacks (in this case) to offset the effect of past informal discrimination against them. On a broader level, affirmative action aims at bringing more of certain categories of people into an organization and then ensuring their representation at all levels (Hacker 1992, 118–23, 124–23).

There are several justifications for affirmative action policies at colleges and universities, of which the following appear to be the most common: (1) to obtain a more diverse student body; (2) to ensure that student body representation roughly approximates the ethnic composition of the overall population; (3) to ensure the enrollment of low-income students; (4) to promote social mobility for an underclass; (5) to redress past wrongs and discriminatory practices (particularly those dealing with blacks); and (6) to ensure the inclusion of a large number of minority group members, particularly blacks. (For a detailed justification of items 3 through 6, see Jencks, 1992; Ezorsky, 1991). Of course, there are proponents and critics of each of these justifications, but their divergent positions go beyond the scope of this book.

On the other hand some writers (particularly whites) either question or negate affirmative action for blacks as an efficacious policy in the interests of either blacks or whites. Taylor (1992) claims that civil rights' reforms have gone far enough and that blacks' excuses and demands for handouts generate self-pity, which in turn generates a denial of individual responsibility. He suggests that blacks emulate Asian immigrants who have succeeded without preferential treatment. In a similar vein, Sykes (1992), in his book *A Nation of Victims: The Decay of the American Character*, finds that "victimism" is now endemic in the United States. He maintains that black Americans have overstated the obstacles they face despite a new atmosphere of tolerance in our economy and culture, and that black leaders made a mistake when they moved from seeking equality under the law to focusing on racism. To Sykes, affirmative action is based on "victimism" because it assumes that many members of a racial group are incapable of meeting existing standards. Therefore, proponents of preferential treatment must deal with the doubt that affirmative action policies stigmatize all successful minority individuals. William Julius Wilson, a black professor of sociology at the University of Chicago, takes a less strident stance in his book *The Totally Disadvantaged* (1987), and in his current, stated political policy he maintains that despite legitimate claims by blacks based on the historical facts of slavery, segregation, and sub-ordination, programs confined to race-specific solutions will have diffi-culty sustaining widespread public support. Wilson presents evidence to show that granting blacks a special status heightens racial antagonisms between different racial groups in the central city and deepens the divide between cities and suburbs. Therefore, he recommends a shift from a race-specific approach to programs in which all races and classes can relate to one another. Programs for the truly disadvantaged, though not specifically applied to blacks, would benefit blacks disproportionately because their needs are greater than those of other groups. President Clinton, who places great store in Professor Wilson's counsel, takes a similar position in his book *Putting People First*, (coauthored with Vice President Gore, 1993), in which the terms "race," "inner city," and "segregation" are rarely mentioned. Clinton's proposals aspire to replace separate treatment with equal treatment based on need.

Affirmative action programs, though legal, remain an issue over which public opinion is sharply divided. A *New York Times*–CBS survey on this topic reports that 71 percent of the black respondents favored some form of preference for their race while only 17 percent of whites favored this position (Hacker 1993).

6

RACE RELATIONS ON FIVE WHITE AND TEN BLACK CAMPUSES

This chapter provides an empirical account of race relations among black and white students and faculty on five white and ten black southeastern campuses. The authors' interest in this area stems from their previous teaching and research experience in the field of race relations on both white and black campuses (see Roebuck and Murty 1990; Murty and Roebuck 1992). This experience, along with a review of the literature in chapter 5, suggested the need for an integrated study of self-reports on campus race relations by student and faculty respondents, representing one set of institutions within a specified time frame. We reasoned that such a study would disclose pertinent data on race relations existing in one set of institutions as well as provide comparative data for similar studies on other campuses. Specifically, we adopted a topical interview schedule to gather data on the following dimensions: (1) respondent's racial identification and self-concept, (2) interracial and intraracial perceptions, (3) interracial and intraracial interactions and relationships, (4) perceived social acceptance, (5) perceived racial conflict on campus, (6) psychological comfort level, and (7) opportunity structure. From our perspective, these dimensions of study cover the focal areas of campus race relations. The topical interview outline draws on the methodology utilized by Smith and Borgstedt (1985) in their seminal study of the adjustments of white faculty on black college campuses.

METHODOLOGY

Topical Definitions and Measurements in Interview Schedule

All topics have four sets of discussion items: one each for black students, white students, black faculty, and white faculty.

Respondent's Racial Identification and Self-Concept

Racial identity herein designates a person's group or collective identity based on that person's perception that he or she shares a common racial heritage with a specific racial group. This significant, dynamic element in one's self-identity (self-concept) is personally constructed from differential group experiences and evolves in reaction to the respondent's perceived racial group membership and belief system. Self-identity is a subjective, reflexive identification that necessarily must be felt by the individual. Self-identity develops from one's social identity and personal identity. Social identity consists of various categories that a person is placed in by society—for example, race, nationality, religion, occupation, and social class. Personal identity refers to the respondent's biographical identity, or identity pegs attached to a unique combination of life-history items, and to his or her presentation of self in everyday life, which involves impression management—that is, techniques to control the impressions that other persons receive of him or her. Although the self is viewed as putting on the performance, the "reality" that supposedly underlies the presentation (and from which the character or dramatic self, the performing self, arises) also rises out of the performance. The presented self, in brief, derives from a performed character. Most important, the identity that a person presents successfully to others comes to be, in time, a part of his or her self-identity. For example, the person who convincingly presents himself as an African American to himself and others actually becomes an African American to himself and others in the process. Obviously, the presenter must have some characteristics of the self that he or she presents. For an elaboration of this definition of identity, see Goffman (1959; 1963).

The reader must keep in mind the fact that racial identity and social class are two separate entities. For example, a person may identify with blacks or black culture without identifying with the middle or upper class and vice versa. It may also be possible for a black person to feel good about herself, while having mixed feelings toward her racial group (Carter and Janet 1988). The ensuing data analysis, however, suggests an association between racial identity and social class.

The review of the literature on campus race relations and the authors' research experience in this area have suggested the formulation of the following sixteen questions. We reasoned that answers to these queries would provide an adequate measure of the existing inter- and intraracial perceptions of students, faculty, staff members, and administrators.

Interracial and Intraracial Perceptions

Black Students:

1. "How do you perceive white students on your campus?"
2. "How do you think white students on your campus perceive you?"
3. "How do you perceive other black students on your campus?"
4. "How do you think other black students on your campus perceive you?"
5. "How do you perceive white faculty on your campus?"
6. "How do you think white faculty on your campus perceive you?"
7. "How do you perceive black faculty on your campus?"
8. "How do you think black faculty on your campus perceive you?"
9. "How do you perceive white administrators on your campus?"
10. "How do you think white administrators on your campus perceive you?"
11. "How do you perceive black administrators on your campus?"
12. "How do you think black administrators on your campus perceive you?"
13. "How do you perceive white staff members on your campus—that is, librarians, secretaries, financial aid employees, housing officials, post office workers, bookstore employees, cafeteria workers, custodial (domestic) service workers, and campus police?"
14. "How do these white staff members perceive you?"
15. "How do you perceive black staff members on your campus?"
16. "How do these black staff members perceive you?"

White Students:

The above questions were posed to white students, substituting "other white students" for "white students" in items 1 and 2 and "black students" for "other black students" in items 3 and 4.

Black Faculty:

The questions above were posed to black faculty, substituting "black students" for "other black students" in items 3 and 4 and "other black faculty" for "black faculty" in items 7 and 8.

White Faculty:

The questions above were posed to white faculty, substituting "black students" for "other black students" in items 3 and 4 and "other white faculty" for "white faculty" in items 5 and 6.

Interracial and Intraracial Interactions and Relationships

Each respondent's interactions, positive and negative personal contacts, verbal exchanges, conversations, and discussions with white students, black students, white faculty, black faculty, white administrators, black administrators, white staff members, and black staff members are examined. All of these encounters are reported as interpreted by the respondent.

Perceived Social Acceptance

This section ascertained each respondent's perceptions of his or her social acceptability to black students, white students, black faculty, white faculty, black administrators, white administrators, black staff members, and white staff members. Social acceptance is determined by the willingness of others to interact with the respondent on an equal, voluntary, personal, informal, communal basis.

Perceived Racial Conflict on Campus

This section specifies each respondent's awareness and knowledge of any racial confrontations, altercations, or incidents on campus and obtains an interpretation and assessment of such events.

Psychological Comfort Level

In this context, each respondent expressed his or her general feelings of ease or unease, sense of belonging or of being out of place because of racial differences, perceptions of being treated or reacted to differently because of race, and perceptions of derogations or humiliations because of racial differences.

Opportunity Structure

Here each respondent assessed the institution in terms of his or her academic and career needs (i.e., faculty competence; curriculum suitability; library facilities; computer facilities and services, including research support; school accessibility and fairness of admissions, financial aid, internship, and grading procedures; campus employment; career placement; accessibility to campus organizations; student activities; and social life.

Study Sample

For reasons of convenience, we selected five white and ten black southeastern campuses with which we were familiar in the states of Alabama, Georgia, Louisiana, and Mississippi. These campuses were convenient in the sense that one or both authors had had prior teaching experience and/or personal contacts with several students and faculty members at all of these schools. Although no attempt was made to select colleges or universities on the basis of type of financial support, the sample includes five black private, five black public, and five white public institutions. All sampled institutions are SACS-accredited, coeducational schools and award at the least a bachelor's degree. The total sample (400 respondents) consists of 250 undergraduate students and 150 faculty members who were selected by a snowball sampling procedure. All student interviewees were sophomores, juniors, and seniors. The student sample is composed of 50 blacks on white campuses, 150 blacks on black campuses, and 50 whites on black campuses. The faculty sample is composed of 25 blacks on white campuses, 75 blacks on black campuses, and 50 whites on black campuses. No white faculty or students on white campuses are included in this study. In terms of gender, the sample consists of 210 males (75 black male students, 30 white male students, 70 black male faculty, and 35 white male faculty) and 190 females (125 black female students, 20 white female students, 30 black female faculty, and 15 white female faculty). For all operational purposes, we define "whites" as native white Americans and "blacks" as native black Americans. Any recorded impressions on foreign students and faculty, black as well as non-black, were volunteered by respondents during the interviews. We did not probe in this area.

All respondents were interviewed between November 1989 and December 1991 at prearranged locales, including our campus office, the respondent's residence or off-campus work place, professional organization meeting sites, and restaurants or bars. A conscious attempt was made not to interview any respondent on his or her campus. The average interview time was approximately one and one-half hours. We assured each respondent anonymity and urged each to keep the interview and its content confidential. We explained each item on the interview schedule to each respondent at the beginning of the interview. Though answers to the questions at times overlapped among the items in the various categories, we did not redirect any question or reorganize the respondent's responses during the interviews. And though we attempted to analyze all verbal responses, the respondents' direct quotes are self-explanatory and revelatory. No tape recordings were made because we did not wish to place any mechanical barrier between ourselves and the interviewees. Each interviewer interviewed one-half of the sample. Following the completion of all interviews, we compared the summaries of responses collected by each of us. This comparison did not yield any significant internal inconsistencies or differential response patterns. This was no surprise because we had collaborated on similar research projects for more than ten years and utilized the same interview style.

As a team, we edited the direct quotes (sparingly) to remove glaring repetitions, awkward speech forms, and a few offensive expletives. In paraphrasing subjects' responses other than direct quotes, we attempted to reconstruct their meanings of social reality—that is, their perceptions, definitions, interpretations, and feelings. We were paramountly concerned with the social actors' perspectives and how they envisioned campus race relations.

DATA ANALYSIS AND STUDY FINDINGS

The results of the data analysis are presented under six categories: (1) black students on white campuses, (2) black students on black campuses, (3) white students on black campuses, (4) black faculty on white campuses, (5) black faculty on black campuses, and (6) white faculty on black campuses.

Black Students on White Campuses

Respondent's Racial Identification and Self-Concept

Thirty-three of the fifty respondents identified themselves as black American students on a white campus. They recognized their social bonds with other black students and noted cultural and physical differences between themselves and whites. Though they viewed themselves as future leaders in the black community, they were middle-class-oriented and emphasized class lines as well as racial demarcations (from whites). All presented themselves as liberal integrationists who understood the need for civil rights organizations and affirmative action programs. All advocated racial integration and equality at the economic (e.g., equal employment), political (e.g., voting rights), judicial (e.g., equality before the courts), public accommodation, educational, and housing levels. Basically assimilationists, they approved of social integration up to and sometimes including courtship and marriage. Simultaneously they preferred to retain a black identity and many elements of black culture.

Nine identified themselves as students whom society had arbitrarily placed in a black racial category (i.e., given a black social identity). Rejecting this label, they presented themselves as liberal "marginal persons," or "biracials" who lived in a "multiracial" and "multicultural" society. Denying the efficacy of black-white racial categories, they pointed out that most so-called blacks in the United States are mixed and overlapped with other racial classifications. All nine verbalized a confused and ambiguous racial identity. Upwardly mobile and white-middle-class-oriented, they hoped to live in a multicultural society where racial lines were no longer important. To them, assimilation, integration, and eventual racial amalgamation are the solutions to racial problems in the United

States. All were more class than race conscious and exemplified little, if any, interest in black causes per se.

Eight were verbally militant (anti-white) and identified themselves as African-American students on a white campus. They clearly separated themselves racially and culturally from white Americans and what they called the white power structure. As one reported:

One must think, act, eat, and live black.

All eight were thoroughly committed to black causes, black organizations, the black community, and black culture—and eschewed the concept of integration. All expressed a strong emotional identification with black culture, but claimed that it was hard to clearly define what they meant by this for whites. Their notions about black culture included black history, black consciousness, black identity, and a revolutionary spirit where white America was concerned. Their concept of black culture involved a demand from whites that blacks be immediately empowered to gain parity with whites in the areas of employment, income, education, housing, health, welfare, and political leadership. They envisioned the tax-paying public and the U.S. government as the instruments to facilitate this empowerment. As one explained:

The white power structure must share the wealth. It is about time we got what is coming to us along with making up for the past. We want everything that the white man has and we want it now.

Beyond affirmative action and civil rights programs, they expressed no concrete action plan to satisfy their demands.

Interracial and Intraracial Perceptions

Perceptions of white students. Most (34) viewed them as a dominant, privileged, and prejudiced student group, the group that the institution was established and functioned for, the group that fashioned the campus scene, and the group that they had to adjust to and compete with. White students were seen as culturally and racially different from themselves— denizens of another world who were more sophisticated, materialistic, and affluent than themselves. They envied these white youth, who had much of what they aspired to. Yet white students possessed "baggage" they could do without. As one asserted:

They got lots of things going for them like money and clothes and good manners. And they are better prepared for college than I am. But they got baggage I don't want. They are wishy-washy and you never know the side they are coming down on. Their jokes don't make me laugh. I feel uncomfortable around them and I get the impression that they are always testing people. And I don't want to be like that.

Though aliens, the white students were not considered enemies. All thirty-four perceived racial barriers between themselves and white students. (Racial barriers connote any perceived obstructions to social interaction that hinder psychological comfort as well as the teaching and learning process.)

Ten regarded them as students like themselves and, though culturally different, as potential friends and allies. One commented:

> We are different in some ways because of segregation. But we are more alike than different. We are both southerners. We eat the same food. Most of us have the same religion. We are here for the same purpose and there is no reason why we can't get along. I know there are some racial barriers but they can come down.

The remaining six perceived them to be alien enemies whom they had to put up with. One reported:

> They don't give a damn about black people. They don't want us here. But they have no choice because I am here. They can go their way and I can go mine. I know my rights and I am going to make sure they are respected.

White students' perceptions of you. Most (44) thought that white students defined them as "affirmative action admits" who were culturally and racially inferior to and less competent academically than whites.

Perceptions of other black students. All characterized other black students as fellow brothers and sisters in the same academic boat. But at the same time they recognized that there were individual differences among them in terms of academic competence, social class affiliation, racial identity, and commitment to the black community.

Other black students' perceptions of you. All reported that other black students recognized them as brothers and sisters in the same academic boat, but at the same time as individuals with different interests and life styles.

Perceptions of white faculty. Most (45) identified the white faculty as a privileged societal group of college professors who were racially and culturally different and remote from themselves. They considered them to be professional, competent, fair, and helpful, but less interested in them than in their white students. Five described them as competent professors, but as racially bigoted, remote, alien, and unfair persons. Forty students perceived some racial barriers between themselves and white faculty.

White faculty's perceptions of you. All surmised that the white faculty regarded them as a culturally and racially deprived affirmative action student group. Most (29) thought that they were portrayed as a problematic group of students in need of remedial education, an education that the white faculty did not have the expertise, inclination, or time to give. Five reported that the white faculty viewed them as "just students."

Perceptions of black faculty. Most (44) viewed them as black professors, similar to the white faculty, but somewhat more accepting and friendlier. Six others evinced an ambivalent attitude toward them and referred to them as "oreo cookies" and "black tokens" on a white campus who acted and thought white. Many students (35) viewed them as belonging to a higher social class. Most (40) portrayed them as accommodators to the white power structure who "bent over backwards" to show that they were not biased in favor of black students. Only fifteen mentioned them as role models.

Black faculty's perceptions of you. Most (44) assumed that the black faculty viewed them as they did white students, with the difference that they were recognized as sharing a racial heritage, a heritage that did not indicate inferiority. Six others assumed that the black faculty considered them to be deserving black students.

Perceptions of white administrators. Black students expressed more negative attitudes toward white administrators than toward white or black professors, though they offered no clear-cut grounds on which to base this distinction. Many predicated their negative views on gossip received from other students and on their general dislike and distrust of white officials. One states:

> I hear a lot of bad things about deans and officials from other students. But I stay clear of them. You don't expect to get anything from a white official.

Twenty said that they were not sure who the administrators were or what they did and that they did not care to know about them one way or the other. Five others, who claimed some idea of who they were and what they did, commented that they did little of anything and that secretaries and clerical help performed most of the administrative work. Thirty depicted them as aloof rulers of a white educational institution who had vested interests in maintaining their positions and not "rocking the boat." Most (40) did not think that the white administrators were committed either to equal educational opportunity or to affirmative action in academia. They maintained that white administrators complied with integration laws and affirmative action mandates in order to receive federal money and to protect themselves from legal action. Most felt that the administration was not seriously interested in their educational welfare and advancement. Ten suspected that most white administrators were racial bigots. All perceived racial barriers between themselves and white administrators.

White administrators' perceptions of you. Most (42) thought that white administrators reluctantly accepted them as "tokens," "affirmative action admits," and "aliens" on a white campus. They also thought that they were considered to be a potentially problematic group that had to be handled with "kid gloves." Eight supposed that white administrators disliked them because they were "black." Only five felt that white administrators were sensitive to the particular needs of black students.

Perceptions of black administrators. Most (40) perceived them to be similar to white administrators, but somewhat less remote. They were seen as black "tokens" who served in middle-management positions to carry out the orders of white administrators, "keep the lid on" potentially black troublemakers, attend to black financial aid needs, counsel black students in trouble, act as minority-student advisors, mediate black grievances, and head and advise Afro-American studies programs. In general, they viewed black administrators more negatively than they did white or black professors.

Black administrators' perceptions of you. Most (40) black students speculated that black administrators were ambivalent toward them. That is, black administrators were pleased to see the students integrated, as they were, into a white institution; but, on the other hand, they perceived them to be a group of educationally deprived and ill-equipped students who posed a racial embarrassment to them. Furthermore, these black students assumed that black administrators were afraid to give them any special attention for fear of being called prejudiced in favor of black students. Additionally, they thought that black administrators considered them a source of campus racial conflict.

Perceptions of white staff members. Black students considered white staff members to be racially prejudiced instruments of the white administrative power structure. They expressed negative views toward many, particularly campus police, housing officials, maintenance personnel, post office workers, and bookstore employees—all of whom they claimed rendered poor service and placed them in an inferior racial category. Secretaries, librarians, financial aid employees, cafeteria workers, and custodial service workers were observed to be more efficient, but cool and aloof. Forty students perceived racial barriers between themselves and the white staff.

White staff members' perceptions of you. They conjectured that white staff members regarded them as problematic alien students whom they had to serve.

Perceptions of black staff members. They defined the black staff as "o.k.," helpful, and considerate, with the exception of the black campus police, whom they viewed as harassers.

Black staff members' perceptions of you. They assumed that black staff members (with the exception of the campus police) were well disposed toward them as a group of fellow blacks. They supposed that the black campus police were ambivalent toward them because the police had to please white employers and white colleagues.

Interracial and Intraracial Interactions and Relationships

White students. Most (45) experienced no significant personal contacts with white students outside the classroom. Verbal exchanges were perfunctory, conventional, and stylized salutations such as "hello," "goodbye," "see you later," "see you in class," "good luck," and so forth. Brief, infrequent conversations and discussions occurred when they encountered each other inadvertently (e.g., at bus stops, outside professors' offices, and in the bookstore, library, post office, secretaries' offices, cafeteria, and campus waiting lines). The verbal content of such encounters focused on safe, everyday, trivial topics such as the weather, sports, the movies, popular music, current news events, routine campus affairs, and gossip (that affected the entire student body). Occasionally information on classroom procedures, assignments, tests, course content, and individual professors (hardness, fairness, and competence) was exchanged. Only three mentioned friendly acquaintanceships with a few white students. Two males dated white females surreptitiously. Interracial dating on all white campuses was tabooed.

Thirty-five reported negative personal and social contacts with white students at the individual or group level, including one or more of the following comments:

1. "They are unfriendly toward us."
2. "They are cold and indifferent."
3. "They ignore us."
4. "They treat us like aliens or foreigners."
5. "They laugh at us."
6. "They put us down in the classroom."

Ten charged that racial slurs were occasionally directed toward them or spoken in their presence—for example, "you jigaboos," "you gorillas," "those house apes," "those niggers."

Most reports revealed that white students interacted with them on a formalized and indifferent basis, as evidenced by one black student's typical statement:

> You know, they don't want us around but they can't do anything about it.
> So they just follow a canned script that all blacks and whites understand.

You know, we talk about some meaningless chit-chat to get through a contact they are really not looking for.

Other black students. Most (35) reported few significant social contacts with other black students aside from casual, brief encounters that transpired in the classroom, in eating places, at the library, in the college union, at local off-campus bars, and at sporting events (as co-players and co-observers). One student explains:

I feel swallowed up on this white campus. You know, everything is set up for white students, but nothing for us. I'm isolated from my friends. I got a lot of acquaintances among my brothers, but few real friends. Man, we just don't have the time or the place to get together. And the activities are for whites. Everybody's too busy trying to make it. And if you hang around together too much on campus, they [whites] see us as ganging up on them. So each brother has to do his own thing. But where and when?

The contacts that did exist were marked by warmth, cheerfulness, acceptance, and understanding—for example, "Hello there!" "Where you been so long?" "No see you in a long time," "We're busy and we got to do what we got to do," "Let's get together soon."

Fifteen enjoyed close personal and social contacts on and off campus with other black students as a result of either intraracial dating or black sorority and fraternity affiliation.

White faculty. Most (40) reported minimal, formalized professional contacts with white professors in the classroom and faculty offices as students vis-à-vis professors. Only ten said they "dropped by" a few white professors' offices for informal chats (about current campus and national news events, career plans, academic matters, and personal problems). Most verbal exchanges dealt with classroom procedures, assigned reading materials, clarification on subject content, and tests and grades. All reported that they said little in the classroom because the lecture method discouraged participation and because they feared being "put down" by white students. Only five said that they volunteered to answer questions. One student's explanation for this situation follows:

We black students let the whites take the lead and only answer up when called on. We fear being put down if we answer wrong. Actually, the professors didn't expect us to say anything. Most of us bunched up together. You know, we usually sat together in class. No one tells you where to sit, but after you choose a seat, you are expected to sit there. Most of the professors didn't seem to treat us much differently from whites. They didn't seem to care too much for any of us anyway.

Ten students claimed their contacts with white professors were chilly and unfriendly. One remarked:

The professors avoided direct contact with us and treated us like numbers. When they did talk to us, we could tell they didn't like us around. Some of them talked down to us like we were inferior and didn't know English. They look at us in a cold way. You can tell by their eyes and cute remarks that they don't like us. But they have to put up with us. You can't go by what they say, but by the way they say it.

All remarked in various ways that they preferred to be treated as individual persons in a familiar way. Two said that white professors met these expectations. The following remark is illustrative:

We African-American students like to be treated like individuals. You know, like persons with a name and some things about us different [sic] from other people. My white professors may be competent and fair in their own minds. But they don't come across to me as very human. They treat me like some kind of object. They are ice men. Man, they live in another world. And they sure as hell don't know anything about my world.

Black faculty. Black students recounted that most of their contacts with black professors were quite similar in kind to those experienced with white professors, albeit there were some qualitative differences. For example, black professors treated them in a more personal and familiar manner during office visits. One student explained:

They mostly acted like white professors to us. But they were not quite so chilly. From time to time when we dropped by their offices, they talked in a friendly way. You know, if no white people were around. I guess they thought they had to put on a white front to everybody lest they be seen as partial to African Americans.

Ten reported close personal contacts with black professors on and off the campus and accepted social invitations to black professors' homes.

White administrators. Very few experienced personal or formal contacts with administrators. Most encounters were with department heads and deans about course scheduling problems, permission to take additional credit hours, acceptance of transfer hours from other schools, class exemptions, scholarships, financial aid, late enrollments, late fees, graduation deadlines, change of majors, and departmental clearances. Some other encounters involved complaints about professors, department heads, and staff; personal problems; and misconduct and disciplinary problems. Most (40) found white administrators to be stuffy, authoritarian, rigid, aloof, and personally detached during their highly structured meetings with them. They were judged to be rigid rule makers and rule enforcers. Ten viewed them as officials "doing their job." As one of these ten said:

They're cool cucumbers just carrying out their duties. You can't expect too much from them. They're doing what their boss told them to do.

Black administrators. Black students reported that their fleeting formal contacts with these few middle-management officials were similar in form and content to those experienced with white administrators, though somewhat friendlier.

White staff members. Most (45) noted that encounters with secretaries, librarians, and financial aid employees were civil, formal, and professional, but lacking in warmth and without extended helpfulness. Five stated that personnel in these three categories were openly hostile toward them at times, as evidenced by a frowning facial expression, a harsh tone of voice, an authoritarian mien, and slow, reluctant service. Most (40) reported negative contacts with maintenance, bookstore, and post office employees and the campus police. These employees frequently treated them as inferiors in a markedly hostile fashion. For example, maintenance men (blue-collar workers) scowled at them from time to time when passing by or when working in their physical proximity, and they exchanged racial slurs among themselves about blacks:

Those niggers think they're it. Why do they want to educate those jiggs?

You niggers think you're it. But no matter how much education you get, you'll still be niggers.

Bookstore and post office employees frequently extended poor, slow service; avoided touching their hands when returning change; watched them closely as if they were thieves; avoided conversation and eye contact, if possible; and slammed down packages and letters on counters before them. Housing officials treated them curtly and were particularly interested in assigning them to black roommates and to off-campus housing in black neighborhoods. White campus police were openly hostile to them in mien (aggressive physical stance and frowning countenance) and in conversation and physical approach. They watched them (particularly males) at all times, were quick to cite them for traffic and other violations (such as possession and use of alcohol on campus), harassed them by demanding that they produce student identification cards and driver's licenses, called them down for loud and boisterous behavior, and rousted them for parking in lovers' lanes. The remaining ten described contacts with employees in the above categories as cool and formal, but without racial overtones.

Black staff members. Contacts with black staff members were reportedly pleasant and helpful, with the exception of those with the black campus police. The black campus police, though not humiliating them as much as the white campus police did, treated them as potential trouble-makers.

Perceived Social Acceptance

White students. None considered themselves socially acceptable to white parties or to close friendship cliques on or off campus. All were excluded from white sororities and fraternities, white friendship circles and social functions, and white bull sessions and from bar-drinking parties off campus (the center of much social life). Most private social get-togethers were also segregated. The black students felt that they were formally socially accepted at public campus functions, such as concerts, lectures, ball games, entertainment performances, and dances (where they danced together). Though church services were available to all students on campus, most black students preferred to worship in off-campus black churches. Only four claimed to have close friendship ties with white students, and these were maintained off-campus.

Black students. All black students ostensibly accepted one another socially on and off campus. However, many black females and some black males drew class lines in dating relationships. Friendships also were based on personal likes and dislikes within the brotherhood. Outside of black fraternity and sorority affairs, social life among blacks tended to be limited and shallow.

White faculty, administrators, and staff members. Black students did not consider themselves socially accepted by these groups outside of public campuswide activities.

Black faculty, administrators, and staff members. Students thought most members of these categories accepted them at the social level on and off campus, but age and occupational status differentials precluded strong personal ties. A few students visited in the homes of members of these categories.

Perceived Racial Conflict on Campus

No black students reported open group conflicts on campus. However, they noted that at one time or another they had encountered hostility from individuals in all white categories, varying from scornful looks, racial put-downs, and avoidance patterns to differential service treatment—all in situations demanding civil conduct, respect, and equal treatment. Most (41) claimed that at one time or another they had been subjected to racial epithets and slurs from whites: nine frequently, twenty-eight occasionally, and the remaining four rarely.

All noted the presence from time to time of derogatory racial graffiti on campus buildings, walls, and bulletin boards, which was erased over and over again only to reappear. Some examples include: "Niggers go home," "Affirmative action babies," "Get lost," "Jungle bunnies don't belong here," "Our niggers won" (following a football game victory), "Niggers run, jump and sing but don't think," "Ain't no sexual harassment necessary among us niggers" (some with and some without attached cartoons).

Psychological Comfort Level

None reported feelings of complete belonging, and all verbalized some alienation and the view that the institution was established by and functioned for whites. Most (41) saw themselves as a small racial minority group surrounded by dominant whites in a situation where they were less prepared for academic success, less numerous, less acceptable, and less powerful than whites. Some few (9) expressed feelings of being accepted on a limited basis by some whites as individuals, but never by whites as a group. Most voiced a sense of uneasiness among whites, where they felt unwelcome, disengaged, and demeaned. About one-half of the sample expressed strong feelings of alienation, sensed ever-present hostility, perceived overt racial discrimination, and felt a lack of cultural integration. These said they had to go back home occasionally for a few days where they could find brothers and black culture and get recharged. These sentiments were succinctly expressed by one student interviewee:

> Man, I had to go back home now and then to get my head straight. I had to get away from all that pain. Without black culture I am nothing. I don't want to go to the funny farm. So I go back home and get recharged.

In cases where students voluntarily mentioned their GPAs, those who were satisfied with their grades expressed less psychological discomfort than did those who were not. (However, we did not consciously collect GPA data from student respondents.)

Opportunity Structure

Most (43) stated that the institution for the most part met their academic and career needs in terms of faculty competence, library facilities, computer services and research needs, student union facilities, the cafeterias, student financial aid, gym and sports programs, and public campuswide entertainment—all accessible to them on an equal basis. Only a few (6), however, expressed any interest in campuswide activities or in organizations and clubs. Most identified these "happenings" as meeting white needs and expectations. Most expressed a need for a strong African-American studies program and more Afro-centric course content in history, languages, and the arts. Only a few attended church services on campus.

Most (33) maintained that the lack of an adequate social life was their main problem on campus. This complaint is illustrated by the following comment by one male student:

> We didn't come here for social life and it isn't here. We found out it is more important than we thought. It's hell to have to wait till you get back home to see real friends. Of course, we know each other here but unless we belong to a fraternity or sorority, we don't see each other much. And the fraternity and sorority social life is really no big thing. Most of us go our separate ways. There is little here to tie us together. What goes on on campus is for whites. The same applies to off-campus happenings. Even the bars off campus are crowded with whites. You just don't belong in them. And the girls won't go to black bars. Really, I don't blame them. The black bars around here don't cater to students, and we don't feel at home there. So we go to white bars and take the . . . hit.

The chief problem with social life for both males and females was dating. On this point, one female commented:

> If you don't belong to a sorority, and I don't, your chances of dating are low. I won't go out with a man just because he's black. He's got to have something going for him. And I know better than to fool around with athletes, and be used and abused. I found out about athletes my freshman year when I didn't know what was happening. There are a few good men around but few places to meet them—and nowhere to go with them. On campus every one is too busy doing his own thing. There is nowhere to go in the black community but churches and bars. I hate to say it, but most social life around here goes on in bars. Blacks and the black community don't bother themselves with us. We're too few and we have different interests. We don't know much about what goes on with them and most of us are not interested. We're tied to our community back home. To those people out there, we're just part of the white college. And they sure don't give a damn about it. Only getting jobs there.

One male commented on this subject:

> I don't belong to a fraternity and don't have much chance with girls. Even some of the girls who aren't in sororities act too snooty. I just don't run into many girls. And those I talk to in the union are just friends. There are not really too many places to go around here. The girls got their heads in the clouds. The good bars are white bars. And that's where the action is. Off campus, there's no place to go but churches and bars. Members of the black community think we act superior and look down on them. We don't, but we just don't have the same interests.

Most (41) attended church services irregularly in off-campus black churches. One female student commented about church services on campus:

I could go to church on campus. Several different services are available. But I just don't feel right in any of them. The preachers lecture, they don't really preach. The music is too formal and leaves me cold. The people in the congregation don't seem to relate to one another or to the minister. And the people don't really seem to be feeling anything. I just don't feel right there. Another thing is, I don't meet many eligible blacks there.

In sum, these students found that neither structured arrangements nor behavior settings (i.e., things to do and places to go were available for a normal and rewarding black social life on or off campus. There was little, if any, integration of the black college students with the black community. Apparently black females were choosier in dating relationships than were black males.

Most (41) proclaimed their willingness to pay the emotional price entailed, as is evidenced by the following sentiment expressed by one male student:

I want to be a professional man and I can get what I want now here. The social life scene is not my thing right now. I'm here whether they want me or not. You face the racial thing everywhere. That's nothing new and no big thing. Sure, women are not easy to get. But I'll first build myself up and then pick and choose later. You know what I'm saying. Knowledge and the piece of paper is the thing.

The remaining nine exhibited an ambivalent attitude toward the school's opportunity structure, expressing both positive and negative views about what it had to offer. They claimed that curriculum content did not include enough about black history and culture and that the subject matter, lecture method, and grading procedures favored whites. However, only three charged that any of their professors had graded them unfairly on the basis of race. Seven of these nine said that they might drop out, get a job, or transfer to a black school.

These students gave one or more of the following reasons for attending white colleges, rather than HBCUs: (1) availability of financial support (e.g., minority scholarships, financial aid, tuition waivers, athletic scholarships, affordable schooling costs), (2) perceived institutional prestige, (3) white recruitment drives and promises, (4) physical proximity and convenience, (5) parental pressure, and (6) self-determination to prove themselves in a white academic world.

Summary and Conclusions

These students for the most part comprised a middle-class-oriented group of liberal racial integrationists. But what they sought was diametrically opposed to what they found on the white campuses they attended.

The overwhelming majority perceived racial barriers between themselves and white students, faculty, administrators, and staff. Many expressed ambivalence toward some members of the faculty and administration. Few experienced close personal contacts or friendly relationships with white or black students, faculty, administrators, or staff. Few considered themselves socially acceptable to whites on or off campus, and all at one time or another had encountered racial epithets and slurs from whites. None felt a sense of complete belonging, and all endured some degree of emotional discomfort at an institution that they said functioned exclusively for whites. Most thought the institution met their academic and career needs, but at the high cost of a meager and constricted social life and an ever-present unaccepting white environment. Most were willing to pay the price.

Should these findings prove to be typical for other white campuses in the South, we recommend that only certain kinds of black students attend them (until white colleges become more psychologically comfortable for black students): (1) those who strongly wish to attend white schools, (2) those who have above average high school grades and high SAT scores, (3) those who are highly motivated academically; and (4) those who have personalities strong enough to withstand alienation. In our opinion, the emotional strain entailed is too great for many black adolescents. All categories of whites on white campuses, particularly students and faculty, must be more accepting of black students and black faculty. In some way, black students who attend white colleges should be integrated in a nearby black community. Finally, white colleges must provide structures for interracial and intraracial campus interactions.

Black Students on Black Campuses

Respondent's Racial Identification and Self-Concept

A majority (132) of the 150 respondents identified themselves as African-American students attending HBCUs and clearly distinguished themselves racially and culturally from white Americans. None believed in or proclaimed a desire for racial integration. Fourteen saw themselves as liberal black American students who supported integration. All of these were middle-class-oriented. The remaining four verbalized an ambiguous racial identification and a middle-class orientation. (Racial identification categories—native white and native black—and definitions for these groups are the same as for the black students on white campuses. See pp. 163).

Interracial and Intraracial Perceptions

Perceptions of white students. Most (120) viewed white students in much the same way as they did foreign non-black students (primarily

Asians)—for example, as "foreigners," "aliens," or "white students."
Though whites were defined as legitimate students, they were irrelevant
to these respondents and their campus activities and life style. White
students were merely sojourners or outsiders on their turf, who were
attending HBCUs as one or more of the following: (1) as better prepared
students who were there to compete for blacks' scarce resources (e.g.,
scholarships, fellowships, financial aid, and honors), (2) as rejects from
white society and white schools, (3) as liberals who wanted to prove how
much they liked blacks, (4) as residents from nearby areas who found it
convenient to commute; and/or (5) as enrollees in desirable professional
programs (e.g., prelaw, premedicine, business, library science) unavailable to them in a nearby white school.

Twenty accepted them without reservation as fellow students and
friends or as potential friends. Ten persons perceived them as aliens and
racial enemies who should not have been admitted to their campus. As
one of these ten commented:

> They don't need to be here taking advantage of the limited opportunities
> that we poor blacks are entitled to. You know, like scholarships, co-ops,
> and tuition waivers. If they are as smart as they think they are, why don't
> they go to a white school and prove themselves there. They don't fit in here
> anyway, so who needs them. If their own kind doesn't want them, why
> should they be dumped on us. Some of them got to be white trash.

In total, 130 students perceived racial barriers between themselves and
white students.

White students' perceptions of you. Most (119) assumed that white
students looked on them as disadvantaged racial inferiors and cultural
aliens. Many others expressed indifference toward how white students
perceived them. One of these explained:

> You know, I really haven't thought about how they see me, but I know
> how they saw us in the past. They have to take me like I am if they want
> to stay here. We just let them be if they don't give us an attitude.

Twenty supposed that white students saw them as fellow students and
potential friends. A few (10) considered them to be racial enemies.

Perceptions of other black students. Most (146) recognized them as a
significant group of students who shared with them a common racial and
cultural heritage. They were brothers and sisters on the same campus;
potential boyfriends, girlfriends, and mates; fellow members of fraternities
and sororities; future partners in the black community beyond the campus;
members of the future enlightened black leadership seeking justice in a
racially segregated society; and future professionals and role models in

the black community. All were aware of individual differences among themselves, such as personality traits, life styles, social class, and academic competence. (They did not use the term "social class" often, but their remarks indicated a keen awareness of what this construct includes. Like whites, they knew about social class, but did not wish to talk about it openly.)

Some black students detected a social and academic hierarchy existing among HBCU students and on specific HBCU campuses. That is, they perceived that some students on some campuses rank others socially and academically. Some members of fraternities and sororities ranked themselves as socially above some other black students. Black foreign students (primarily from Africa and the Caribbean) were generally ranked as an intermediary group between themselves and white students. Racially, they were more acceptable than whites, particularly in the area of close personal relations such as dating. Some native black females considered many foreign black males to be more chauvinistic than native black males.

Other black students' perceptions of you. They thought that other black students perceived them in the same way they were perceived. They conjectured that foreign black students accepted them as fellow students and racial equals, but as culturally different from themselves in courtship and marriage customs, parenting, gender role differentiation, diet, and so on. Many expressed indifference to all foreign students' assessments of them, particularly the assessments of non-black foreigners.

Perceptions of white faculty. Most (135) visualized white faculty as fair, friendly, and competent professors to whom they could turn for group or individual academic assistance (including remedial instruction and career counseling). This was particularly the case for those white faculty who did not deal with subject matters concerning African-American issues and race relations. One student explained:

> I have no problems with them so long as they don't try to teach me about my culture. They are good teachers and the race thing between us doesn't matter. They do a good job and that's what they are here for. But I don't want them telling me anything about my culture.

Fifteen expressed ambivalent attitudes toward white professors, most of whom they defined as good, fair, and helpful teachers, but still aliens out of place on a black campus. Though they reported no classroom or academic barriers, they were somewhat reluctant to seek white faculty members out for counseling or to drop by their offices for private chats. They also wondered why the white faculty members were not on white campuses: Did they have job opportunities elsewhere? Were they there to prove something? Were they deviant in some way? As one student explained:

I have some good white professors but they seem to be a little strange here. It's hard to explain but I don't feel exactly comfortable with them. You know, if it's not about class work. I relate better to a black professor than to a white professor. I wonder sometimes why they are here and not on some white campus. They got to be different from most white people. But what that difference is beats me. They could be rejects, or a bunch of white do-gooders. So what, most do their job and that's what counts.

These fifteen reported some form of racial barrier between themselves and white faculty.

White faculty's perceptions of you. Most (129) observed that the white faculty perceived them to be worthy students with whom they could enjoy a professional as well as a friendly relationship. That is, they were primarily students and secondarily black students. One commented:

I think they look at us as students. You know, college students who they are prepared to teach. And they can counsel too. Sure we are black and they know that. But teaching is teaching, and I think they see us like they see other college students. I don't let the race thing get in my way. All that jazz about it takes blacks to teach blacks doesn't make a lot of sense to me.

Twenty voiced mixed opinions about how they thought they appeared to the white faculty. All of these twenty assumed that they were considered to be culturally and educationally deprived students of another race and that some white faculty took a condescending missionary position toward them. One student explained:

You know, they think it's their moral duty to upgrade us, save us and make us like them. I'm black and that's the way I'm going to be. But some don't get it. And no one can change it.

Others of this persuasion thought they were seen as instruments necessary to the white faculty's career. One typical comment follows:

They wouldn't be here if it wasn't for us. They got Ph.D.s to teach, and they got to teach somebody. Maybe this job is the only one they can get. We're necessary for their career.

Only five said that the white faculty disliked them. As one of these stated:

They put on a show. Who are they kidding? They don't really like us. But they got to eat.

Perceptions of black faculty. A majority of the black students perceived "their" black faculty as friendly, accepting, helpful, competent, and empathetic professors; worthy counselors and mentors; intellectual and moral role models; professionals in their fields; prestigious honorable blacks with a high social position; and big brothers and surrogate parents in academia and in the wider community. A few of them (10) expressed doubts about some faculty members' dedication and commitment to Afrocentric philosophy, although they admired them in other ways. Eleven black male students commented that a few of their black female teachers were militant feminists. As one asserted:

> I know I'm black enough and that I'm not a sexist. But a few of my female teachers tell me I'm a sexist and not black enough in my approach to things. I don't like this but what can I do.

A few others felt the faculty tried to "puff them up" too much. As one student complained:

> Some faculty are always trying to puff us up. They tell us how fortunate we are and how important it is to be black. And that we must come up to their expectations. I know I am somebody and that I come from a good family. But you know, we all can't be doctors, lawyers, and Martin Luther Kings. I want to do my thing in my own way and for my own reasons.

Black faculty's perceptions of you. They supposed that the black faculty doted on them as worthy black students, surrogate children, and an enlightened generation; future professionals and leaders in the black community; future friends, supporters, alumni, and colleagues; and the preservers and carriers of black culture. A few (5) remarked that some of their teachers did not think they were "black enough."

Perceptions of white administrators. The few white administrators (usually at the middle-management level) were observed to be competent subordinates of black administrators. Most appeared indifferent toward them. One student exclaimed:

> Man, they mean nothing to me. I guess they do their jobs, but I don't know what they are supposed to do.

White administrators' perceptions of you. They assumed that they were looked on as students, tuition payers, and a source of income.

Perceptions of black administrators. Most (139) admired black administrators as the successful "big shots" on campus, caretakers of black education and culture, well-wishers and advocates, and educational leaders and role models. They made more positive statements, however, about professors than about administrators, whom they considered aloof at times. As one student explained:

They are the cream of the crop and I'm proud of them. But we don't see much of them because they're too busy. I get to see my dean once in a while. You have to be a student leader or in big trouble to see the higher-ups. I see my department head more as a professor than as an administrator.

Black administrators' perceptions of you. Most (142) assumed that black administrators considered them to be worthy black students enrolled at the right place (i.e., at an HBCU geared not only to their chosen fields, but also to black history and culture). Some thought too much was expected of them. One student's comments are illustrative:

Man, they value us but they sure want to puff us up. You know, make us aware of black culture, and proud of being black. Some of us are already puffed up enough, but they are doing the right thing because they want us to be prepared for future leadership.

Eight students thought that administrators looked on them as necessary career instruments, tuition payers, a source of income, and future alumni contributors. They also expressed the view that administrators desired them to "stay clean," be cooperative, "be quiet," and "stay out of their way."

Perceptions of white staff members. Black students considered the few white staff members to be acceptable, competent, civil, alien workers on a black campus who played no significant role in their campus life. They were no more than instrumentalities, people who had just happened to find jobs at an HBCU. One student commented:

They are here to do a job and I think most of them are o.k. Most of them are locals who find it convenient to work here. I hope they are not taking away black people's jobs.

White staff members' perceptions of you. They assumed that white staff members deemed them student clients who required the adjunct services they delivered.

Perceptions of black staff members. Most defined the white-collar personnel, particularly librarians and secretaries, as competent, cooperative, friendly, and helpful. Librarians were portrayed as important aides in helping them prepare classroom assignments. They said that some secretaries were their informal advisors, troubleshooters, friends, and liaisons between them and the administration—as well as their agents and advocates at times. Most reported blue-collar workers to be friendly and competent. A minority of nine said blue-collar workers were competent, but distant, members of the black brotherhood. One of these stated:

They do what they're supposed to do but they treat us as if we are different. They act as if we think we are better than they are. Some of them think we have it easier than they did when they were students here. Others who didn't go to college think we are uppity.

Most got along well with younger members of the campus police, some of whom were students and many of whom had some college training. They respected middle-aged and older campus police, but considered them to be too bossy and authoritarian, but never unfair or brutal. All expressed hostility toward law enforcement personnel off the campus. As one student commented:

> We get along fine with the campus police, especially the younger ones. The older campus police are o.k. but too nosy and bossy. We call them "Pops" sometimes. Police off the campus are something else. We don't like them because they harass us. You know they stop us for nothing and are always looking for something to pin on us. But what can you expect from rednecks.

Black staff members' perceptions of you. Most thought they looked on them as worthy students, an enlightened generation, and privileged members of the wider black community. Some few believed that some blue-collar staff thought they were snooty.

Interracial and Intraracial Interactions and Relationships

White students. Most (142) experienced few personal contacts with white students outside the classroom. Moreover, they did not pursue contacts or relationships with whites and considered any interaction with them inconsequential. They exchanged inane chitchat and formal greetings and good-byes when they found themselves inadvertently in the presence of white students on the campus, at bookstores, in classroom building halls, at cafeterias, and so on. Eight reported acquaintanceship and friendship ties with a number of whites, but none of these relationships appeared to be deep, meaningful, or durable. All were reluctant to discuss these so-called friendships other than to say "they shot the bull together" and talked about campus activities and class assignments. Three black males dated three white females sub rosa. Open interracial dating between white and black students was tabooed, but interracial dating among native blacks, foreign blacks, and foreign non-blacks was acceptable and occurred occasionally.

Other black students. All enjoyed personal contacts with many other black students on and off campus, resulting in acquaintanceships, friendships and friendship networks, sorority and fraternity affiliations, courtship ties, campus work ties, church memberships and church service fellowships, friendly classroom participation groups, study groups, and sports and athletic activities. Many participated together in a host of well-integrated, campuswide activities and celebrations (e.g., homecomings, commencement exercises, church services, concerts, lectures, seminars, black history month, founders day, Martin Luther King's birthday, and programmed entertainment), and many belonged to clubs, associations, and organizations of one kind or another (e.g., Black Caucus, Southern Christian Leadership Conference, African People's Organization, African Caribbean Society, Black Students in Psychology, Black Students' Association, African Men of Impact, Pan African Students' Organization, All African People's Revolutionary Party, African American Women's Association, Regional Association of Black Sociologists, National Association of Blacks in Criminal Justice, Black Students Union, Association for Black Accountants, NAACP, Black Urban League, and National Organization of Black Law Enforcement Executives). Furthermore, a wide variety of campus activities were available (e.g., band, glee club, debating clubs, sports activities, honor clubs, religious clubs, and sororities and fraternities), which made it possible for students to participate in any one or a number of different activities.

Most remarks and accounts about on- and off-campus contacts and associations made it clear that they lived in a black campus community that fostered camaraderie, engagement, connection, emotional support, and encouragement. Although they claimed to be more egalitarian in their social relationships than are white students, they acknowledged limiting their close personal contacts and intimate associations with others on the basis of a similarity of interests, life style, and family background. They said fraternity and sorority members restricted much of their social life to activities among themselves. Furthermore, their remarks indicated that those with middle-class family backgrounds usually associated with other middle-class individuals. This was especially the case with black females. One woman asserted:

> Because we're all black, we socialize a lot on that basis. We have to in this segregated society. But there are other things besides race. You usually like to go out with people who have interests like yours. If you don't, what can you do together? What can you talk about? I like to be around people who have things in common with me. Then I can feel comfortable. The bottom line is when you date seriously, you must be around somebody who shares your way of thinking. You know, like being career oriented, and being able to fit in with respectable people. What I'm saying is he has got to be more than just black. He's got to have something going for him. Like, you know, a mind and having some ambition. I am looking for a winner, not a loser. Sex is not the only thing.

A male student spoke to this point:

> Man, most of these girls are materialistic. They don't like to go out with you unless they think you got something going. They might date you once

or twice, but after that, they have sized you up. And if you don't make the grade, forget it. I know where I'm coming from. You know, a poor family. And I know, I'm never going to be a hot shot lawyer or doctor. I may not even make the pros, but I'll be o.k. So you see I'm not looking for one of those high class sorority girls. I'll find me a real down home girl with some of my basic values.

White faculty. Most (135) related pleasant, friendly contacts and associations with white faculty inside and outside the classroom situation and found them readily available at all times. Encounters usually centered on academic matters, but occasionally involved personal problems, career plans, and counseling. Only a few (7) reported limited contacts with white faculty. These said that they felt awkward and ill at ease with whites in general. Eight thought that frequent contacts with white professors were inevitable because of extensive reading and writing assignments that required out-of-class consultations. One student comments:

> We stop by the white professors' offices when we feel like it. They treat us as good as anybody. The race thing didn't make any difference. I'm sure these white professors are different from those whites I run into off campus. And I think they are different from white teachers on white campuses. I hear some bad things about them.

Ten recalled that they visited some white faculty members at their homes.

Black faculty. All reported pleasant and close personal contacts with black faculty, paralleling the plethora of data on this subject found in the literature. Encounters in and out of the classroom included rewarding intimate relationships, counseling sessions, role modeling, classroom assignments, remedial education, and surrogate parental relationships. The content of frequent encounters in faculty offices ran the gamut from academic matters (e.g., classroom subject matter, grades, and academic progress) to current events (e.g., religion, career choices, black culture, personal problems, and race relations in the United States). Verbal exchanges often focused on black consciousness, racial identity, racial politics, and the black community. Black faculty frequently commingled with them at social functions on and off campus (e.g., at dances, barbecues, eateries, picnics, bars, professional meetings, church services, and athletic events). Furthermore, some black faculty frequently entertained them in their homes.

White administrators. Contacts with the few white administrators were rare, brief, civil, and formal.

Black administrators. Contacts with black administrators for the most part were limited to encounters with deans and department chairs. Encounters with deans were infrequent, brief, and formal and generally centered on academic problems and clarification. Contacts with department chairs were frequent and friendly with open agendas. Chairs were perceived to be advisors, teachers, mentors, problem solvers, career counselors, and job placement aides. In fact, they were looked on more as faculty than as administrators. Some occasionally entertained students at their homes. (The authors note the overt exuberance and affection that black administrators display toward black students on the platform at commencement exercises when the diplomas are handed out—where administrators and students exchange pleasantries, congratulations, warm handshakes, and occasional embraces and kisses.)

White staff members. On-campus contacts with the few white staff members were brief, courteous, and formal. There were no off-campus contacts with members of this category.

Black staff members. Contacts with the white-collar black staff, though service-oriented and professionally focused, were friendly and highly personalized. Formal encounters were frequently extended in time and content beyond their manifest purpose and often resulted in personal relationships. This was particularly the case with librarians and secretaries. Librarians went beyond their call of duty by assisting them with locating documents, periodicals, and microfiche; initiating computer-based literature searches; and obtaining materials through interlibrary loan. Departmental secretaries frequently performed many services for them far beyond what was called for in their job descriptions: for example, typing and duplicating class materials beyond the limits of official approval; typing personal letters and written communications; permitting unauthorized telephone usage; assisting them with the selection of courses and registration; and acting as liaisons between them and department heads as well as other administrators, particularly in problem situations. These personal relationships at times circumvented formal, legitimate bureaucratic channels and obviated students' contacts with the administrators. Contacts with the black blue-collar staff were usually formal, precise, service-connected, and limited in time and content.

Perceived Social Acceptance

White students. Most (135) considered themselves socially acceptable to white students on campus. Fifteen thought they were socially acceptable in a limited way to liberal white students off the campus—for example, in private social relationships, in bars, and at particular weddings, funerals, and church services.

Black students. In principle, all perceived themselves to be socially acceptable to other black students on and off campus. They recognized, however, that social acceptability was a matter of degree and did not depend solely on race and that one's individual traits, interests, life style, and social background were important considerations in determining who is acceptable to whom. One male student spoke to this point:

We certainly are equal in the eyes of God. And we blacks know we should not rank each other socially. That's the white man's game. But we choose our friends and who we associate with for a lot of reasons. We all have likes and dislikes and differences. From a social view, we can't deny that some of us are more equal than others. And you know, that birds of a feather flock together. But we don't make as big a deal about the class thing as whites.

(The authors' experiences with black and white students suggest that, in fact, both groups draw class lines to the same degree. White and black Americans, particularly females, are well aware of social class lines and socialize accordingly—while simultaneously denying that social classes exist in the United States.)

White faculty, administrators, and staff members. Most (141) considered themselves to be socially acceptable to white faculty, administrators, and staff on campus, whereas only nine felt they were socially accepted by a few members of these categories off campus (in informal settings inside and outside their homes).

Black faculty, administrators, and staff members. All perceived themselves to be socially acceptable to all black categories on and off campus.

Perceived Racial Conflict on Campus

None perceived any overt interracial group conflict on campus. Some (18) expressed resentment of white American and white foreign students who they felt should be enrolled in white schools. Some others (10) reported a few incidents of individual and isolated rivalries and conflicts concerning interracial dating situations. For example, some black males verbally berated non-black males (whites and Asians) for dating native black women, though it was acceptable for black males to date white females. Eleven black students expressed resentment over what they termed "unfair competition" for grades between themselves and whites. They based this complaint on the fact that white students were better prepared academically than were black students.

Psychological Comfort Level

The overwhelming majority reported comfort on their campuses where they felt a sense of belonging. They said that they were at ease on an HBCU campus where the curriculum was geared to the specific needs of blacks and where they could interact with fellow blacks in a setting removed from the hassles, prejudices, and discriminations of the white world. Accounts indicated their social ease in an insular milieu freed from white domination. The comfort level was greater for those students who had attended white schools at one time or another (37) than for those who lacked such experience.

Eleven expressed mild mixed feelings about their comfort on campus and mentioned one or more of the following negative sentiments:

1. Too much emphasis is placed on black identity, black consciousness, and black culture by professors, students, and administrators. One of these students remarked in regard to this point:

   Too much emphasis is placed on race. We are Americans first, and we live in a multiracial society. More emphasis should be placed on integration and less on the mosaic idea. You know, with blacks at the top. It's poor racial politics, too, because of the backlash that's bound to come.

2. There is a dearth of white students. Another student commented:

   We need more white students because we should have a good mix. We have to compete in a white world. We must learn how to compete now. It may be too late later on. We really have a segregated school and that's not what integration is all about. If we get more white students, we will get more financial support.

3. Library holdings are inadequate. Another student remarked:

   I got a library card which cost me $50 but I've got to go all over town to find the books and journals I need to write term papers. Sometimes I have to order the books through interlibrary loans but they don't always come before the deadline for my papers. This affects my grades and peace of mind.

4. The curriculum is inadequate, and the offerings are inconvenient. Yet another student complained:

   We have good teachers. But we don't have enough choices. And you know, enough academic programs. Especially in the sciences. I can't get a degree in chemistry here. They list a lot of courses in the catalog but many of them are never offered. Some courses I'm interested in but I can't take because they conflict with my work schedule. Another problem I have is getting to the professors when I need them. They are too busy with their on- and off-campus commitments, and I can't always see them during their office hours because of my work schedule.

Opportunity Structure

Most asserted that their academic needs, career needs, and social needs were being fulfilled for the most part. All reported that they had been treated fairly and kindly by other students, faculty, administration, and staff most of the time and that their campus experiences had given them the buffer zone necessary between the black community in which they had grown up and the white world in which they would have to compete. Some (29) mentioned mild complaints about one or more of the following: (1) high tuition fees; (2) inadequate and deteriorated physical facilities (classrooms, dormitories, etc.); (3) the dearth of adjunct student facilities (e.g., student union, post office, bank, cafeteria, housing); (4) delays in processing financial aid papers; (5) class schedule conflicts with their off-campus work agenda; (6) inadequate library and computer facilities and support services; (7) insufficient course offerings in certain areas, especially in the sciences and the public health fields; and (8) weak job placement services.

Most were convinced that the HBCU they attended provided them with a more wholesome and beneficial campus life than they could have found on a white campus. They also claimed that the HBCU faculty was its greatest asset and of immense help to them.

Summary and Conclusions

These students for the most part made up a group of African Americans who professedly had given up on integration and who took great pride in their racial identification. They viewed HBCU campuses as "their turf" and considered whites there, with the exception of white faculty, as aliens. They perceived some racial barriers between themselves and all white categories, excluding white faculty. Few interacted with white students, administrators, or staff on any personal meaningful basis, and people in these three categories were of little relevance to them. On the other hand, they lauded white professors with whom they experienced friendly and wholesome relationships. The reason for these exceptional relationships with white professors is unknown. Perhaps the answer lies in the dedication of white liberal professors, the mutual respect developed during a shared educational experience, and the ambiance of an integrated campus.

All enjoyed close personal contacts with other blacks in all campus categories, particularly with black students, faculty, and secretaries. Social interaction occurred on a highly personalized basis within both formal and informal encounters. Students were individuals to one another and to others. They enjoyed a special student–surrogate-parent relationship with the black faculty and some departmental secretaries, as well as with administrators in a more generalized and less personal sense.

Black faculty utilized supportive and apparently successful teaching methods uncommon on white campuses. Furthermore, a rich social life was available to all within the cultural contest of an accepting extended black family. They felt emotionally at ease on a campus that met their academic, career, and everyday living needs.

On the basis of these findings, we recommend that most black youth attend HBCUs when feasible. Many white youth could also benefit from adjusting to the different set of race relations and different teaching methods found on an HBCU campus. The teaching techniques utilized by black HBCU faculty members should be researched from a strictly empirical and practical stance, rather than from a formalized theoretical approach, to find out why they are apparently so successful with the average and below-average college student. The authors speculate that the key probably lies in the black HBCU professor's personal, friendly, and supportive relationship with students. Black campuses have never accepted the old principles that exist on many white campuses: that the professors demand the respect of the student, that subject matter is to be taught on an objective basis without regard to student-professor personal relationships, and that the professors are not concerned with whether the students like them or not. Black professors at HBCUs know these practices will not work with black adolescents. Moreover, they know that in the long run, if not the short, respect for the teacher is necessary, but not sufficient. If students like the professor, they will do better; and if they like the professor *and* respect him or her, they will do even better—and this applies to all students, whatever their academic strengths. Of course, the black HBCU professor's teaching methods, on which we comment later in this chapter, are worthy of consideration beyond HBCU campuses.

Two criticisms that black students make of HBCUs should be attended to: inadequate library holdings and an insufficient number of professors. Finally, HBCUs should in some way integrate outside-the-classroom activities of black and white youth. This would probably eliminate some racial barriers.

White Students on Black Campuses

Respondent's Racial Identification and Self-Concept

All identified themselves as white students attending HBCUs. Fifteen of the fifty presented themselves as white liberals who believed in racial integration and equality at the economic, political, judicial, public accommodation, educational, and housing levels. They also accepted in principle voluntary racial social integration up to courtship and marriage. Five accepted courtship and marriage. All fifteen expressed a compassion for blacks, who they thought had been grossly mistreated in the past, and advocated tax-supported governmental social programs such as affirmative action to bring them up to parity with whites.

Twenty-four presented themselves as white conservatives who accepted legal racial integration, but not social integration. Eleven called themselves southern conservatives. None of the thirty-five in the last two categories accepted affirmative action or other governmental programs to bring blacks up to parity with whites. All professed equality before the law. As one commented:

> We should all be treated equally before the law. But I'm not responsible morally or financially for any transgressions against any group by the government, or by any individuals in the present or in the past. I don't want

to hear that junk about white racial guilt. I have none. We should all be treated equally and no group should have any legal advantages over another group for any reason.

Interracial and Intraracial Perceptions

Perceptions of other white students. Most white students (35) viewed most other white students as sojourners like themselves on an HBCU campus when they would have preferred to be on a white campus. Residential proximity, enrollment problems at white schools of their choice, and financial constraints made it convenient, if not necessary, for them to attend an HBCU. One student commented:

> I live off campus and commute. Most of us do. I don't really belong here but there is no four-year school close by. It is much easier for me financially and more convenient to get a degree from here. If I had my way, I would go to a white school. But I don't spread this around.

The members of this group referred to the liberal white students who espoused racial equality and social integration as "liberal fools"—fools who might stir up racial problems by trying to force their views on non-liberal black and white students. They devalued this group and looked on them as deviants and racial renegades.

The minority of fifteen liberal white students perceived the conservative group of white students as misguided and ill-informed "rednecks." (See Roebuck and Hickson, 1984, for a definition of rednecks—i.e., under-educated, churlish, violent, and bigoted working-class white southerners.) One of these commented:

> I think some of the white students feel like me. I am not a racist who believes in all that superiority stuff. I believe in racial equality. We should all be students together. You know, be friends and get along. We are certainly more alike than different. We've a moral duty to get immersed in the black culture on campus so we can understand blacks and become their friends. We must also educate the "rednecks" in the right direction. But it takes time, and they won't talk to us.

Other white students' perceptions of you. Most assumed that other white students viewed them as reluctant aliens like themselves who were trying to "make it" on a black campus without getting involved in campus affairs or interracial difficulties. As one commented:

> I have never taken a poll, but I am sure most feel out of place here just like I do. Most of us are just trying to make it. And really it's not all that bad. We're treated o.k. No big problem. It's those fool white liberals that bother me. I'm afraid they might stir up some trouble.

Perceptions of black students. Most (35) viewed black students as members of a nationwide racial and cultural minority group. They also saw them as the dominant student group on campus, the group they had to adjust to. This categorization resulted not only from an individual penchant, but also from formal segregation and group dynamics. This is demonstrated by the fact that most white students noted individual differences among black students, although they still tended to visualize them as a category. One white student's comment illustrates and explains this tendency:

> I know they are all not the same. Some of them are better students than others. And I like some of them as individuals. As individuals, they are a lot like other people I know, but when they get together in a group they change. They get loud and pushy. I'd rather deal with them as individuals. But that's impossible. I know some of them like me, but we're both under pressure to be what we are. You know, act white or black. If we don't do that, we are not loyal to the group we belong to. Every time I start looking at a pretty black girl or talking to her, the brothers take notice and stand around. Forget it. Who needs the hassle?

Most looked on foreign black and non-black students as a racial and cultural minority group on the campus. The minority group of fifteen liberal white students viewed all black and foreign students as potential friends and allies whose hoped-for support and cooperation would make racial integration possible. In the final analysis, the thirty-five conservative white students perceived racial barriers between themselves and black students.

Black students' perceptions of you. Most (31) assumed that they were defined as a tolerable, inconsequential, and non-threatening alien group. Fifteen thought that they were seen as fellow students and potential friends. Only four thought that they were rejected as racial enemies.

Perceptions of white faculty. Most (42) portrayed white faculty members as liberals and as competent, fair, unbiased, and helpful instructors. They also saw them as an asset to and a bulwark of the HBCU they attended in terms of the enhancement of faculty strength, student advising, grantsmanship, student recruitment efforts, research, and training. The remaining eight rated them as less competent than white counterparts on white campuses and noted them to be subservient to black students, black faculty, and black administrators. As one of these stated:

> I've got nothing against them but I think they are a bunch of liberal flunkies to the blacks. The black faculty and administrators run all over them and don't pay any attention to what they say. If they weren't liberals who like blacks, they wouldn't be here. They're afraid to give black students low grades but they give them to me. They're too busy with black students to

give me much help. Every time I go to see one he is busy with other students. If you don't get it in class, forget it. But I should have expected all this before coming here. But any way, I can get it for myself.

White faculty's perceptions of you. Most (40) thought the white faculty welcomed them as worthy students and as allies and friends in the furtherance of HBCU racial integration and academic strength. A minority gathered the impression that they were acceptable, but not as important as black students. One student commented:

On this campus we are a minority group to the liberal teachers and everybody else. My white professors seem to like me but they don't think I'm as important as black students. They get what they want right away but I have to wait. I understand their position. They have to play the game if they want to keep the job.

Perceptions of black faculty. Most (40) found the black faculty to be civil, competent, fair, and helpful. Some others observed that they were competent, but more dedicated to the education of black students than to themselves. For example, they said that professors were friendlier to black students than to themselves and spent more office time with them than with white students. A few rated them as less competent than white counterparts on white campuses, but on par, if not superior to, white professors on their campus. Only four perceived some racial barriers between themselves and black faculty.

Black faculty's perceptions of you. Most (30) assumed that the black faculty viewed them as worthy students. Eleven felt that they were perceived as worthy students on a contingency basis—pending adjustment to the campus environment. Six thought that they were seen as regular students. Three were convinced that some black faculty members did not like them because they were white.

Perceptions of white administrators. Most (46) described the few middle-management white administrators they knew about as competent administrators and as liberals. The remaining four regarded them as "hired help" to black administrators. One of these four stated:

I don't see many of them around. They got to be hired help to keep the show going. They got to be liberals too or they would not be here.

None viewed administrators (white or black) in as favorable a light as they did professors.

White administrators' perceptions of you. Most (39) reported that they did not know how they were perceived by this group. Eleven assumed that they were seen as alien students on an HBCU campus.

Perceptions of black administrators. Administrators, other than chairs and deans, made up an unfamiliar group. Chairs were viewed more as faculty than as administrators. Higher administrators were referred to as "VIPs," "wheels," "decision makers," and "CEOs." Most were judged to be competent, fair, and helpful, but also officious and aloof. An illustrative comment by one student follows:

> Really I don't know much about them. I do know the dean of my college. He's o.k. He's straight and fair. I guess the others are managers . . . like most wheels they are distant and like to tell people what to do. I hear they like to throw their weight around.

Black administrators' perceptions of you. Most were not sure about how administrators perceived them. Some (23) thought that they were viewed as necessary aliens on the campus. As one of these explained:

> You know integration works both ways. We have as much right to be here as they do on white campuses. They are required by law to have some white soul brothers on this campus. And the more students they have, the more money they get.

Perceptions of white staff members. White staff members were viewed as liberals and as competent allies who had adjusted well to all black and white categories on campus.

White staff members' perceptions of you. They assumed that white staff members accepted them as they did other students (i.e., as student clients in need of their services).

Perceptions of black staff members. With a few exceptions, they found black staff members to be competent, helpful, and unbiased, but less friendly toward them than toward black students. A few perceived a few secretaries to be prejudiced toward them and toward white people in general, but not discriminatory. Only five perceived racial barriers between themselves and black staff members.

Black staff members' perceptions of you. Most assumed that black staff members saw them as legitimate alien students. One student commented:

> They don't have much to say to us. They see us as out of place. We're here because the school accepted us and this doesn't have anything to do with them.

Interracial and Intraracial Interactions and Relationships

Other white students. Most (39) did not maintain personal contacts with other white students outside the classroom beyond brief communications at public accommodations on the campus. Neither friendship cliques nor organized groups existed among them on or off campus. As one student pointed out:

Some of us are acquainted and we shoot the breeze now and then in the halls or on the campus. But none of them are my personal friends. The only time I see them is on the campus. We just don't get together. Now, if we were on a white campus, it would be a different story. But I got other friends and going to school here is like going to work.

Black students. A majority (36) maintained few contacts with black students beyond the classroom, other than chance meetings on campus. Classroom contacts were formal and shallow. Less formalized contacts elsewhere, though civil, were confined to polite salutations and brief inane exchanges about the campus (class scheduling, holidays, exams, concerts, and sport events). Other topics of conversation were safe and trivialized (e.g., the weather and current events). They entered into classroom discussions only if they were called on in order to "stay safe." For the most part they did not participate in campuswide organizations or clubs or engage in student activities. As one student put it:

We're on their turf, so we let them have it. All we want to do is just take the classes and stay out of trouble. We don't say much in class because we don't want to get involved in any racial arguments. Most of the black students are polite. They go their way and we go ours. This keeps the slate clean. Once in a while one will give you a hard look or make a smart remark. We just ignore it.

A few (14) claimed to have personal contacts with a number of black acquaintances and friends on and off campus. Members of these friendship cliques interacted inconspicuously in dormitories and apartment houses. Some also socialized at campus public accommodations, public bars and restaurants, and private dwelling units off campus. One student commented:

We have a number of black friends. You know, black guys that we hang out with. But we don't go in for campus clubs and organizations. We keep our social life to ourselves. We would feel out of place at open affairs.

Three white females covertly dated black males, and one white male dated black females.

White faculty. Most (36) reported pleasant and helpful campus contacts with white faculty. None reported other than chance contacts off campus. Fourteen dropped by their offices for chats or met them outside the classroom. Encounters tended to be formalized and restricted to academic matters. One illustrative comment follows:

You see, they're in the classrooms or in their offices. They don't move around much on the campus. So we usually find them in the classroom.

> That's o.k. because we don't need to see them anyway. They're foreigners like us. Every time I go by their offices I see them helping a bunch of black students. I couldn't wait so I left.

A few claimed that they were expected to meet higher classroom standards (e.g., on exams and written reports) than were their black classmates. One student commented:

> I always felt like many white teachers expected me to do better than black students. They all gave us good grades, but I worked hard to earn mine.

Black faculty. Most (33) characterized their contacts with black faculty, on the whole, as pleasant and helpful. Contacts beyond the classroom, other than scheduled office visits, were infrequent, despite the professors' open door policy. One student elaborated:

> As far as I know we all lived off campus, so we're always coming and going. Basically we had the same type of contacts with them as we did with white professors. And you know the same kind of relationship. They treated us well but they spent more time with black students than with us. We didn't go to their offices much because they were too busy with other things and helping others.

Thirteen reported that they were treated as friendly as black students were. One typical comment follows:

> They treated me just like they did black students. I didn't even think of race with them. And I don't think they did either. I never hesitated to go to their office when I wanted to. I just knew I could go by whenever I needed. I had friendly chats with them outside the campus, too. Some of them invited me to their homes, and I went and had a good time.

Only four expressed negative views toward them. Their complaints included (1) the black professors' failure to acknowledge reasonable answers in class and (2) their failure to give white students proper attention during office visits (e.g., they spent too long talking on the telephone and conversing with others during what the students considered their time).

White administrators. On-campus contacts with the few middle-management white administrators (other than department heads) were infrequent, brief, civil, and formal. Contacts with white chairs were frequent, pleasant, and productive.

Black administrators. Contacts with black administrators were similar to those with white administrators, but more frequent and friendlier. A few (5) found black administrators to be rigid, authoritarian, and unreceptive. A few others, however, visited in black administrators' homes.

White staff members. Contacts with white staff were professional, goal-oriented, civil, friendly, helpful, and limited to on-campus encounters.

Black staff members. Contacts with the black white-collar staff were similar to those with the white white-collar staff. Contacts with the black blue-collar staff were formal and somewhat strained. No off-campus contacts were reported.

Perceived Social Acceptance

White students. They considered themselves socially acceptable to most other white students on and off the campus. Social interaction among them, however, was at a minimum.

Black students. Most white students (36), in accordance with prevailing customs in a segregated society, considered themselves excluded from black students' social cliques, intimate friendship circles, and fraternities and sororities and from black organizations. They assumed themselves to be socially acceptable at all campuswide events. Fourteen said that they were socially acceptable to some black students on and off campus.

White faculty, administrators, and staff members. They deemed themselves socially acceptable to all white categories on and off campus, although they noted few off-campus encounters with members of these categories.

Black faculty, administrators, and staff members. Most (41) saw themselves as socially acceptable to these black categories on campus, and nine considered themselves socially acceptable to some members of these categories off campus. A few visited in the homes of selected members of these categories.

Apart from race, differences in age, student status, and life style precluded appreciable social interaction between students and faculty, administration, and staff members.

Perceived Racial Conflict on Campus

These students perceived no overt racial group conflict on campus. The fifteen liberal integrationists and thirty-five conservatives clashed ideologically and engaged occasionally in one-on-one arguments, but never faced off in an open forum.

Psychological Comfort Level

Most (44) reported a satisfactory accommodation and emotional adjustment, though they experienced some campus alienation and some problems adjusting to a different set of race relations. They said that they compartmentalized their lives into (1) a segmented, goal-oriented campus life and (2) life among significant others beyond campus. The remaining six expressed emotional discomfort because of one or more of the following reasons: (1) perceived reverse racial discrimination; (2) inability to accept a more egalitarian racial scene than they were accustomed to; and (3) ridicule by friends, family, and community for attending an HBCU. Despite these discomforts, only three mentioned the likelihood of transferring to a white college.

Opportunity Structure

Most (42) asserted that the faculty, academic programs, curriculum, and support services met their current academic and career needs. Eight complained about one or more of the following: (1) slow paper work connected with admission, registration, and financial aid; (2) insufficient library holdings; (3) inadequate security measures; (4) inadequate computer services; (5) limited academic offerings; (6) high student-faculty ratio; (7) high tuition fees (particularly at private HBCUs); (8) inadequate physical facilities; (9) inadequate classroom facilities (e.g., visual aids, lab equipment, instructional supplies, space); and (10) campus organizations and activities that were exclusively geared to black students. Most found the HBCU campus more congenial and helpful than they had initially expected. Most mentioned the faculty as the HBCU's greatest asset.

Summary and Conclusions

These students fell into two groups: a majority group of conservatives and a minority group of liberal integrationists. Conservatives accepted legal racial integration, but decried affirmative action policies or any other civil rights programs that provide more than strict equality for blacks vis-à-vis whites. Liberal integrationists expressed compassion for blacks and supported affirmative action programs to bring them up to parity with whites. The conservatives perceived social barriers between themselves and white liberals, as well as racial barriers between themselves and black students. They were indifferent toward all other white and black categories on campus, except white and black faculty members whom they looked on as worthy, respectable, competent, and friendly teachers. Conservatives said that they avoided close contacts with black students for two reasons: "pressure from a segregated society" and "a desire to stay clear of racial trouble." Contacts with black and white faculty were pleasant, professional, and helpful. Few experienced social contacts with others outside the classroom situation because they were commuters and had little interest in campus activities. They viewed the campus as "black turf" and avoided all activities unrelated to the classroom.

The liberal students attempted, with some success, to adjust to a black ambiance and fit into an integrated scene. Both groups accommodated to the campus situation, though utilizing two different approaches. Both groups found that the HBCUs met their academic and career needs and were more congenial than they had initially expected. Psychological discomfort was at the minimum. Although black students considered white students aliens, they accepted them as legitimate persons on campus. White students appeared to have developed more respect for blacks than they had before attending an HBCU.

We recommend that white students continue to enroll in black colleges. Difficulties are likely to arise in the foreseeable future, however, if white students should come to outnumber black students at any one HBCU. In fact, such has already been the case on some HBCU campuses. While balancing policy must be developed to meet this problem, this extends beyond our research project and our expertise. The most important finding was the congenial, helpful, and professional relationship that existed between these students and the white and black faculty. Obviously, the methods utilized by the black faculty with students at HBCUs might work with white students attending white colleges as well. According to these white students, the white and black faculty members taught them in the same manner. This question then arises: Do the white faculty members at HBCUs learn new methods of teaching from black HBCU faculty or from their teaching experience with black students? Perhaps white professors and colleges have something to learn from HBCUs. As will be discussed in more detail later, the key appears to lie in three areas: (1) personal relationships involving emotional support between faculty members and students, (2) faculty expectations of students' success, and (3) teaching techniques beyond the lecture method. Finally, HBCUs should develop strategies to integrate the activities of black and white students and make the two groups aware that HBCU campuses exist for all races.

Black Faculty on White Campuses

Respondent's Racial Identification and Self-Concept

All twenty-five recognized themselves as black professors who were teaching on a predominately white campus. Though aware of the fact that HBCUs were in desperate need of black professors, they rationalized away their choice of a white campus on the basis of salary, career opportunities, and job offers. In brief, they described themselves as professionals who were prepared to teach on any reputable campus. They presented themselves as liberals and professed racial equality and racial integration up to the social level. They were equally divided on interracial courtship and marriage. All identified with the black middle class and its value system of respectability, marriage, two-parent families, family values, home ownership, religiosity, ambition, education, hard work, getting ahead, and a defensive life style (risk avoidance). Their remarks divulged a strong awareness of class lines as well as race consciousness. Three presented themselves interchangeably as black Americans or African

Americans. Most viewed themselves as worthy role models for white as well as black youth. All mentioned the necessity of adjustment to a multiracial and multicultural society. Five appeared to possess a marginal and ambiguous role identity.

Interracial and Intraracial Perceptions

Perceptions of white students. Most identified them as worthy students who now occupied a status level similar to the status they had had and who exhibited a life style similar to the life style they had had a few years ago, as youth they had prepared themselves to teach, and as key figures in their academic careers. Secondarily, they recognized them as members of a different and advantaged racial group, as the dominant campus student group, and as their potential admirers and critics. They were also seen as potential allies in a reciprocal, challenging educational pursuit. A few noted some arrogant and critical white students, who were difficult to teach, but not beyond control and redemption. Most perceived few racial barriers between themselves and white students, whom they regarded as students rather than as members of a racial category.

White students' perceptions of you. All assumed that most white students perceived them to be worthy faculty, similar in all respects, other than race, to other faculty. They also thought that white students, with few exceptions, perceived no racial barriers between themselves and their black professors. A few (6) thought some accepted them on a contingency basis, pending their teaching performance. Two faculty members thought that some white students found them undesirable on a white campus. Five surmised that a few white students wondered about their presence on a white campus: For example, why did they choose a white campus? Were they recruited because of affirmative action?

Perceptions of black students. All, in the first instance, viewed them in a fashion similar to the way they perceived white students. Secondarily, they recognized them as fortunate black allies who were similar to themselves in background, values, motivation, aspirations, and expectations. In this sense, black students comprised a special group of whom they were proud. A few (4) feared that some unprepared black students might embarrass them in the eyes of white professors and students by a poor academic performance. These four voiced a demand for stricter admissions criteria.

Black students' perceptions of you. All supposed that they were envisioned as worthy black professors, as an educated elite who had demonstrated racial parity in a segregated society, and as their mentors and role models.

Perceptions of white faculty. Most (14) viewed the white faculty as the dominant and most prestigious group on campus, as those who set the academic pace, and as the group they desired as peers. They considered them to be worthy, competent, and cooperative, though at the same time cool and impersonal in demeanor. Nine deemed them competent, civil, and professionally correct colleagues, but also ruthless competitors. It should be noted here that white faculty members can be extremely competitive, cool, and aloof toward one another and that white academia is, indeed, a very competitive and rigorous enterprise, where faculty members vie with one another for salary, tenure, and promotion—all involving publication records which are hard to come by. As one black faculty member commented:

> My white colleagues are competent and civil but they seem to be at each other's throats. They fight like dogs to get tenure and promotion. I think they could be more cooperative.

Two viewed white professors as camouflaged, alien enemies—outwardly civil, but inwardly hostile. As one of these two stated:

> They put on a good show up front but I know they would be the first ones to get me out of here, if they could. They don't think I can write articles in their journals. And they don't recognize black journals.

In total, eleven black professors perceived racial barriers between themselves and white professors.

White faculty's perceptions of you. Fourteen surmised that most white professors welcomed them as fellow faculty members, allies, and potential friends, and they perceived no racial barriers between them. Some (9) assumed that they were acceptable colleagues, pending their adaptability as well as research and publication performance. Two were certain that they were judged to be incompetent aliens.

Perceptions of other black faculty. They recognized them as worthy fellow black faculty members and potential allies on a white campus.

Other black faculty's perceptions of you. They assumed that they were viewed as worthy black colleagues and allies on a white campus.

Perceptions of white administrators. They expressed mixed feelings and assessments of white administrators. Some remarks indicated they thought that most were anti-racist, competent, and fair and that they treated black professors in the same way as white professors. Other remarks by the same respondents portrayed some administrators as self-serving, capricious officials who complied with civil rights laws and affirmative action policies in order to avoid litigation and campus unrest. Still other remarks characterized them as racist to some degree. As one faculty member remarked:

> Generally they are o.k. But at times they are hard to figure out. Sometimes I think they want to do the right thing by us. Other times I don't know. But

they still see us as black professors on a white campus. But they know they have to have some of us around. You can't tell what's on their mind and what they are likely to do. The chairs and the deans place too much emphasis on publication but they don't give us credit for publications in black journals. The higher-ups don't want to promote you or give you tenure until they see you aren't a potential problem.

Finally, they thought that white administrators made conscious attempts to avoid any racial barriers on the campus scene. Despite this fact, many perceived racial barriers between themselves and white administrators.

White administrators' perceptions of you. They were uncertain about the perceptions of white administrators. Some remarks indicated they thought that the administrators viewed them as worthy professors who required their support in adjusting to a white campus. Other comments indicated that some of them thought that they were seen as a problematic group (i.e., a group requiring special attention in order to gain their cooperation in avoiding litigation and campus unrest), as necessary tokens less qualified than white professors, and as unappreciative and disgruntled black faculty members who demanded preferential treatment. One faculty member's comments are illustrative:

I think they see us as a group they must handle with kid gloves. I know some of them think of us as tokens but I'm fully qualified for this job. They may know some whites who are more qualified but I know some whites who are not. Some of them think they can never satisfy our needs. Some think we want the moon because we're black. The bottom line is they must treat me with respect and dignity like any one else. If they treat us right, they don't have to fear us.

In addition, some believed that white administrators perceived them as role models for black students, as well as allies in maintaining racial peace on campus.

Perceptions of black administrators. They considered black administrators to be worthy allies on campus and in the black community and to be similar to themselves racially and culturally. Some of them were former friends and colleagues as well as neighbors in the same residential area.

Black administrators' perceptions of you. They assumed that black administrators looked on them as worthy and competent faculty members and as potential allies.

Perceptions of white staff members. They reported white-collar staff, particularly librarians, supervisors, and secretaries, to be competent, co-operative, civil, and formally polite, but aloof. Blue-collar workers were described as civil and aloof, but occasionally hostile. They perceived some racial barriers between themselves and blue-collar workers.

White staff members' perceptions of you. They thought that white staff

defined them as respectable alien faculty members whom it was their duty
to serve.

Perceptions of black staff members. They saw all black staff members
as worthy, competent, and friendly staff on a white campus.

Black staff members' perceptions of you. They assumed that the black
staff viewed them as competent black professors on a white campus whom
it was their duty to serve.

Interracial and Intraracial Interactions and Relationships

White students. Most (21) noted friendly, professional, and helpful encounters with white students in their classrooms and offices. All said that
contacts elsewhere on and off campus were inadvertent, brief, and polite.
Some (4) mentioned that a few white students dropped by their offices
occasionally for chats on a myriad of subjects. Most encounters dealt
with professional and academic matters. Close personal ties were rarely
formed.

Black students. Most (21) related on-campus contacts similar to those
they experienced with white students. Four recalled frequent friendly
chats with black students in their offices, focusing on career plans, personal problems, and race relations. Some (10) reported frequent off-campus personal contacts with black students at their (faculty) homes and at
churches.

White faculty. Most (19) reported civil, cooperative, and professional
contacts with white colleagues on campus. Meetings elsewhere were un-
planned, infrequent, and polite. Three said some white faculty avoided
off-campus contacts with them. The remaining three said they engaged
in friendly relations with white faculty on and off campus, including an
exchange of home visits. Only two of them shared research interests with
white faculty. All of them, however, served with white professors on
departmental and campuswide committees. Close personal friendship ties
were rare.

Other black faculty. On-campus contacts, with the exception of research activities, were similar to those with white faculty, though somewhat friendlier. Most enjoyed close friendly relationships off campus,
including home visits. Many were neighbors in the same residential area.

White administrators. All experienced civil, cooperative, professional
contacts with white administrators on campus. Contacts with chairs and
deans were more frequent and friendlier than were those with other administrators. A few (3) interacted on a friendly and personal basis with
some chairs and deans off campus (i.e., in their homes, restaurants, and
bars). However, close personal friendship ties were rare.

Black administrators. All noted civil, cooperative, friendly, and professional contacts with black administrators on campus. Some interacted

with black administrators on a personal and friendly level off campus, including home visits.

White staff members. Most (21) said that their contacts with white white-collar staff were civil, cooperative, and formalized. On the other hand, four stated that some of their contacts with some white white-collar staff were unsatisfactory; for example, some white staff occasionally glared at them in a hostile fashion, avoided physical contact, and made indirect racial slurs about them to others. One of these related the following comment by one secretary to another in his presence:

> You know how those people are lazy, uppity, and disorganized.

Most contacts with blue-collar staff were cool, strained, and occasionally unpleasant. For example, one black faculty member overheard the following comment directed by one maintenance man to another in his presence:

> You know how those darkies are. You know, lazy and stupid with no morals. Even the educated ones are still niggers.

None had off-campus contacts with white staff members.

Black staff members. On-campus contacts with black staff were formal, pleasant, and professional. Their off-campus contacts were infrequent, but friendlier and more personal than were their on-campus contacts.

Perceived Social Acceptance

White students. Most (20) considered themselves socially acceptable to most white students on campus. Only five thought that they were socially acceptable to white students on and off campus.

Black students. All considered themselves to be socially acceptable to black students on and off campus. Unlike at HBCUs, the black faculty socialized at a minimum with black students on and off campus.

White faculty, administrators, and staff members. Most (21) saw themselves as socially acceptable to many members of these three categories (except blue-collar staff) on campus. Only four thought that they were socially acceptable to some members of these categories off campus. All campuswide activities, social functions, and public accommodations were perceived as available to all black and white categories.

Black faculty, administrators, and staff members. All considered themselves socially acceptable to all these categories on and off campus. There was, however, much less on- and off-campus socializing among the members of these three groups than was the case at HBCUs.

Perceived Racial Conflict on Campus

Though none reported overt racial group conflict, all had experienced passive racial rejection at one time or another and had been occasionally subjected to indirect racial slurs. All, of course, noted racist graffiti on campus at one time or another.

Psychological Comfort Level

Most (15) communicated mixed feelings about psychological comfort and ease and had experienced temporary discomfort and anxiety at times when they were the objects of racial avoidance, social rejection, and derogation. According to them, they had managed to rationalize away these transgressions and humiliations as a consequence of what they termed "penetrations from the outside segregated community." One of these fifteen commented:

> I know we catch it once in a while, but what can you expect from a seg-
> regated society. You know, the society where those people who put us
> down come from. The campus has no invisible walls. Anyway, I've heard
> that trash all my life. It's much better here on the campus than out there
> in the white community.

Some others (4) expressed negative feelings about campus life, but vacillated from a state of ease to one of unease, depending on perceived incidents of mistreatment. All of these voiced some anxiety about what they termed the prevailing "cool atmosphere," the "impersonal rela-tions," and the "cutthroat competition" among professors and students. One of these four commented:

> People here treat each other as objects. I like to be treated for who I am.
> But to these people, you are what you produce. And that changes. You
> know the professors act like it's a zero-sum game. I want no part of it.

These four maintained that they were trying to adjust to the white campus situation. As one put it:

> I have good and bad days, and sometimes I feel like an alien in another
> country. But it's my career. You have to learn how to play their game.
> Maybe I can handle it. The publication thing worries me more than anything
> else. I can put up with all that other junk.

Two suffered appreciable psychological discomfort as a result of what they perceived to be the coldness of the white campus. They planned to seek positions at HBCUs. One of these two commented:

> From what I know and what my friends tell me, things are different at a
> black college. There everybody is a family and the faculty is more teaching
> oriented. They treat each other like people, not like objects.

Opportunity Structure

Though assessments differed in this area as well as others, most (15)
rated overall career opportunities from fair to average in terms of salary
scale, promotion, and tenure; fringe benefits (health and life insurance,
retirement plan, etc); teaching load; student advising load; research and
computer services; library holdings; and physical facilities. Six expressed
doubts involving one or more of the following focal concerns: (1) inadequate social life, (2) cold colleague relationships, (3) impersonal relationships campuswide, (4) overemphasis on publications, and (5) uncertainty
of promotion and tenure. All mentioned the lack of an opportunity structure on or off campus to facilitate interracial or intraracial association and
interaction among black and white students as well as faculty members.

Summary and Conclusions

These black professors formed a professional, middle-class group of
liberal integrationists who were prepared to teach on any available reputable campus. To them, students were students, though they recognized
a common racial heritage with other blacks. They related to students in
a fashion similar to that of white counterparts on a white campus where
social distance was observed between student and professor. Contacts
with students, other professors, and staff tended to be civil and professionally correct, but lacking in warmth and emotional depth. Most important, their relationships with black students, though academically
acceptable, did not appear to be as strong as those found between professors and students on HBCU campuses. As was the case with black
students on white campuses, all perceived racial barriers on and off campus, experienced social rejection, and were occasionally subjected to
racial slurs. They found the prevailing atmosphere bearable, but chilly
and uninviting. Relationships with colleagues were tenuous and highly
competitive, and encounters with administrators were ambiguous and
unassuring. Some felt they were black tokens. Despite these conditions,
most were determined to hang on and adjust themselves to a system where
the criteria for the success did not bode well for them. It should be noted
here that white faculty on white campuses compete fiercely among themselves for appointments, promotions, and tenure. (Unlike M.D.s and attorneys, who at graduation are considered equal to all other M.D.s and
attorneys, Ph.D.s must continue to struggle first for appointments, then
for promotion to associate professor and tenure, and finally for full pro-
fessorships. The course is long, arduous, and unending—and usually re-

quires continual publication in scholarly research journals. Many full professors continue to compete. Many professors drop out, and many who stay the course never become full professors.)

Should these findings prove typical, and should white campuses not become more accepting of black faculty, we suggest that black professors seek employment at HBCUs where they and their students would be better off. For those who are highly motivated to become research scholars, a white campus may be a choice. Furthermore, a few HBCU campuses stress research and publications.

Obviously, most white institutions must become much more accepting of black professors if racial integration in higher education is to be more than a dream. White campuses need a racial mix among the faculty like that now found at HBCUs. Finally, as alluded to before, white faculty on white campuses could profit from a knowledge of the teaching methods utilized at HBCUs.

Black Faculty on Black Campuses

Respondent's Racial Identification and Self-Concept

Most (44 of the 75 interviewed) identified themselves as African-American professors teaching at HBCUs and maintained that most black youth could be better educated at HBCUs than on white campuses, that they could teach more effectively at an HBCU than at a white college, and that they preferred to teach at an HBCU. They claimed to play a unique role in higher education within a racially segregated society, which enabled them to provide formal education to black youth; to transmit black culture and instill black consciousness; to prepare future professionals for service and leadership roles in the black community; to serve as mentors, surrogate parents, and role models for black youth; to offer special assistance and emotional support to many culturally deprived youth; to act as educational liaisons between academia and the surrounding black community; to better focus on black issues as members of an organized academic entity; to function as elites, intellectuals, and leaders in the black community on and off campus; and to serve as agents of social change in a racially segregated society. They presented themselves as respectable middle-class citizens entitled to equal opportunity rights and privileges in a "political democracy." They dismissed racial integration as utopian ideology and emphasized race as more important to their self-identification than social class. All were committed to uplifting the black underclass through and by tax-supported governmental programs.

Twenty-one identified themselves as black American professors and liberals who held respectable and important positions at HBCUs. They saw themselves and their roles in a fashion similar to that of the African

Americans in certain respect; they were, however, proponents of racial integration at all levels. They saw their role as the preparation of minority youth for life in a multiracial and multicultural society. To them, social class lines were more important than were racial demarcations in the long run, and they advocated voluntary social integration up to and including courtship and marriage. They recommended HBCUs for many black youth, particularly those who desired to attend them and those who were not adequately prepared for college.

The remarks of six of the remaining ten disclosed a militant African-American identification. To them, racial and cultural distinctions were far more important than was class orientation. They emphasized black consciousness and black culture and urged all African Americans to adhere to their heritage by thinking, acting, and living black. They perceived their role functions as similar to those noted by the African Americans, but they were more committed to Afro-centrism, separatism, and a confrontational stance with respect to the white power structure. As one member of this group explained:

> I play my role as a college professor within an African-American context. In order to maintain a balance of power we have to stand up to and be willing to fight the white power structure. The white man has never given us anything anyway. They responded to civil rights legislation because they had to, not out of any goodness in their hearts. Integration is only wishful thinking. People like me don't care about integration. I see society as a racial mosaic and African Americans must possess their niche on an equal basis with whites. If we keep playing this integration game, we lose our African-American identity. And we never can obtain white identity. To fight for a white identity is to lose both ways. Even if they offer me a white identity, I wouldn't go for it. I don't think any real African American would go for it either. We're different and we should be proud of it.

Four female faculty members identified themselves as African-American women who were discriminated against on and off campus by whites on the basis of race and gender and by blacks on the basis of gender. They saw themselves as fighting a two-way battle of sexism and racism. One of these four declared:

> I get tired of being treated like an inferior person by both whites and African-American males day in and day out on and off campus because I'm a black female. It's bad enough to be treated low by whites and it is even worse when you get treated by black males as inferior because you are a female. I end up fighting with both of them.

Interracial and Intraracial Perceptions

Perceptions of white students. Most (42) regarded them as "different," but worthy, legitimate students on an HBCU campus. Along with some others, they wondered about their presence at an HBCU. Twenty saw them in the same way they saw other students. As one of these 20 remarked:

> White students, black students, what's the difference? You take them where you find them like Booker T. Washington says. We're here to teach and they're here to learn. They're two racial groups but they are much more similar than different. Whites are integrated students too. So we teach them the same way we teach our own. It's really a good thing to have them. We need a good mix.

Some (8) accepted them as questionable, but legitimate alien students on a contingency basis. As one of these remarked:

> If they are here to study and fit in, o.k. But if they are here to prove how liberal they are, or how superior they are, or how much they like blacks, they are off base. But I shall still do my duty by them. That's what I'm paid for.

The remaining five thought that most white students were alien enrollees who were at HBCUs because of either convenience or inability to gain admission to white schools of their choice. One of these five commented:

> I don't think that some of them really want to be here. Either they live nearby or they couldn't get in any white school. Or couldn't get the program they wanted. We don't need these students.

Thirteen perceived some form of racial barriers between themselves and white students.

White students' perceptions of you. Most (66) supposed that white students assessed them as competent, pleasant, fair, and respectable faculty members and did not perceive any racial barriers between themselves and black faculty. Six assumed they were respected, but not rated as highly as were white faculty members on the campus. Three opined that some white students did not like them.

Perceptions of black students. Most considered them their pride and joy; students with a status level they once occupied; future black professionals, leaders, and role models in the black community; future proponents of civil rights and affirmative action; potential members of the black middle class; future neighborhood friends and supporters; a more enlightened and privileged generation than their own; and, finally, surrogate children.

Black students' perceptions of you. Most thought that they were visualized as competent and helpful professors; successful black professionals; members of the black educated elite; patient and caring counselors and mentors; role models; and older black brothers, sisters, or surrogate parents.

Perceptions of white faculty. Most (61) recognized them as welcome, worthy, competent professors; anti-racist liberals; and allies and potential (if not current) friends. They perforce noted racial and cultural differences between themselves and the white faculty, but did not regard these differentials as barriers to social interaction or to cooperation in a common educational endeavor. They observed and emphasized many similarities among themselves and white faculty, such as educational background, goals, professional interests, and social class. One acknowledged:

> There are differences but there are also more similarities. We all have Ph.D.s and come from middle-class backgrounds. Certainly, they aren't racists. If they were, they wouldn't be here. Many of them are my friends. Of course, some are not. But then, I'm not friends with some black faculty either. We need all the good faculty we can get. A good mix makes for a better academic atmosphere.

Most important, they recognized white faculty members at both the individual and the group levels. Others (11) saw them as worthy colleagues, but not as close friends. As one of these commented:

> I have no problem with them on campus and we work well together. In fact they are good colleagues. But that's enough. Who's kidding who? We're brought up in two different groups in a segregated society. This has made us different in many ways and I like my ways better. Once we leave campus, we go our separate ways. That's too bad. But that's the way it is.

Only three rejected them as unacceptable aliens on a black college campus. As one of these three stated:

> I don't spend time thinking about these unrealistic things. I guess they know what they're doing. If they don't, the administrators need to worry about it, not me. I stay out of their way, and I expect them to stay out of my way. In my opinion, they don't belong here.

Fourteen perceived some racial barriers between themselves and white faculty.

White faculty's perceptions of you. Most (62) assumed that they were considered to be worthy, cooperative, competent, and friendly allies in a common educational pursuit where no significant racial barriers existed. Others (11) thought that they were accepted as competent colleagues, but not as close friends. Only two speculated that many white faculty members disliked them because of racial differences.

Perceptions of other black faculty. They perceived them, first, as loyal, worthy black colleagues and allies in the education of black youth. Second, they recognized them as members of an extended campus family, including all black categories. Third, they saw them as members of a network of friends and acquaintances on other HBCU campuses and in the local black community. Fourth, they knew them as members of a known and elite circle of educated blacks who transcended geographical areas. All belonged to the black middle class, but were divided into different camps on social and political issues; for example, full integrationists, partial integrationists, vacillators between full and partial integration, and African-American separatists were represented. All perceived them as black brothers and sisters in the struggle for racial equality and, at the same time, as individuals who possessed different personality traits and life styles.

Other black faculty's perceptions of you. They supposed that other black faculty had a mirror image of them.

Perceptions of white administrators. They viewed white administrators as welcome, competent allies of an aides to higher-echelon black administrators. They observed no racial barriers between themselves and these employees.

White administrators' perceptions of you. They assumed that they were viewed as worthy, competent black faculty members.

Perceptions of black administrators. Most alluded to them as educational leaders and successful fellow blacks with backgrounds similar to their own. Though acknowledged as college officials and as their superiors, they were also cooperative and friendly allies in a common educational enterprise. Many administrators were recognized as former faculty colleagues and students, as well as neighbors and friends in the black community. They also noted a keen sense of competition within the administrative circle, and some thought that there was too much turnover among deans, vice presidents, and presidents. Some also reported that some top administrators assumed too much power and dealt with the faculty in an arbitrary manner and that they were overpaid in comparison to faculty. (Both of these complaints are quite common on white campuses as well.)

Black administrators' perceptions of you. They thought that they were seen as worthy members of one of the two most important academic groups, professors and students. Some conjectured that certain administrators at times considered faculty members to be disgruntled malcontents and opponents of the administration.

Perceptions of white staff members. White staff members were viewed as welcome, anti-racist, and competent persons who rendered necessary support services to their institution.

White staff members' perceptions of you. They supposed that they were seen as competent, worthy black professors on HBCU campuses and as the major category they were employed to serve.

Perceptions of black staff members. They looked on black staff members, particularly white-collar staff, as competent, friendly, fellow black allies who played a key role in the smooth function of the institution. Many staff members were seen as members of the extended family system on campus.

Black staff members' perceptions of you. They assumed that black staff members viewed them as respectable, competent, worthy, and learned professors who were promoting the best interests of the future black generations. They also thought that they were seen as friendly superiors and allies.

Interracial and Intraracial Interactions and Relationships

White students. Most black professors (61) reported friendly, informal, and professional contacts with white students in their classrooms and offices. For the most part off-campus contacts were inadvertent and insignificant. Only a few (6) claimed personal and friendly off-campus contacts. These included informal chats and home visits. They reported that nearly all white students were commuters who lived off campus. When classes were over, they usually departed the scene because they had work schedules to meet and because they did not become involved in extracurricular activities. This situation precluded frequent personal encounters.

Five reported few contacts outside the classroom. Only four reported that racial barriers appeared to block their informal encounters with white students. All professors, however, claimed an open-door policy for all students.

Black students. All black professors reported frequent and friendly formal and informal meetings with black students on campus. One professor explained this, and more:

> We seek out our students on the campus and off the campus. We want them to know we love them, we care for them, and we are behind them in every way. We try not to have pets. And we don't rank them in class. And we don't let them rank other students. We teach them to cooperate and we give them many assignments where they have to cooperate. We want them to succeed and we tell them to follow their dreams. We don't give up on any of them. We tell them if they try hard, they can make it. If they don't know how to read, we teach them. If they don't know how to spell, we teach them. We take them as they are and try to improve them.

Classroom work and encounters, vital forms of interaction, involved question-and-answer periods, call-and-response sessions, oral reports, group discussions, individual assignments, team assignments and presentations, role playing, sociodrama, map and chart reading, use of the library and audiovisual aids, and etiquette and social education. Teaching styles and methods emphasized the exchange of subject matter, ideas, beliefs, opinions, and impressions of topics under discussion. Each student was treated as an important person and encouraged to express his or her views in an open format. Instruction was structured and adjusted in accordance with student responsiveness, comprehension, and preparedness within a context of patience, understanding, and emotional support. The level of instruction was geared toward the academic level of individual students and adjusted to their knowledge and learning ability. Students were consistently encouraged, as individuals and as groups, to visit with the instructor in his or her office where any topics were open for discussion. Topics of discussion included subject matter, remedial instruction, assignments, personal matters, campus events, current events, race relations, economic conditions, political events, organizational activities, career plans, and so on. Professors held individual and group counseling sessions with students in their offices. They permitted students who were academically behind to make up deficiencies in several ways: retake exams, complete take-home exams, make additional classroom presentations, prepare additional literature reviews on mutually agreed upon topics, and do other extra work within the students' capabilities.

Off-campus encounters occurred at home entertainments, sports activities, church services, and black community meetings.

White faculty. Black professors' contacts with white faculty, for the most part, were friendly and cooperative, though generally limited to on-campus encounters. Off-campus contacts with white faculty were usually infrequent, brief, and limited to professional activities. A few (10) socialized with white faculty in one another's homes. Thirteen noted some racial barriers that impinged on their formal and informal contacts. Fourteen avoided close personal contacts with white professors on and off campus.

Other black faculty. Contacts with other black faculty on and off campus were frequent, friendly, pleasant, and cooperative. They interacted with one another on a highly personal level. Their conversations during these encounters covered a wide range of topics, varying from professional matters (such as student counseling, teaching style, scholarships, grants, research interests, administration policies, salary scale, promotion and tenure, hiring practices, and campus social relationships) to gossip and deep personal concerns. These encounters existed within a campuswide extended family context. One faculty member elucidated:

> We are different from white campuses. We're like a family here. We're concerned about each other's welfare and the welfare of our kids. We stick

together and fight for a common cause. Publications may be important, but taking care of our younger generation is more important. We devote our main efforts to teach these children.

White administrators. Contacts with white administrators were infrequent, brief, civil, and formal and were generally limited to on-campus meetings.

Black administrators. For the most part contacts with this group were friendly, pleasant, cooperative, and professional in nature. Some interacted with them on a more personal level, particularly those with whom they had former collegial relationships and those who were neighbors in the same residential area. Most of them had experienced unpleasant meetings with some black administrators at one time or another (involving disagreements on promotion and tenure recommendations, salary and pay raise issues, hiring practices, budgetary matters, policy making, lack of faculty input, teaching load requirements, etc.). They reported that during these unpleasant encounters, the administrators were frequently rigid and authoritarian.

Some maintained close personal ties with many black administrators off campus, including, but not limited to, home visits.

White staff members. Contacts with white staff members were civil, formal, brief, and professional and were usually related to on-campus activities.

Black staff members. Contacts with black staff members were frequent, pleasant, familial, and egalitarian. Conversations during these encounters covered personal as well as professional matters.

Perceived Social Acceptance

White students. Most saw themselves as socially acceptable to most white students on campus, and a few considered themselves to be socially acceptable to some white students on and off campus.

Black students. They all considered themselves socially acceptable to black students on and off campus.

White faculty, administrators, and staff members. Most considered themselves to be socially acceptable to these categories on campus and to some white faculty and administrators (but not to staff) off campus.

Black faculty, administrators, and staff members. All supposed themselves to be socially acceptable to these three categories on and off campus.

Perceived Racial Conflict on Campus

None reported any overt racial group conflict on campus. They did note media accounts of racial conflicts on many white campuses throughout the United States and sympathized strongly with the black students involved.

Psychological Comfort Level

Most reported that they were comfortable where they were for many of the same reasons mentioned by black students on HBCU campuses: (1) a sense of belonging on a campus that focused on the needs of black youth; (2) insulation from prejudice and discrimination they would face on a white campus; (3) respect and high status on campus and in the black community; (4) accessibility of and immersion in African-American culture; and (5) professional ease and security where teaching, service, and leadership, rather than research and publications, were emphasized. A few active researchers (3) were not comfortable with the lack of recognition they received for their publication records. Some faculty felt uneasy about the perceived authoritarianism and rigidity in the administrative structure.

Opportunity Structure

Most (71) were satisfied with the existing opportunity structure because they were able to: (1) find psychological comfort within a secure academic career; (2) play a role in preparing black youth for professional service and leadership in the black community; (3) act as surrogate parents and role models for black youth; (4) be a member of a black institution that provided channels for voicing Afro-centric concerns and views regarding civil rights, affirmative action, and racial equality; and (5) experience a rich social life involving professional membership in HBCU networks.

Some (14) mentioned a few career disadvantages (e.g., inadequate physical facilities, poor campus security, limited library holdings and computer services, heavy teaching loads, wide salary differentials, an oversized administration in relationship to student enrollment, institutional financial restraints, and an authoritarian administration). On this last point, it should be noted that academic institutions have never been democratic. They evolved from church-centered universities within the rigid, hierarchical scholastic system of medieval Europe. Furthermore, the struggle for power between the professors (the practitioners) and the administrators (the professional educators) is endemic to academia in the United States. The balance of power between these two shifts from one institution to another, and usually the more prestigious the institution, the greater the power of the faculty. Whatever the power considerations, the administrators invariably reap the higher financial rewards. In contrast to academia, M.D.s, the practitioners in hospitals, have unchallenged power and prestige and receive higher financial rewards vis-à-vis the medical administrators and other managerial support staff. Although college professors teach and write about administrative structure and process, perhaps they could learn something from M.D. practitioners, who neither teach nor write about administration.

Summary and Conclusions

This group includes professors with three different racial identities: African Americans, black Americans, and militant blacks. All were strongly committed to HBCU institutions and to the educational preparation of black youth, their surrogate children. Seeing themselves more as teachers, role models, active liaisons to the black community, and agents of social change than as research scholars per se, they were unconcerned with what they called "the white man's rat race game" or the "zero-sum publication game." Ensconced in a secure teaching career, they belonged to an extended-family academic group wherein they sensed feelings of success, psychological comfort, and belonging. Most accepted white professors and students as long as they tried to fit in; accommodated themselves to a black cultural scene; and refrained from attempting to alter the HBCU's educational goals, policies, curriculum, and teaching methods. Personal contacts and relationships varied in kind and degree among them and the white faculty, and some racial barriers existed between them. Effective professional relationships were the rule. Their relationships with the administration were as a rule congenial; at times, however, they thought that administrators were too rigid, domineering, and authoritarian.

Significantly, the relationships they developed with black students and the apparent effectiveness of their teaching methods transcended all other interracial or intraracial interactions. These relationships and teaching methods should continue on HBCU campuses and perhaps be duplicated, in part, on white campuses—particularly with students who perform below the average. These relationships and teaching methods are a metaphor for HBCUs. The number of black professors must be increased on black as well as white campuses. The problem is that not enough are available and not enough are being trained in graduate schools. More U.S. government funds could be made available for black graduate students who are interested in becoming college and university professors.

One problem is the usual requirement of a Ph.D. for college teaching. We suggest that teaching doctorates be established in each academic discipline alongside the Ph.D. for those who plan to teach, rather become research scholars. The Ph.D. is first and foremost a research degree, but many graduate students who must earn Ph.D.s because they would like to teach in college are not interested in research careers. Furthermore, most Ph.D.s who now teach in colleges do little research and publish few articles. The teaching doctorate curriculum for each discipline would focus on course content, rather than on research and methodology. For example, the curriculum for a teaching doctorate in history would deal with historical facts and interpretations, rather than historiography. The teaching doctorate would probably attract more students and certainly require less time to complete than the Ph.D. This would facilitate the preparation of more black professors to meet HBCU teaching needs.

In addition, black campuses must work to eliminate the perception that white faculty and students are not treated equally vis-à-vis black faculty and students on HBCU campuses. Finally, the HBCU administrative structure should be decentralized to some extent on those campuses where it is perceived to be too authoritarian.

White Faculty on Black Campuses

Respondent's Racial Identification and Self-Concept

All fifty respondents identified themselves as white, middle-class, liberal professors teaching on a black campus. All professed racial equality and supported integration at all levels up to courtship and marriage. Twenty accepted interracial courtship and marriage, nineteen disapproved, and eleven were undecided. The majority (34) defined themselves as professionals who said they were pursuing an academic career on whatever campuses were available to them. Currently they saw themselves not only as professors, but also as agents bridging the gap between two racial and cultural groups. Twelve others saw themselves as anti-racists dedicated to the education of blacks in a racially segregated society. The remaining four conceived of themselves as "hired help" and unequals on a black campus. One of these four protested his low status and vulnerability on an HBCU campus:

> I work hard and do a better job than many of them. Still I don't get treated the way I ought to be socially, professionally, or financially. They see me as an unwelcome outsider and a competitor who comes here to share their wealth. They ought to know the historical and current roles of whites at HBCUs. You know, how they got established and funded to date. We whites should always have equal rights and a respectable place on these campuses. ... That includes the right to share the wealth. I have a legitimate reason to be here and deserve every penny I'm making. After all, I'm not looking for a handout. HBCUs don't belong to any one group. All schools are integrated now. Blacks have equal rights on white campuses. Then why shouldn't I have equal rights on a black campus?

Interracial and Intraracial Perceptions

Perceptions of white students. Most (35) defined white students as members of a worthy minority group on a black campus who are similar to themselves in many respects. They also viewed white students as allies and friends in the further integration of black schools—assets in and of themselves as well as agents in bridging the gap between the black and the white worlds. In brief, they saw these students as real white integrationists. They realized, however, that many white students attended HBCUs for convenience, rather than for altruistic reasons.

White students' perceptions of you. Most (37) assumed that white students defined them as liberals and as a competent group of worthy, friendly white professors on an HBCU campus. They also thought that many students wondered about their presence on a black campus: Are they here because they are liberals and anti-racists with a mission, because they were unable to find a job on a white campus, or because they were drawn by job availability or job inducement? Some others (13) believed that white students viewed them as regular faculty members without concern about their racial identification.

Perceptions of black students. Most (36) considered them to be the dominant and most important group of students on campus, the major group they had been employed to teach, support, and assist. They assumed that some black students were culturally deprived, required remedial education, and needed to feel that the faculty liked them. One white professor commented:

> I was employed to teach black students and knew full well that some of them would need remedial work and individual attention. And that I would be expected to render them extra service. I also knew that I had to present myself a little differently to black students—that I had to make an extra effort to show them I liked them, and wanted to help them. I also had to see each student as an individual, rather than as a racial category. They will accept you if they know you accept them. And they know that many whites do not accept them.

The remaining fourteen professed a more objective, but ambiguous, teaching stance. One of these remarked:

> I see them as students, not as blacks or special cases in any way. I teach them like I do other students . . . the same way I would teach white students on a white campus. Anytime you lose sight of this objective approach you are not doing anybody any good in the long run. But one thing is for sure, you must relate to black students. If not, you teach them little. This is true to some degree for white students. But many of them will learn whether they like you or not. Respect goes a long way. Black students must like and respect you. And if you don't like them, they will know.

Most (38) perceived that black students liked them, and they noted no racial barriers between themselves and black students.

Black students' perceptions of you. Most (37) remarked that black students perceived them to be a competent, helpful, unbiased group of worthy white professors on a black campus. A minority (13) thought that they were viewed as regular faculty without concern for racial identification. One explained:

Forget race. They see us for what we are, faculty. And that's what we are.

Five thought that a few black students rejected them because they were white.

Perceptions of other white faculty. They observed them to be a group of fellow competent, liberal professors who, like themselves, taught on an HBCU campus. As one of these stated:

I don't get hung up on race. We are all faculty members engaged in a common enterprise.

Other white faculty's perceptions of you. Most (42) inferred that they were seen in the same light as they viewed themselves: as liberal, competent professionals. A minority (8) thought that they were seen as "just faculty members."

Perceptions of black faculty. All observed that black faculty comprised the dominant, favored faculty group on campus. Although they recognized racial and cultural differences between themselves and the black faculty, most (33) did not think that such differentials precluded cooperative professional interaction. Some (9) viewed black faculty as professional allies, colleagues, and potential friends. Others (8) took them to be professional colleagues, but ruled out friendship ties. One of this latter persuasion commented:

I can see them as colleagues but never as close friends. We travel in different social circles off campus. Why should we or they pretend all of this phony friendship jazz. Even if I wanted to be a close friend, they would not let me in. And I can understand why.

More than half (31) believed that the black faculty was favored over them in terms of recruitment, promotion, tenure, salary range, appointment to administrative positions, faculty organizational roles, chairmanships, and so on. A few (7) found black faculty to be overtly cold and aloof toward them during formal and informal interactions. Only eight reported racial barriers that precluded effective professional relationships.

Black faculty's perceptions of you. Most (30) thought that they were considered to be a competent, civil, cooperative, professional group, though racially and culturally different. Fifteen supposed that they were seen as anti-racist allies, friends, or potential friends. Eight sensed rejection and thought that they were viewed as racial aliens and unwanted competitions. One of these eight explained:

> I know they don't like me because I'm white. They probably think that I've no other place to go. I do the best job I can and try to stay out of their way. I may have to look for a job somewhere else.

Perceptions of white administrators. Most (29) defined them as a necessary support group to the top black administrators and referred to them as "hired help," "troubleshooters," "problem fixers," and "brain feeders." Twenty-one defined them as administrators like those of any other race.

White administrators' perceptions of you. Most (41) thought that these administrators viewed them as competent, worthy faculty members. Nine thought that they were seen as "hired help."

Perceptions of black administrators. Most (42) saw them as a competent, altruistic, fair, and talented group of educational leaders, who were fulfilling important roles on an HBCU campus. The remaining eight suggested that they performed more effectively when aided by committed white assistants in bridging the gap between the black and the white worlds. Some called them authoritarian administrators within a centralized power structure in the campus administration. These felt that racial barriers at times interfered with their effective communication with some black administrators.

Black administrators' perceptions of you. Most (29) supposed that they were viewed as competent faculty and as a necessary element of the educational mix (white and black faculty), to be treated fairly and evenhandedly. Others (11) thought that they were looked on as necessary fill-ins, pending the availability of suitable black professors. Still others (10) thought that they were viewed as "tokens" to satisfy racial integration requirements at HBCUs and/or as "cheap hired help." One of the last group offered the following statement:

> I suffer under no illusions. Most of us are either tokens or cheap hired help. Sometimes both. They have to have some of us around to meet their quotas. With my credentials if I were black, I would be making more money here. Discrimination is a two-edged sword. They should not be able to have it both ways. Black and white professors on all college campuses should be treated equally.

Perceptions of white staff members. They considered them to be competent employees who performed essential support services reasonably well. They also saw them as being on campus because of job availability and convenience. One white faculty member commented:

Staff is staff and they take jobs where they can find them. We are in short supply here. The college hires a lot of local people. Most white staff members live nearby.

White staff members' perceptions of you. All thought that they were viewed by white staff members as competent professors on an HBCU campus.

Perceptions of black staff members. Most (45) viewed black staff as competent skilled workers. This was particularly the case with white-collar workers (e.g., supervisors, secretaries, and librarians). As one white faculty member commented:

> The black staff, especially the secretaries and supervisors, carry a lot of weight. At times they have as much input as faculty and mid-level administrators. Of course, some of them are more important and powerful than we are. We have to get along with them. If we don't, things just don't get done.

Five considered a few black secretaries to be hostile and racially prejudiced against them. One of these reported:

> The departmental secretary doesn't like white professors. So she doesn't do much for them. My typing comes last and my telephone calls are not always passed on.

These five perceived racial barriers between themselves and black staff members.

Black staff members' perceptions of you: Most (45) thought that they were seen as competent and respectable white faculty. A few (5) thought that some staff members considered them to be white aliens and "hell raisers."

Interracial and Intraracial Interactions and Relationships

White students. They reported few contacts with white students in or out of the classroom because, as they explained, most of them were commuters who spent little time on campus. Many were employed off campus, which left them little time to spend with faculty. Although encounters were limited, they were characterized as pleasant and friendly. One faculty member explained:

> They come to classes and then disappear. Because they assume a low profile in class there is little interaction between us. I will have to admit, though, I'm usually busy with other students when they do drop by my office.

Black students. All white faculty members reported frequent, pleasant, and friendly contacts with many black students in their classrooms and offices. Classroom exchanges focused on the subject matter, question-and-answer sessions, volunteered remarks, group discussions, and oral reports. Office talk and counseling sessions covered a gamut of topics—subject matter tasks, personal problems, term papers, and career plans—as did friendly chats. They claimed a strong rapport with most and friendships with many. Fifteen white faculty members entertained some black students in their homes. A few faculty members, however, acknowledged some strained and problematic relationships with a few black students over grades. Most of these students earned low grades from both white and black faculty. They noted that these black students placed more pressure on them for grade changes than they did on black professors. One white professor declared:

> The hell we catch about grades comes from poor students who don't do well in any class taught by a white or a black professor. They know we are more vulnerable. You know, to charges of racial prejudice. Therefore they think they can pressure us more for better grades than their black professors.

With a few exceptions, the white faculty did not perceive racial barriers between themselves and black students.

Other white faculty. On-campus contacts among white faculty members were infrequent because they comprised a minority group that was distributed throughout campus programs. Contacts were brief, pleasant, and concerned primarily with academic matters. They did maintain friendly and personal relationships off campus through an informal news grapevine and support system.

Black faculty. All noted frequent, everyday professional contacts with black faculty made necessary by the daily academic round centering on the common tasks of teaching, advising, assisting, and counseling students. These encounters required face-to-face personal contacts and shared duties. Accounts about these contacts varied in nature and point of view.

Most (32) claimed pleasant, cooperative, friendly, and rewarding encounters with their black counterparts. As one remarked:

> We did all sorts of things together like team teaching, counseling, working on committees, student advisement, redoing curriculum, scheduling classes and working registration. You name it, we did it together. And we forgot about race in the midst of these duties. We were just fellow faculty members and students were just students.

Some of these (15) exchanged home visits with black faculty.

Of the remaining eighteen, fourteen described their contacts as civil, pleasant, cooperative, and professionally correct, but shallow at the deeper interpersonal level. One of these explained:

They are pleasant and friendly acting and we get things done together. But we don't discuss off-campus personal matters. We work well together and respect each other but I can tell they don't want to be our close friends. And really I think the chance of real friendship for any of us in this segregated society is slim.

None of these interacted with black faculty members off campus.

A few others (4) characterized their contacts with black faculty as impersonal, strained, and chilly, but usually professionally correct. One of these four commented:

We managed to cooperate and put on a good show. But I knew most of them didn't really care for me. The disapproving expressions on their faces at times told me the story. They acted real cool toward me when we were alone. When we were in interracial groups, my presence was totally ignored in their discussions. And they made a few snide remarks about white people which I overheard. We are not really friends and never will be. But we can work together.

White administrators. Personal contacts with the few white administrators were pleasant, but infrequent, brief, and formal. None claimed close friends among white administrators. A few administrators, however, belonged to the informal white faculty support system.

Black administrators. All had occasional personal contacts with black administrators (primarily with department chairs and school deans), which they described as pleasant and satisfactory, for the most part, though conventional in form and content. At times discussions with some deans and chairs were friendly and informal. Some few (5) reported unpleasant encounters with chairs and other officials when dealing with such matters as grading procedures, students' complaints, teaching methods, tenure, promotions, salary raises, faculty salary differentials, and merit assessments. According to them, some administrators were blunt, authoritarian, rigid, and biased. None reported off-campus social contacts.

White staff members. Encounters with white staff were pleasant, brief, formal, and limited to on-campus meetings.

Black staff members. All experienced frequent contacts with the black white-collar staff and occasional contacts with black blue-collar employees. Most interactions with secretaries and librarians were reported to be pleasant and friendly; they found that other white-collar workers varied from pleasant, but formally polite, to coolly indifferent. Interactions with blue-collar workers were mixed, varying from civil exchanges to problematic and unpleasant situations. One faculty member explained:

Black secretaries and librarians usually treat us with respect but some are friendlier than others. Contacts with the blue-collar workers are usually service-oriented. Sometimes they are rude, but it is hard to tell if it's race or class dislike.

Overall, racial barriers between them and black staff members were minimal.

Perceived Social Acceptance

White students. All perceived themselves to be socially acceptable to white students on and off campus, but they experienced little social interaction with them on or off campus.

Black students. They considered themselves socially acceptable to most black students on campus, but only to a minority off campus.

White faculty, administrators, and staff members. They considered themselves socially acceptable to all these categories on and off campus. Off-campus social contacts, however, were maintained only with other white faculty members.

Black faculty, administrators, and staff members. Most viewed themselves as socially acceptable to most black faculty and administrators on campus. A few thought that they were socially acceptable to some members of these two categories off campus. Most said that they were socially acceptable to white-collar staff on and off campus. They were indifferent to their social acceptability to the blue-collar staff on or off campus.

Perceived Racial Conflict on Campus

None noted any manifestations of open group conflict on campus. Some white faculty members said that they had encountered racial hostility from a few individuals, including black faculty members, black secretaries, and black blue-collar staff members, involving what they perceived to be "professional jealousy" and/or "racial animosity"; for example, they were called derogatory nicknames, blacks exchanged indirect racial slurs in their presence, they were the objects of direct professional put-downs, blacks made discrediting remarks about white faculty scholarship, and blacks used avoidance patterns. One who perceived individual racial conflict explained:

> There is no way to win for a white on a black campus. If you try to be nice, they think you want something from them. If you act neutral about the race question, they accuse you of insensitivity. If you sympathize with them, you are patronizing. If you criticize them, you are a racist. If you publish and try to be a scholar, you are a smartass. And if you don't, you are a loser and a white reject. If you speak good English, you have no appreciation for black English. And if you don't speak good English, you are a redneck.

Despite these subjective feelings on the part of a few, most black and white faculty members reported pleasant interactions.

Psychological Comfort Level

Most (29) reported feeling comfortable without reservations; eighteen reported that they felt comfortable most of the time, but uneasy and irritated at times when they encountered rejection and professional put-downs. A few (3) reported feeling uncomfortable and alienated for a good part of the time as a result of what they called "reverse racial prejudice."

Opportunity Structure

Most (35) were interested in teaching, rather than research and publications, and foresaw a rewarding career opportunity where they were. Some others (9) were reasonably satisfied, but also somewhat concerned about what they perceived to be the "favored position" of black counterparts with reference to professional advancement. These reasoned, however, that the differentials were not rigidly systematized and could, and would, be erased in time. Others (6) perceived an unequal opportunity structure as a part of the campus culture. Those few engaged in research and publications thought such achievements were rewarded or unrewarded at the discretion of the administration. Those who perceived reverse discrimination did not wish to teach at an HBCU in the first place and did not wish to stay if they had a choice. Some complained about the existing heavy teaching load, low salary, inadequate library holdings and computer services, poor physical facilities, and lack of research opportunities. Some also noted that being white blocked them from obtaining top-level administrative positions. On the other hand, some noted, to their advantage, that the competition for external funding was less at an HBCU than that existing at predominately white universities.

Summary and Conclusions

Most of these middle-class liberal professors were professionals pursuing academic careers on whatever campuses were available to them. A minority were specially dedicated to the education of black youth. We found no "Morons" or "Messiahs" in this study. Some were guilt-ridden, and some were "Marginal Men." Most felt a compassion for blacks. All reasoned that they should be afforded respect and an equal opportunity structure at an HBCU. All perceived respect, but many thought that the black faculty was favored over them, particularly where promotions and accessibility to administrative positions were concerned. Some faculty perceived that a number of black faculty and students wondered about their presence on a black campus; they maintained that they had as much right to be on HBCU campuses as black faculty had to be on white campuses.

Some suggested the need to approach black students in a different way from white students; others professed more objective teaching positions; still others were undecided about what approach to take. All noted that rapport with black students is crucial to the learning process and that one must be liked in order to teach them effectively. Most perceived acceptance by students, faculty, administration, and staff. Most important, they had a stronger rapport with black students than with white students, white faculty, or black faculty. They maintained cooperative professional relationships with the black faculty. The competition between white and black faculty on an HBCU is much less than that among white faculty on white campuses. One reason for this is probably the relative absence of pressure on HBCU campuses to publish.

Interactions and relationships with black faculty at the personal and social levels were ambivalent and shallow. Black and white faculty attributed these impersonal relationships to two interrelated conditions: (1) differences in culture, racial identity, and world view; and (2) societal racial segregation, particularly at the social level. Most were more comfortable than they had expected to be on an HBCU campus, but perceived occasional reverse racial prejudice and racial put-downs. Most, to reiterate, envisioned an unequal opportunity structure and wondered at times if they were tokens or hired help.

We recommend that HBCUs continue to employ white professors and that the current racial balance between white and black professors be continued. This healthy mix should provide a model for white campuses. White professors should seriously consider teaching careers at HBCUs, should they possess an anti-racist perspective, a willingness to teach underprivileged and unprepared students, and an ability to effect a rapport with black youth. Finally, steps should be taken to eliminate some white professors' perceptions of unequal opportunity structures at HBCUs.

7

SUMMARY AND CONCLUSIONS

SUMMARY

Historically black colleges and universities (HBCUs) were established following the Civil War to provide elementary, secondary, and post-secondary education for freedmen and to prepare them to teach other blacks. The initial impetus giving birth to these schools was ignited and implemented during Reconstruction (1863–1877) by northern missionary groups, the Freedmen's Bureau, and black churches and social associations. The mission of these HBCUs included religious, moral, citizenship, and secular educational components. An overwhelming number of these institutions were private schools operated by white faculty and administrators. Following the passage of the Morrill Act of 1890 and the extension of black public school education, public HBCUs were established as land-grant colleges—primarily to provide segregated agricultural, mechanical, and engineering training. During the period from 1896 through 1954, a segregated public school and higher education system, including both private and public HBCUs, was further developed within an atmosphere of southern white hostility.

Funding from the state and federal levels was meager, and considerable financial support was provided by organized philanthropy. Since the 1940s, the private HBCUs have received additional financial help from the United Negro College Fund. Despite many difficulties during this long segregated period, HBCUs became complete higher education institutions that provided both academic and professional training. Secondary education programs at HBCUs were discontinued before the end of this period, and great strides were made in curriculum development, faculty improvement, and accreditation.

The period from the 1960s through the 1970s was marked by the integration of most black students into predominantly white institutions at the cost of HBCU enrollments—and many would claim at the cost of the alienation of many black students on white campuses. The proponents of HBCUs argued that the preservation of black colleges and universities was essential to the higher education of black youth. During the late 1970s and 1980s, black educators and leaders shifted their emphasis from strict integration at the higher education level to a policy of educational pluralism, a policy that the U.S. government has endorsed, though with much ambiguity. According to this new policy, black students must still have the option of attending white colleges and universities, but at the same time HBCUs must be *preserved and strengthened* for the black students and faculty who opt for them.

Several conditions fostered this pluralistic stance: (1) the dramatic drop in HBCU enrollments (though from 1986 to 1990 enrollments at both public and private HBCUs rose by 15 to 16 percent); (2) the fear that integration and mergers of state colleges and universities would swallow up many HBCUs; (3) the failure of the integration dream; (4) the increasing alienation and difficulties many black students have encountered on white campuses since the 1970s; (5) the growing conviction that HBCUs can best prepare black students for service and leadership roles in the black community; (6) the belief that HBCUs can be the best means of preserving black culture, black history, and black identity; and (7) the failure of white institutions to provide black faculty and students with an opportunity structure and a comfort level on par with those at HBCUs.

Black educators, the black community, some white educators, and the federal government are committed to the preservation and improvement of HBCUs in the foreseeable future. Throughout their existence HBCUs have contributed significantly to the efforts of black, low-income and educationally disadvantaged Americans to attain equal opportunity through post-secondary education. The estimated median family income of students attending private black colleges in 1991 was $33,823, only three-fourths of the $44,485 median income for families of students at all four-year private colleges. In 1991, over one-fourth of all students attending private black colleges came from families with incomes of less than $20,000. (These median estimates were obtained from the Atlanta UNCF office.) As is generally known, the cost of education is higher at private than at public HBCUs. Furthermore, more emphasis is placed on black history, black culture, black consciousness, and black identity at private HBCUs than at public HBCUs.

HBCUs continue to function as institutions necessary for the education of many students who otherwise would not obtain college degrees. Our findings, as well as those of others (see Pascarella and Terenzini 1992) disclose many positive features of an HBCU education for black students. To highlight some of these:

1. Black students feel more acceptable, more comfortable, and less alienated on HBCU campuses than they do on white campuses.
2. Black students make a better overall adjustment at HBCUs than they do at white colleges.
3. Black students on HBCU campuses, unlike those on white campuses, are not subject to racial prejudice, racial discrimination, or racial slurs.
4. Black students are less likely to drop out of college if enrolled at black colleges than if enrolled at white colleges.
5. Undergraduate attendance at HBCUs has a more positive effect on the later educational attainment of black students than does attendance at white undergraduate schools.
6. Black students perform better academically at HBCUs than they do at white schools.
7. Black students receive more emotional support from various groups on HBCU campuses than they do on white campuses.
8. Black students experience a much more satisfying social life on HBCU campuses than they do on white campuses.
9. Black students at HBCUs are more thoroughly integrated into and active in the total campus scene than they are at white schools.
10. Black students enjoy a closer relationship with HBCU faculty than they do with faculty at white schools.
11. Black students enjoy a higher level of psychological comfort at HBCUs than they do on white campuses because of the presence of the black cultural milieu.
12. The opportunity structure for black students at HBCUs is more rewarding than is that at white schools.

Though white students on black campuses consider themselves to be aliens, they experienced congenial relationships with black and white faculty, and they were satisfied with the HBCU opportunity structure. Most developed more respect for blacks than they had had before attending HBCUs. Black faculty on white campuses feel alienated from white faculty and did not perceive the campus opportunity structure to be rewarding. Black faculty on black campuses adjusted well in a familiar milieu that met their personal, social, and career needs. White faculty on black campuses perceived that they were accepted by most students, faculty, and administrators. Some, however, felt somewhat alienated from black faculty and black administrators. The overwhelming number experienced pleasant working relationships with black students. Most white faculty had mixed feelings about the HBCU opportunity structure, which was perceived to be geared to the advantage of black professors. The most important finding on campus race relations was that interracial relationships between students and faculty were more accepting and wholesome than were interracial relationships among faculty, or among students, or between faculty and administrators.

HBCUs, in addition to offering a wholesome, accepting, and rewarding atmosphere, provide adequate undergraduate and professional programs within a variety of accredited private and public institutions (see chapter 3). To their credit, several HBCUs have received high national academic ratings. Recent enrollment patterns show that more students from third world countries, students from other U.S. minority groups (e.g., Hispanics and Asians), and native white students are enrolling at HBCUs. Native black students continue to enroll at higher rates than they did in the 1970s, and many black administrators expect these enrollments to soar within the next few years. This mixture of HBCU students from various ethnic groups should prove valuable in our multicultural and multiracial society.

CONCLUSIONS

We maintain that HBCUs' present and future raison d'être rests on three major functions: (1) to carry out the central mission of educating black youth, (2) to provide unique student-teacher relationships and teaching methodology, and (3) to offer a rich archival source for black scholarship and to become centers for black cultural studies (see chapter 4). HBCU student-teacher relationships are based on mutual respect, acceptance, and love and on a teaching methodology that embraces cooperative learning by doing in an accepting classroom setting. These elements could be profitably adopted by other colleges and universities.

The major challenges as we view them are as follows:

1. More non-black students must be enrolled, while simultaneously maintaining a black identity and the central function of educating black youth. This will require an ingenious balancing act.

2. HBCUs need to reach farther out to the local, off-campus black, community and to provide a multitude of services to them. The people and the activities of these two entities should be further integrated. Currently the chasm between town and gown is too great.

3. Library holdings and research facilities must be increased.

4. Faculty research and publications must be expected, required, and rewarded without impairing the current emphasis on teaching and counseling. Perhaps two sets of professors could be employed for two different purposes. In any event, in the opinion of some, black professors and administrators do not appreciate enough the scholarly output of individual faculty members. To them,

many HBCU professors do not publish frequently, and those who do are insufficiently rewarded.

5. Black faculty must be increased.

6. The number of black male students must be increased in order to balance the current campus sex ratio (i.e., the number of males is small in comparison to that of females.

7. HBCUs need to address the perceptions of some white HBCU faculty that they do not have equal opportunity rights vis-à-vis black faculty.

8. HBCUs need to address the perceptions of some white students at HBCUs that they are not as acceptable as black students are.

9. HBCUs need to address the perceptions by some HBCU faculty members that HBCU administrators are too authoritarian.

Finally, our research findings clearly demonstrate that HBCUs must continue to play a vital role in our diversified higher education system. HBCUs are no longer special-purpose institutions. They are now essential multipurpose colleges and universities.

REFERENCES

Alba, D. R. *Ethnic Identity: The Transformation of White America.* New Haven, Conn.: Yale University Press, 1989.

Allen, H. L. "The Mobility of Black Collegiate Faculty Revisited: Whatever Happened to the 'Brain Drain'?" *Journal of Negro Education* 60, no. 1 (1991): 97–109.

Allen, W. R. "Black Student, White Campus: Structural, Interpersonal and Psychological Correlates of Success." *Journal of Negro Education* 54, no. 2 (1985): 135–147.

———. *Gender and Campus Race Differences in Black Student Academic Performance: Racial Attitudes and College Satisfaction.* Atlanta: Southern Education Foundation, 1986.

———. "Black Colleges vs. White Colleges." *Change* 30 (1987): 28–39.

———. "The Color of Success: African-American College Student Outcomes at Predominantly White and Historically Black Public Colleges and Universities." *Harvard Educational Review* 62, no. 1 (1992): 26–43.

Allen, W. R., E. G. Epp, and N. Z. Haniff, eds. *College in Black and White: African American Students in Predominantly White and in Historically Black Public Universities.* Albany: State University of New York Press, 1991.

American Association of State Colleges and Universities. *The Lurking Evil: Racial and Ethnic Conflict on the College Campus.* Washington, D.C.: the Association, 1989.

American Council on Education. *American Universities and Colleges.* 13th ed. New York: Walter de Gruyter, 1987.

American Council on Education, Office of Minority Concerns. *Minorities in Higher Education: Sixth Annual Status Report.* Washington, D.C.: American Council on Education, 1987.

———. *Minorities in Higher Education.* Washington, D.C.: American Council on Education, 1988.

———. *Minorities in Higher Education: Ninth Annual Status Report.* Washington, D.C.: American Council on Education, 1990.

Atlanta University Center, Inc. *Strength through Cooperation.* Atlanta: Atlanta University Center, 1987.

Ayers, E. L. *The Promise of the New South: Life After Reconstruction*. New York: Oxford University Press, 1992.

Baker, P. S. "Federal-State Relations." In *Encyclopedia of Southern Culture*, edited by C. R. Wilson and W. Ferris, 229–50. Chapel Hill: University of North Carolina Press, 1989.

Barthelemy, S. "The Role of Black Colleges in Nurturing Leadership." In *Black Colleges and Universities*, edited by A. Garibaldi, 14–25. New York: Praeger, 1984.

Becker, J., and R. Weiner. "Minority Educators Skeptical about SAT Revisions," *Black Issues in Higher Education* 7, no. 19 (1990): 1, 16.

Benjamin, L. *The Black Elite: Facing the Color Line in the Twilight of the Twentieth Century*. New York: Nelson-Hall, 1992.

Berlin, I. *Slaves Without Masters: The Free Negro in the Antebellum South*. New York: Pantheon Books, 1974.

Billingsley, A. C. "Building Strong Faculties in Black Colleges." *Journal of Negro Education* 51, no. 1 (1982): 4–15.

Blackwell, J. E. *Mainstreaming Outsiders: The Production of Black Professionals*. New York: General Hall, 1981.

Blumenstyle, G. "Cavazos Names Businessman-Turned-College-Official to Direct Bush's Efforts to Help Black Institutions." *Chronicle of Higher Education* 35, no. 45 (1989): A14–A17.

Bowles, F. D., F. A. Decosta, and K. S. Tollett. *Between Two Worlds: A Profile of Negro Higher Education*. New York: McGraw-Hill, 1971.

Braddock, J. H. "Racial Ideology: Toward a Multidimensional Approach to Measurement." Paper presented at the Southern Sociological Society, Atlanta, 1974.

Branson, H. R. "The Hazards in Black Higher Education: Program and Commitment Needs." *Journal of Negro Education* 56, no. 2 (1987): 129–36.

Brazziel, M. E., and F. W. Brazziel. "Impact of Support for Graduate Study on Program Completion of Black Doctorate Recipients." *Journal of Negro Education* 56, no. 2 (1987): 145–51.

Brown, C. I. *The White Presence of Traditionally Black Public Colleges and Universities: A Synopsis 1837–1980*. Durham: North Carolina Central University, 1980. (ERIC Document Reproduction Service No. ED), 286-403.

Browning, J., and J. Williams. "History and Goals of Black Institutions of Higher Learning." In *Black Colleges in America*, edited by C. V. Willie and R. R. Edmonds, 68-93. New York: Teachers College Press, 1978.

Bullock, H. *A History of Negro Education in the South, From 1619 to the Present*. New York: Praeger, 1970.

Bunzel, J. H. "Black and White at Stanford." *Public Interest* 105 (1991): 61–77.

Carter, R. T., and E. H. Janet. "The Relationship between Racial Identity Attitudes and Social Class." *Journal of Negro Education* 57, no. 1 (1988): 22–30.

Cash, W. J. *The Mind of the South*. New York: Knopf, 1941.

Clinton, W., and A. Gore. *Putting People First: How We Can All Change America*. New York: Times Books, 1993.

Cohen, D. K. "Segregation, Desegregation and Brown." *Society* 12 (1974): 34–40.

Collison, M. N. K. " 'Fight the Power': Rap Music Pounds Out New Anthem for Many Black Students." *Chronicle of Higher Education* 36, no. 14 (1990): A29.

———. "Colleges Have Done a Bad Job of Explaining Affirmative Action to Students, Critics Say." *Chronicle of Higher Education* 38, no. 22 (1992): A37–A38.

Daubenmier, J. "Berry Says College Racism Still Pervasive." *Black Issues in Higher Education* 7, no. 11 (1990): 25.

Davis, K., and J. Swartz. *Increasing Black Students in Predominantly White North Carolina Colleges and Universities*. Research Report no. 2. New York: College Entrance Examination Board, 1972.

Dawkins, M. P., and R. L. Dawkins. "Perceptions and Experiences as Correlates of Academic Performance among Blacks at a Predominantly White University: A Research Note." *Journal of Colleges and Universities* (Winter 1980): 171–80.

DeLoughry, T. J. "Presidents of Black Colleges Press Congress for Money to Improve Teaching, Expand Graduate Programs." *Chronicle of Higher Education* 37, no. 16 (1990): A18–A19.

Deskins, D. "A Regional Assessment of Minority Enrollment and Earned Degrees in U.S. Colleges and Universities, 1974–84." In *Colleges in Black and White*, edited by W. R. Allen, E. G. Epp, and N. Z. Haniff, 17–39. Albany: State University of New York Press, 1991.

Diener, T. "Job Satisfaction and College Faculty in Two Predominantly Black Institutions." *Journal of Negro Education* 54, no. 4 (1985): 558–65.

DuBois, W.E.B. *Souls of Black Folk*. Chicago: A. C. Clurg, 1903.

DuBois, W.E.B., and A. C. Dill. *The College Bred Negro American*. Atlanta: Atlanta University Press, 1910.

Dupre, B. B. "Problems Regarding the Survival of Future Black Teachers in Education." *Journal of Negro Education* 55 (1986): 56–63.

Dyer, T. G. "Education." In *Encyclopedia of Southern Culture*, edited by C. R. Wilson and W. Ferris, 237–41. Chapel Hill: University of North Carolina Press, 1989.

Edwards, H. *The Revolt of the Black Athlete*. New York: Free Press, 1970.

Ehrlich, H. J. *Campus Ethnoviolence and the Policy Options*. Washington, D.C.: National Institute against Prejudice and Violence, 1990.

Elam, J. C., ed. *Blacks on White Campuses: Proceedings of a Special NAFEO Seminar*. Washington, D.C.: NAFEO Research Institute, 1983.

Exum, W. H. "Climbing the Crystal Stair: Values, Affirmative Action, and Minority Faculty." *Social Problems* 30, no. 4 (1983): 383–99.

Ezorsky, G. *Racism and Justice: The Case for Affirmative Action*. Ithaca, N.Y.: Cornell University Press, 1991.

Fleming, J. "Stress and Satisfaction in College Years of Black Students." *Journal of Negro Education* 50, no. 3 (1981): 307–18.

———. *Blacks in College*. San Francisco: Jossey-Bass, 1984.

Foner, E. *Reconstruction: America's Unfinished Revolution, 1863–1877*. New York: Harper & Row, 1988.

Fordyce, H. R., and A. L. Kirschner. *1990 Statistical Report*. New York: United Negro College Fund, Inc., 1990.

Franklin, J. H. "The Two Worlds of Race: A Historical View." In *The Negro American*, edited by T. Parsons and K. B. Clark, 413-23. Boston: Houghton Mifflin Co., 1975.

Gamson, Z. F. "Four Institutions: Racial Climates, Responses and the Future." In *Black Students on White Campuses: The Impacts of Increased Black Enrollments*, edited by M. W. Peterson et al., 279–91. Ann Arbor: University of Michigan, 1978.

Gibbs, J. T. "Patterns of Adaptation among Black Students at a Predominantly White University." *American Journal of Orthopsychiatry* 44 (1974): 728–40.

Gibbs, N. "Bigots in the Ivory Tower: An Alarming Rise in Hatred Roils U.S. Campuses." *Time*, May 6, 1990, 104–106.

Gless, D. L., and B. H. Smith. *The Politics of Liberal Education*. Durham, N.C.: Duke University Press, 1989.

Goffman, E. *The Presentation of Self in Everyday Life*. New York: Doubleday Anchor, 1959.

———. *Stigma: Notes in the Management of Spoiled Identity*. Englewood Cliffs, N.J.: Prentice-Hall, 1963.

Goodenow, R. K. "Black Education." In *Encyclopedia of Southern Culture*, edited by C. R. Wilson and W. Ferris, 151–53. Chapel Hill: University of North Carolina Press, 1989.

Gurin, P., and E. G. Epps. *Black Consciousness, Identity and Achievement: A Study of Students in Historically Black Colleges*. New York: Wiley Press, 1975.

Hacker, A. "Trans-National America." *New York Review of Books* 37, no. 18 (1990): 19–24.

———. *Two Nations: Black and White: Separate, Hostile, Unequal*. New York: Charles Scribner & Sons, 1992.

———. "The Blacks and Clinton." *New York Review of Books* 40, no. 3 (1993): 12–15.

Harlan, L. R. *Booker T. Washington: The Making of a Black Leader, 1856-1901*. New York: Oxford University Press, 1972.

———. *Booker T. Washington: The Wizard of Tuskegee, 1901-1915*. New York: Oxford University Press, 1983.

Harvey, W. B., and L. E. Williams. "Historically Black Colleges: Models for Increasing Minority Representation." *Education and Urban Society* 21, no. 3 (1989): 328–40.

Hemmons, W. M. "From the Halls of Hough and Halstedt: A Comparison of Black Students on Predominantly White and Predominantly Black Campuses." *Journal of Black Studies* 12 (1982): 383–402.

Hodgkinson, H. *All One System*. Washington, D.C.: Institute for Educational Leadership, 1985.

Howard, E. D. "Extremism on Campus: Symbols of Hate, Symbols of Hope." *Christian Century* (July 15–22, 1987): 625–28.

"In Brief." *Chronicle of Higher Education* (April 15, 1992): A5.

Jackson, J. "Alienation and Black Political Participation." *Journal of Politics* 35 (1973): 849–85.

Jacques, J. M. "The Split Labor Market and Ethnic Antagonism: A Case Study of Higher Education." *Sociology of Education* 53 (1980): 225–36.

Jaschik, S. "Court's Desegregation Ruling Has Black Colleges Worried about Winning Support from State Legislators." *Chronicle of Higher Education* 34, no. 19 (1988): A21–A25.

———. "Black Colleges Back Revival of Bias Lawsuit, But Seek to Shift Focus from Desegregation." *Chronicle of Higher Education* 35, no. 30 (1988): A19–A22.

———. "After the Adams Case: Civil-Rights Groups Are Concerned as 14 States Regain Responsibility for Desegregation of Public-College Campuses." *Chronicle of Higher Education* 36, no. 10 (1990): A21–A22.

———. "White House Eyes Change in Approach to Black Colleges: Controversial Plan

Would Divide Campuses into Separate Categories." *Chronicle of Higher Education* 37, no. 17 (1991): A1, A18, A19.

———. "High-Court Ruling Transforms Battles over Desegregation at Colleges in 19 States." *Chronicle of Higher Education* 38, no. 44 (1992): A16–A18.

Jaynes, G. D., and R. M. Williams, Jr., eds. *A Common Destiny: Blacks and American Society.* New York: National Academy Press, 1989.

Jellema, W. W. *Higher Education Finance: A Comparative Study of Matched Samples of Black and White Private Institutions.* Atlanta: Southern Regional Education Board, 1972.

Jencks, C. *Rethinking Social Policy: Race, Poverty, and the Underclass.* Cambridge, Mass.: Harvard University Press, 1992.

Jencks, C., and D. Reisman. *The Academic Revolution.* New York: Doubleday Anchor, 1968.

Jenkins, M. D. "Problems Incident to Racial Integration and Some Suggested Solutions: A Critical Summary." *Journal of Negro Education* 21 (1952): 411–21.

Johnson, C. S. "Some Significant Social and Educational Implications of the U.S. Supreme Court's Decision." *Journal of Negro Education* 23 (1954): 364–71.

Johnson, G. "Desegregation in Southern Higher Education." *Higher Education* 20 (June 1964): 5–7.

Jones, E. P. "The Impact of Economic, Political, and Social Factors on Recent Overt Black/White Racial Conflict in Higher Education in the United States." *Journal of Negro Education* 60, no. 4 (1991): 524–37.

Jones, J. *The Dispossessed: America's Underclass from the Civil War to the Present.* New York: Basic Books, 1992.

Jones, M. "The Responsibility of the Black College to the Black Community: Then and Now." *Daedalus* 100 (1971): 732–34.

Jones, S. J., and G. B. Weathersby. "Financing the Black College in America." In *Black Colleges in America*, edited by C. V. Willie and R. R. Edmonds, 313-27. New York: Teachers College Press, 1978.

Jordan, V. E., Jr. "Blacks in Higher Education: Some Reflections." *Daedalus* 104 (1978): 160–65.

Junod, J. X. "Are Black Colleges Necessary?" *Atlanta Magazine* 27, no. 6 (1987): 78–119.

Kantrowitz, B., and B. Turque. "Blacks Protest Campus Racism: A Rash of Incidents." *Newsweek*, April 6, 1987, 30.

King, R. H. *A Southern Renaissance: The Cultural Awakening of the American South, 1930–1955.* New York: Oxford, 1980.

Krippendorff, K. *Content Analysis: An Introduction to Its Methodology.* Beverly Hills, Calif.: Sage Publications, 1980.

Kropp, A. J. "Colleges Must Find Ways to Eradicate Racial Divisions." *Chronicle of Higher Education* 38, no. 33 (1992): B3–B4.

Law, W., and V. Clift. "Education: Colleges and Universities." In *Encyclopedia of Black Americans*, edited by W. Law and V. Clift, 338–51. New York: McGraw-Hill, 1981.

Leatherman, C. "Louis Farrakhan's Controversial Campus Visits: Inspirational for Blacks, Abhorrent to Jews, a Headache for College Officials." *Chronicle of Higher Education* 35, no. 36 (1989): A35.

Lederman, D. "Special Admissions Treatment for Athletes Widespread at Big-Time-Sports Colleges." *Chronicle of Higher Education* 37, no. 33 (1991): A1, A31.

Levy, C. *The Process of Integrating White Faculty Members into a Predominantly Negro College*. Washington, D.C.: U.S. Department of Health, Education, and Welfare, 1967.

Lomotey, K., ed. *Going to School: The African American Experience*. New York: State University of New York Press, 1989.

Loo, C. M., and G. Rolison. "Alienation of Ethnic Minority Students at a Predominantly White University." *Journal of Higher Education* 57, no. 1 (1986): 58–77.

Louis, E. T. "Racism on Campus: Learn How to Fight Back." *Essence*, August 1987, 53, 120–22.

McGrath, E. G. *The Predominately Negro Colleges in Transition*. New York: Teachers College Press, 1965.

McMillen, L. "Mellon Foundation Gives United Negro College Fund $2.6 Million to Recruit New Faculty Members." *Chronicle of Higher Education* 36, no. 18 (1990): A31–A32.

Meharry Medical College. *Meharry Medical Fact Sheet*. Nashville: Meharry Medical College, Office of the President, 1990.

Melish, I. H. "Attitudes toward the White Minority on a Black Southern Campus: 1966–1968." *Sociological Quarterly* 11, no. 3 (1970): 321–30.

Meyers, M. "For Civil Rights or Compromise: Racism and Black Colleges." *Los Angeles Times*, December 26, 1978.

Mingle, J. R. "Faculty and Departmental Response Patterns: Individual and Contextual Predictors." In *Black Students on White Campuses: The Impacts of Increased Black Enrollments*, edited by Marvin W. Peterson et al., 261–77. Ann Arbor: University of Michigan Press, 1978.

Moore, W., Jr., and H. L. Wagstaff. *Black Educators in White Colleges*. San Francisco: Jossey-Bass, 1974.

Morris, E. W. "The Contemporary Negro College and the Brain Drain." *Journal of Negro Education* 41 (1972): 309–20.

Moss, A. "Northern Philanthropy." In *Encyclopedia of Southern Culture*, edited by C. R. Wilson and W. Ferris, 651–53. Chapel Hill: University of North Carolina Press, 1989.

Murty, K. S., and J. B. Roebuck. "The Case for Historically Black Colleges and Universities." *Journal of Social and Behavioral Sciences* 36, no. 4 (1992): 171–92.

Myers, S. L. "What Is a Black College?" *NAFEO Inroads: The Bimonthly News Letter of the National Association for Equal Opportunity in Higher Education* 1, no. 5–6 (1987): 1–24.

———. "What Is a Black College?" *NAFEO Inroads: The Bimonthly News Letter of the National Association for Equal Opportunity in Higher Education* 6, no. 5 (1992): 1–5.

National Association for Equal Opportunity in Higher Education (NAFEO). *Historically and Predominantly Black Colleges/Universities*. Washington, D.C.: NAFEO Research Institute, 1988.

———. "Black Higher Education Center." In *Institutional and Presidential Profiles of the Nation's Historically and Predominantly Black Colleges and Universities*, 12. Washington, D.C.: NAFEO Research Institute, 1991.

————. *Factbook on Blacks in Higher Education and in Historically and Predominantly Black Colleges and Universities* edited by A. M. Elam. 3 vols. Washington, D.C.: NAFEO Research Institute, 1991.

National Center for Education Statistics. *Digest of Educational Statistics.* Washington, D.C.: U.S. Office of Education, 1972.

National Commission on Testing and Public Policy. *From Gate Keeper to Gateway: Transforming Testing in America.* Boston: Boston College, 1989.

Nettles, M., ed. *Toward Black Undergraduate Student Equality in American Higher Education.* Westport, Conn.: Greenwood Press, 1988.

New York State Department of Education. *A Curriculum of Inclusion.* New York: New York State Department of Education, 1988.

Niba, J. N., and R. Norman. *Recruitment and Retention of Black Students in Higher Education.* Washington, D.C.: NAFEO Research Institute, 1989.

Nicklin, J. L. "Black-College Fund Says It Has Raised $86-Million." *Chronicle of Higher Education* 37, no. 28 (1991): A30.

Nieves, L. *The Minority College Experience: A Review of the Literature.* Princeton, N.J.: Educational Testing Services, 1977.

Office for the Advancement of Public Black Colleges. *A National Resource for Historically Public Black Colleges and Universities.* Washington, D.C.: OAPBC, 1985.

O'Neil, R. M. "Point of View." *Chronicle of Higher Education* 38, no. 14 (1992): A40.

"Opinions in Supreme Court's Decision on Mississippi Desegregation." *Chronicle of Higher Education* 38, no. 44 (1992): A19-A24.

Orfield, G., and F. Monfort. *Racial Change and Desegregation in Large School Districts.* Washington, D.C.: National School Boards Association, 1988.

Pascarella, E. P., and P. T. Terenzini. *How College Affects Students.* San Francisco: Jossey-Bass, 1992.

Patai, D. "Minority Status and the Stigma of 'Surplus Visibility.' " *Chronicle of Higher Education* 38, no. 10 (1991): A52.

Patel, N. H. *Student Transfers from White to Black Colleges.* Washington, D.C.: NAFEO Research Institute, 1988.

Pruitt, A. S., and P. D. Isaac. "Discrimination in Recruitment, Admission, and Retention of Minority Graduate Students." *Journal of Negro Education* 54, no. 4 (1983): 526–36.

Quarles, B. "History of Black Education." In *United Negro College Fund Archives: A Guide and Index to the Microfiche,* edited by United Negro College Fund, New York: University Microfilms, 1985.

Raboteau, A. G. "Black Religion." In *Encyclopedia of Southern Culture,* edited by C. R. Wilson and W. Ferris, 191–92. Chapel Hill: University of North Carolina Press, 1989.

Randolph, E. "And That's the Way He Is." *Washington Post Magazine,* July 8, 1990, 12–17, 27–31.

Randolph, L. B. "Racism on College Campuses: Racial Prejudice Makes Resurgence at Predominantly White Institutions." *Ebony,* December 1990, 126, 128–30.

Rice, M. F., and C. A. Bonnie. "A Preliminary Analysis of Black Undergraduate Students' Perceptions of Retention/Attrition Factors at a Large, Predominantly White, State Research University in the South." *Journal of Negro Education* 58, no. 1 (1989): 68–81.

Richardson, R. C., and W. B. Louis. *Fostering Minority Access and Achievement in Higher Education*. San Francisco: Jossey-Bass, 1987.

Roebuck, J. B. "Sociability in a Black Outdoor Drinking Place." In *Symbolic Interaction: A Research Annual, Part A*, edited by N. K. Denzin, 61–197. Greenwich, Conn.: JAI Press, 1986.

Roebuck, J. B., and M. Hickson. *The Southern Redneck: A Phenomenological Class Study*. New York: Praeger Press, 1984.

Roebuck, J. B., and K. S. Murty. *The Role of Historically Black Colleges and Universities in Higher Education*. Washington, D.C.: National Institute on Drug Abuse, 1990. (Written for the National Institute on Drug Abuse as a part of Clark Atlanta University grant no. 271-89-8015 entitled "HBCUs Examine Drug Abuse among Black Youth").

Roseman, C. C. "Migration Patterns." In *Encyclopedia of Southern Culture*, edited by C. R. Wilson and W. Ferris, 551–52. Chapel Hill: University of North Carolina Press, 1989.

Schuman, H., and S. Hatchett. *Black Racial Attitudes, Trends and Complexities*. Ann Arbor, Mich.: Institute for Social Research, 1974.

Selected Data on Historically Black Colleges, Academic Year 1986-87. Washington, D.C.: National Science Foundation, 1987.

Sharpe, S. A. "Hampton Institute." In *Encyclopedia of Southern Culture*, edited by C. R. Wilson and W. Ferris, 288–89. Chapel Hill: University of North Carolina Press, 1989.

Shingles, R. D. "College as a Source of Black Alienation." *Journal of Black Studies* 9, no. 3 (1989): 267–85.

Simmons, H. L. "The Accreditation Process as a Factor in the Improvement of Traditionally Black Institutions." *Journal of Negro Education* 53, no. 4 (1984): 400–405.

Sleeper, J. *The Closest of Strangers: Liberalism and the Politics of Race in New York*. New York: Norton, 1989.

Smith, A. W., and W. R. Allen. "Modeling Black Student Academic Performance in Higher Education." *Research in Higher Education* 21, no. 2 (1984): 210–25.

Smith, D. H. *Admissions and Attrition Problems of Black Students at Seven Predominantly White Universities*. Washington, D.C.: National Advisory Committee on Black Higher Education and Black Colleges and Universities, 1980.

———. *Admissions and Retention Problems of Black Students at Seven Predominantly White Universities*. Washington, D.C.: National Advisory Committee on Black Higher Education and Black Colleges and Universities, 1981.

Smith, H. D., and B. M. Baruch. "Social and Academic Environments of Black Students on White Campuses." *Journal of Negro Education* 50, no. 3 (1981): 299–306.

Smith, S. L., and K. W. Borgstedt. "Factors Influencing Adjustment of White Faculty in Predominantly Black Colleges." *Journal of Negro Education* 54, no. 2 (1985): 148–62.

Southern Education Foundation. *Small Change: A Report on Federal Support of Black Colleges*. Atlanta: Southern Regional Education Board, 1972.

Sowell, T. *Black Education: Myths and Tragedies*. New York: McKay, 1972.

Spearman, L. H. O. "Federal Roles and Responsibilities Relative to the Higher Education of Blacks since 1967." *Journal of Negro Education* 50, no. 3 (1981): 285–98.

Standley, N. V. *White Students Enrolled in Black Colleges and Universities: Their Attitudes and Perceptions*. Atlanta: Southern Regional Education Board, 1978.

Stewardt, R. J., M. R. Jackson, and J. D. Jackson. "Alienation and Interactional Styles in a Predominantly White Environment: A Study of Successful Black Students." *Journal of College Student Development* 31 (1990): 509–15.

Suen, H. K. "Alienation and Attribution of Black College Students on a Predominantly White Campus." *Journal of College Student Personnel* 24 (1983): 117–20.

Sykes, C. J. *A Nation of Victims: The Decay of the American Character*. New York: St. Martin's Press, 1992.

Synnott, M. G. "Desegregation." In *Encyclopedia of Southern Culture*, edited by C. R. Wilson and W. Ferris, 248–49. Chapel Hill: University of North Carolina Press, 1989.

Taylor, J. *Paved with Good Intentions: The Failure of Race Relations in Contemporary America*. New York: Carrol and Graf, 1992.

Thomas, E. G., and J. McParttland. "Have College Desegragation Policies Threatened Black Student Enrollment and Black Colleges? An Empirical Analysis." *Journal of Negro Education* 53, no. 4 (1984).

Thomas, G. E. *Black College Students and Factors Influencing Their Major Field Choice*. Atlanta: Southern Education Foundation, 1984: 389–99.

Thompson, D. C. *Private Black Colleges at the Crossroads*. Westport, Conn.: Greenwood Press, 1973.

———. "Black College Faculty and Students: The Nature of Their Interaction." In *Black Colleges in America: Challenge, Development, Service*, edited by C. V. Willie and R. R. Edmonds, 180–95. New York: Teachers College Press, 1978.

———. *A Black Elite: A Profile of Graduates of UNCF Colleges*. Westport, Conn.: Greenwood Press, 1986.

Tifft, S. "Bigots in the Ivory Tower: Racial, Religious, and Sexual Prejudice Make a Campus Come Back." *Time*, January 23, 1989, 56.

United Negro College Fund. *Profiles of Past and Present UNCF Member Colleges and Universities*. New York: United Negro College Fund, Inc., 1985.

U.S. Bureau of the Census. *U.S. Census of Population: 1970, General, Social and Economic Characteristics*. Washington, D.C.: U.S. Government Printing Office, 1972.

U.S. Department of Education. "The Traditionally Black Institutions of Higher Education: Their Development and Status, 1860 to 1982." In *Historical Report*, Washington, D.C.: National Center for Educational Statistics, 1985.

U.S. Equal Employment Opportunity Commission. *Summary of 1989 EEO-6, Historically Black Colleges and Universities*. (Obtained through personal communications with Joachim Neckere, Division Director, Program Research and Surveys, Washington, D.C., May 1992.)

Walters, R. "A Cultural Strategy for the Survival of Historically Black Colleges and Universities." Paper presented at the annual conference of the National Council for Black Studies, Atlanta, March 1991. Mimeo.

Warnat, W. I. "The Role of White Faculty on the Black College Campus." *Journal of Negro Education* 45, no. 3 (1976): 334–38.

Washington, B. T. *Up from Slavery*. Reprint, orig. pub. 1901. New York: Dell, 1974.

Washington, J. L. "Black Students, White Campuses: The Plight, The Promise." *Black Collegian* 27, no. 1 (1988): 48–50, 120–21.

Wells, A. "Facing the Current of Campus Racism." *Journal of the National Society of Black Engineers* 4, no. 1 (1988): 36–40.

West, E. H. *The Black American and Education*. Columbus, Ohio: Charles E. Merrill, 1972.

Wiener, J. "Racial Hatred on Campus: Reagan's Children." *Nation* 12, no. 2 (1989): 260–64.

Willie, C. V. *The Ivory and Ebony Towers*. Lexington, Mass.: Lexington Books, 1981.

———. "Black Colleges Should Recruit and Admit More White Students." *Chronicle of Higher Education* 37, no. 6 (1991): A18.

Wilson, C. R. "Religion and Education." In *Encyclopedia of Southern Culture*, edited by C. R. Wilson and W. Ferris, 259–61. Chapel Hill: University of North Carolina Press, 1989.

———. "New White-Student Unions on Some Campuses Are Sparking Outrage and Worry." *Chronicle of Higher Education* 36, no. 29 (1990): A1, A36.

Wilson, W. J. *The Totally Disadvantaged*. Chicago: University of Chicago Press, 1987.

"Wrong Message from Academe." *Time*, April 6, 1986, 57.

Wymes, A. D. "The Atlanta University Center." *Dollars and Sense* 18, no. 2 (1992): 27–37.

INDEX

About the Authors

JULIAN B. ROEBUCK is Research Professor in the Criminal Justice Institute at Clark Atlanta University. He is the author of more than ten books, including *The Redneck Southerner* (Praeger, 1982).

KOMANDURI S. MURTY is Associate Professor and Chairman of the Criminal Justice Department at Clark Atlanta University and is the author of numerous articles and book chapters.